A *New York Post* Required Reading book

PRAISE FOR CIVIL WARS

"A thoroughly engaging narrative that is poignant and provocative." —*The Baltimore Sun*

"A tribute to what can happen when Americans of deep but differing convictions struggle to engage in a dialogue that is honest, informed, and respectful—one that strives, in the end, to recognize 'our common humanity.' As such, *Civil Wars* is a heartening book, and tonic for these politically polarized times." —*Kentucky Courier-Journal*

"This book, written in the sparely elegant style that characterizes Moats's editorials and public-radio commentaries, does more than document a historic event. It is valuable reading for anyone who wants to understand one of the central issues of our time." —*Yankee Magazine*

"As the case moves from its preliminary stages through the courts and legislature, Moats ratchets up the suspense. . . . Like a nonfiction version of Harper Lee's *To Kill a Mockingbird,* he avoids preaching, instead letting the case's rich characters and inherent tension do the bulk of the dramatic work. The result is that *Civil Wars* is a page-turner that may have readers so engrossed in its storytelling, they forget the controversial nature of its subject matter." —*Nashville Scene*

"Gripping. Moats has an incisive writing style that in bursts of short but emotionally charged sentences details the tricky jobs of uniting a state with a range of lifestyles and ideological fault lines as complicated as California. Shrewd analysis."
—*Bay Area Reporter*

"If you did not know the outcome, *Civil Wars* would be a cliffhanger, a legal thriller down to the final vote. Instead of turning to the last page to see how the story ends, you are drawn in to see how it unfolds."
—*Out in the Mountains*

"A remarkable drama of democracy in action. Moats' mesmerizing depiction of queer activism, citizen participation, and one state's unusual tolerance for the rights of others may well become as central to the issue of gay marriage as Allan Berube's *Coming Out Under Fire* was to gays in the military, or Randy Shilts' *And the Band Plays On* was to the early days of AIDS."
—*In Newsweekly*

"A riveting analysis . . . Moats' fervid storytelling lends tremendous appeal and suspense which will keep readers eagerly turning pages, even though the outcome is known before you read the first word. . . . Moats must also be commended for telling the story in human terms, putting fully dimensional characters on the pages."
—*Echo Magazine*

"A deftly detailed, dispassionate, and eminently rational account of the messy, moving way in which history was made in the Green Mountain State. Moats neither demonizes nor lionizes all of the proponents of same-sex marriage, choosing instead to present their humanity, a simple fact those on both sides of this continuing national debate would be well-advised to acknowledge."
—*Courier-Post* (New Jersey)

"A timely reminder that the gay community is no stranger to violence and even murder; and that despite that cruelty, or perhaps because of a growing understanding on the part of ordinary Americans of just what that hatred means, there may be hope for people who are asking nothing more than to live out their lives in peace with the people they love." —*Legal Times*

"Moats is a master at making courtroom maneuverings, judiciary proceedings, and congressional power plays plain and simple when the legal and political wranglings were anything but. He is also a historian . . . especially good at painting life portraits of the leading figures in this story."

—*The Memphis Flyer*

"Timely, insightful, and often moving, Moats' book benefits from the same fundamental decency that animated his eloquent series of same-sex marriage editorials in the *Rutland Herald*. *Civil Wars* is impressive not only for its similarly calm and commonsense tone, but for the depth of its reporting about the judicial, legislative, and political processes, as well as for its vivid portraits of those who fought for and against the civil unions measure." —*Blade*

"An emotionally moving story . . . [with] many political profiles in courage." —*The Star-Ledger* (New Jersey)

"Offers up a plethora of amazing stories, all brought together by the common thread of an ordinary state being ripped apart—and sewn together—by an extraordinary court case. . . . The book should be studied as a guide to the political and personal turmoil behind the argument for any gay marriage legislation, but it should also be kept in mind as we approach the 2004 presidential election." —*MGW Newspaper*

CIVIL WARS

THE BATTLE FOR GAY MARRIAGE

DAVID MOATS

A HARVEST BOOK
HARCOURT, INC.
ORLANDO   AUSTIN   NEW YORK   SAN DIEGO   TORONTO   LONDON

Requests for permission to make copies of any part
of the work should be mailed to the following address:
Permissions Department, Harcourt, Inc.,
6277 Sea Harbor Drive, Orlando, Florida 32887-6777.

www.HarcourtBooks.com

Sharon Underwood's op-ed piece used courtesy of Sharon Underwood
and the *Valley News* of Lebanon, New Hampshire.

Library of Congress Cataloging-in-Publication Data
Moats, David.
Civil wars: a battle for gay marriage/David Moats.—1st ed.
p.   cm.
ISBN 0-15-101017-X
ISBN 0-15-603003-9 (pbk.)
1. Same-sex marriage—Vermont. 2. Same-sex marriage—Law and legislation—
Vermont. 3. Gay couples—Legal status, laws, etc.—Vermont. 4. Same-sex
marriage—United States. 5. Same-sex marriage—Law and legislation—United
States. 6. Gay couples—Legal status, laws, etc.—United States. I. Title.
HQ1034.U5M62   2004
306.84'8'09743—dc22   2003019811

Text set in Dante MT
Designed by Linda Lockowitz

Printed in the United States of America

First Harvest edition 2005
A C E G I K J H F D B

For my parents,
Loraine H. Moats
and the late William L. Moats, Sr.

As our case is new,
so we must think anew and act anew.

—ABRAHAM LINCOLN

A movement that changes
both people and institutions is a revolution.

—MARTIN LUTHER KING, JR.

CONTENTS

PROLOGUE

I WAS IN California for a short time, visiting with four old friends. We were having dinner at a restaurant in Oakland, and I was trying to explain the fury that had overwhelmed my state. In leaving Vermont behind for a week, I felt I had escaped a war zone. It was a political, social, and cultural war unlike anything I had ever experienced.

You must have heard about it, I said to them, Vermont's new civil unions law, the equivalent of marriage for gays and lesbians. And now—it was October 2000—the state was embroiled in the bitterest election campaign anyone could remember.

Oh, yes, they'd heard about it. Interesting. How did such a thing happen in Vermont?

We poured some more wine. John, Maria, Craig, and Susan were old friends. I had been to college with two of them. We had experienced the turmoil of the Vietnam War era, and after college we were living together at the time of Watergate. We knew about turmoil.

But I remember the frustration I felt trying to convey the full scope of the upheaval that had overwhelmed Vermont during those months. Vermont is a distant corner of the nation, an idiosyncratic combination of the old and the new. How could I make my friends understand what was going on there? I was the editorial page editor for the *Rutland Herald,* and I had written dozens of editorials on the battle then under way. I was yearning to tell them the story that night; though later, as I began to look into it more deeply, I realized that I still didn't know what kind of story I wanted to tell.

What we had experienced in Vermont was the latest tumultuous chapter in a decades-long struggle for civil rights in America. The gay rights movement had emerged later than the movement for racial equality, but both were aimed at securing the dignity of previously scorned minorities. Both confronted ancient prejudices and ignited fierce, sometimes violent, opposition. As author Andrew Sullivan has pointed out, the bar against the freedom to marry in both cases was one of the final taboos to fall.

As I began research for this book, I saw Vermont's civil unions law to be the culmination of a history reaching back at least thirty years. I heard stories of enormous courage and commitment on the part of people struggling during that time to expose a bias that was both politically and personally oppressive. The success of the struggle in Vermont depended on an extraordinary cast of characters, all of whom were essential to the final outcome. They included the six people who brought the lawsuit that was the catalyst for events, their dedicated legal team, the justices of the Vermont Supreme Court, the legislators, a governor, the activists, and the ordinary people from all walks of life who recognized a claim to equality that could no longer be denied.

Ultimately, civil unions in Vermont did not represent victory for the freedom-to-marry movement. It was an important step but also a difficult compromise for those seeking the right to marry, and that battle has continued in other states. As of this writing, the Supreme Judicial Court in Massachusetts was expected to rule at any time in a case similar to that in Vermont.

Even if the men and women seeking the right to marry settled for a half measure in Vermont, they learned something that was an important lesson for the nation as a whole: That what Harvey Milk had said back in the 1970s was true. Milk, the slain San Francisco city supervisor, had urged gays and lesbians across America to stand up openly, with dignity and pride. They would provoke bigotry, of course, but in doing so they would also expose bigotry to the light, touching the conscience of their neighbors in a surprising and gratifying way. It was a truth understood by Martin Luther King, Jr., and a truth that Vermonters put into practice in the battle over gay marriage.

I had come to this story by history and by luck. Like many of my generation, I had been touched early by the power and moral force of the civil rights movement. Hosea Williams, an early associate of King's, made an appearance at my university in 1965, and his call to conscience was compelling enough for me to ask myself why I had cocooned myself within a comfortable college rather than riding a freedom bus to the South. In 1968, following King's assassination, I marched arm in arm with hundreds down State Street in Santa Barbara, singing a hauntingly mournful version of "We Shall Overcome."

But it was also by chance that I happened to witness the story of civil unions in Vermont. I did not come to the issue as a gay man. I came to it as a journalist discovering the most extraordinary story I had ever covered. I had gay and lesbian friends, of course, and, like anyone who manages to look beyond the distinctions of sexual orientation, I was able to see a truth that becomes increasingly plain as the curtains of bias are pulled aside. When love shows up, it does not always obey arbitrary social conventions. It is up to us to follow where it leads. If it is love, it will not be sinful, abusive, or otherwise wrong.

I wrote numerous editorials on the civil unions debate and about the election that followed, and then I went back to learn what had really happened, discovering who brought about the story and what they went through from a personal and political point of view. In my view, the Vermont story ranks, not just with the Stonewall riots and the murder of Harvey Milk as landmarks of gay history, but with Birmingham and Selma as landmarks of our growth toward a more complete democracy.

The result was this book. It was the story I would have told my friends that night at the restaurant in Oakland. It was the story of a historic moment in a small place that echoed widely with a lesson of courage and compassion.

CHAPTER ONE

OUR COMMON HUMANITY

I.

BETH ROBINSON did not expect the call to come that Monday, but at 10:55 A.M. on December 20, 1999, the court clerk was on the line. It could mean only one thing. The Vermont Supreme Court had reached a decision.

The struggle for gay marriage had been waged fitfully for nearly thirty years in courtrooms across the country, gaining a short-lived victory six years before in Hawaii. But Hawaii eventually reversed course, and no jurisdiction in the country had established that gays and lesbians had a right to marry equal to that of heterosexual couples.

Now the Vermont Supreme Court was in a position to lead the way. Robinson had argued the case thirteen months before, urging the court to establish for the first time anywhere in the United States that gay and lesbian couples had the right to marry. For the past year, she and supporters all across the country had been waiting for the outcome.

The court customarily released its decisions on Fridays, and for the last six months Robinson had worn specific outfits to work each Friday to be ready for the press conference that would follow an announcement of the ruling. In the spring and fall she had worn an electric blue suit. For the summer she had a black and white outfit. But Friday had passed three days before without a ruling, only a hint: The court had sent out a message that because of the holidays it might release rulings the following week on a day other than Friday.

Robinson was a 34-year-old lawyer with one of Vermont's most prestigious firms. She was trim and athletic, with an intense gaze, an incisive intellect, and a devotion to the rigors of the law. She had been working on the freedom-to-marry issue for four years, and she knew that people all across the country who had struggled against the indignities of a second-class status had pinned their hopes on her. She had heard the stories of insults endured and rights denied, and she had drawn inspiration from the commitment of people who were willing to fight for legal recognition of their intimate relationships. Since the dawning of the gay rights movement thirty years before, gays and lesbians had been engaged on numerous fronts to establish protections against harassment and hatred, to secure equal rights, and to live with dignity. Now the issue of gay marriage was at the vanguard of the struggle. The decision Robinson waited for on the telephone in Middlebury could well be a landmark in that struggle.

Each of the participants in this political drama had followed a different path to this moment. Some of them were born and raised in Vermont. Others came from as far away as California. Some were gay. Some were straight. Many of them had emerged from the 1960s and 1970s with an idea of Vermont as a community where the individual still mattered.

Vermont was, perhaps, an unlikely setting for such a drama. This was not Castro Street or Christopher Street, the neighborhoods in San Francisco and New York where gay America had staged its sometimes flamboyant, sometimes violent, coming out. This was South Pleasant Street, a shady avenue in Middlebury, a picturesque town of 8,000 where

Robinson was a partner at Langrock Sperry & Wool. It was a practice that handled all the affairs, grand and small, of a small town in a rural state. Peter Langrock, the founder of the firm, had written a book of tales from his practice that included a story about the disputed ownership of a stuffed fish.

The Langrock office was housed in a stately white nineteenth-century house situated between another law practice in another white house and the gray stone Baptist church. A florist's shop, where high school kids bought corsages for their proms, was across the street. Three buildings down, overlooking the green, was the elegant mansion built in 1802 by Gamaliel Painter, the pioneer who was one of Middlebury's founders. During the early decades of the nineteenth century Painter, a signer of Vermont's first constitution, was able to look down from the third-floor monitor—a kind of widow's walk—onto the green, the shops, and mills of the village he had helped to establish on the falls of Otter Creek.

LARRY ABBOTT was the court clerk who had called Robinson that day. He was authorized only to tell Robinson the outcome of the case, in which the Supreme Court was ruling on a lower court finding that the law limiting marriage to heterosexual unions was constitutional.

This is what he read: "The judgment of the superior court upholding the constitutionality of the Vermont marriage statutes under Chapter 1, Article 7 of the Vermont Constitution is reversed."

Robinson felt a surge of elation. She had won. The lower court had been reversed, and excluding gay and lesbian couples from marriage was now unconstitutional.

But Robinson listened with dismay as Abbott continued to read. "The effect of the Court's decision is suspended, and jurisdiction is retained in this Court, to permit the Legislature to consider and enact legislation consistent with the constitutional mandate described within."

Robinson was astounded.

"Larry, what does that mean?"

It was not Abbott's job to tell her what it meant. He told her the ruling would be on the court's Web site at 11 A.M.

To Robinson this was devastating news. It seemed to her like the cruelest defeat. Even so, her mind was already racing ahead. She hung up the phone and broke in on Susan Murray, who was meeting with clients in the adjacent second-floor office. Murray, 41, and Robinson had founded the Vermont Freedom to Marry Task Force four years before, and since then she and Robinson had mapped out a careful legal strategy and had worked assiduously to cultivate grassroots support for their cause.

They had won, Robinson told Murray, but the court had handed the issue to the Legislature. The two lawyers didn't have time to dwell on their joy or their disappointment. Pandemonium broke out at Langrock Sperry & Wool. Months ago Robinson and Murray had made arrangements with the Ramada Inn in South Burlington to use a conference room for a press conference. The whole world would know about this ruling as soon as it appeared on the court's Web site. In the next three hours they had to get up to South Burlington, thirty-five miles away, but they didn't have a clue what they were going to tell the press.

Murray, tall and affable, with flecks of gray in her dark hair, had been at Langrock Sperry & Wool since 1984. She quickly joined Robinson in trying to figure out what to do next. The two staff assistants who were prepared to help them with the press conference were both out with the flu, so the lawyers enlisted other staff members to download a copy of the ruling, get in touch with the Ramada Inn, notify the press, and track down the six plaintiffs.

Murray and Robinson represented one gay and two lesbian couples who had gone to their town and city clerks seeking marriage licenses. The clerks had politely denied all three couples, citing Vermont law and an opinion from the Vermont attorney general's office. The six had sued, and their case had ended up before the Vermont Supreme Court. These six were the public faces of the case, and they needed to be at the press conference.

Robinson and Murray decided the lawyers and clients would have to meet at the firm's Burlington office before the press conference so they could decide what to say about this mystifying decision. In the meantime, Robinson and Murray would have to read the court's ruling. The court had affirmed their clients' right to marry but had suspended its decision. It seemed they had won a victory. But what kind of victory? The news of the decision would soon be on the airwaves nationwide, but the lawyers who had won the case were caught between the joy of victory and the despair of victory deferred.

THAT MORNING Holly Puterbaugh had left her home on Lake Champlain in South Burlington, heading north to pick up her daughter. She had an inkling the court might act this week. Why else would the court issue that peculiar warning last Friday? What case could it have been talking about but theirs?

Holly and her partner, Lois Farnham, had been living together for nearly thirty years, most of that time in Milton, a rural town north of Burlington. Everyone knew them as Lois and Holly, a couple, a part of the community. They ran a Christmas tree business and had served on a variety of town boards and committees. Holly had been deacon of the United Church of Milton, and Lois was head of the women's society at the church. They were also dedicated fund-raisers. They bicycled across the country in 1987 to raise money for the American Lung Association. Six years later, they completed a journey on a tandem bicycle from the Gulf of Mexico to the Canadian border to raise money for a children's camp.

They had met in 1972 when Lois sat down in the front row of a classroom at the University of Vermont where Holly was teaching a class in statistics. "It was love at first sight," Holly remembered, "except at that time I had zero clue that such a thing as a lesbian existed."

Lois had grown up one of twelve children on a farm in the northern Vermont town of Jay. Holly had grown up in a suburb of Dayton, Ohio. After they began their relationship, Lois took Holly to the farm in Chittenden where her family had moved, and Holly got a taste of the farming life. She helped bale hay and butcher a steer. Eventually, they bought a house in Milton and established a life for themselves. If their neighbors in Milton had wanted to think about it, they might have guessed they were lesbians. But if they thought about it, they didn't let on.

Lois and Holly took in fifteen foster children over the years, and in 1994 they adopted one of them, thirteen-year-old Kimberly Farnham. Now, five years later, Kimberly had finished her first semester at Johnson State College about forty miles northeast of Burlington. Lois and Holly had received a call from Kimberly. It was a college freshman's desperate call for clean laundry and home-cooked food, and Holly agreed to come up that Monday and bring Kimberly home.

Holly, 53, was a lecturer in mathematics at the University of Vermont. She was 4 feet, 10½ inches tall, with brown hair, long in back and short in front. Lois was a fifty-five-year-old registered nurse with short-cropped white hair who worked for the public schools in nearby Essex. At about 11 A.M. Lois was still home, and she received a message on her pager to call Langrock Sperry & Wool. When she got through to the law office, the receptionist put Lois on hold, unaware that upstairs the lawyers and their assistants were desperately trying to reach her. After waiting on hold, Lois hung up, and the telephone rang. It was a reporter from WCAX-TV, the CBS affiliate in Burlington.

"What do you think of the decision?" the reporter asked her.

"I don't know anything about it," she said.

She hung up and called Langrock back. She asked the receptionist for either Beth or Susan.

"They're awfully busy," the receptionist said. "What is your interest in the case?"

"I'm a plaintiff!" Lois insisted.

Finally, Beth Robinson got on the phone with Lois and told her the court's decision was both good and bad. Lois could sense Robinson's distress. They would have to meet at Langrock's office in Burlington at 1 P.M. so they could orchestrate their public reaction.

Meanwhile, Holly found Kim at her dorm room and telephoned Lois, but her line was busy. Before heading south, they stopped at a gas station so Holly could call again. The line was still busy, and Holly was beginning to think her instinct about the court decision was right. She had promised she would take Kim out to lunch, but now she thought they ought to head right home.

It was a raw, gray day with a possibility of rain, sleet, or snow, but so far the bad weather had held off. Finally at a gas station near Essex Junction, Holly got through to Lois. It was a win, but it wasn't a win.

It was infuriating to Holly that the state had recognized her and Lois as parents but not as partners. She could only wonder why something as blessed as her relationship with Lois would be so difficult for other people to accept or understand.

NINA BECK and Stacy Jolles were running errands in Burlington on the morning of December 20. Just a month before, Nina had given birth to Seth, their second child, and she was enjoying this chance to get out of the house with Stacy and the baby.

Nina and Stacy had signed on to the case in part to protect their joint parental rights. Their first son, Noah, had died from the effects of a heart defect at the age of two and a half in the summer of 1997 shortly after the lawsuit in their case had been filed.

After Noah died, their lawyers and the other plaintiffs told them that if they didn't want to continue with the case, they didn't have to. Overwhelmed with grief, they withdrew from discussions of the case or public appearances, but they insisted on staying with it. It was the darkest time of their lives, but the loss of Noah had made the case even more compelling for them. Both Nina and Stacy were daughters of Holocaust survivors, and both women were martial arts experts who had taught aikido and kung fu. They thought of themselves as fighters, and they were not about to give up on the case.

Then Nina had conceived again, and on November 20 Seth was born. Now Seth was part of the reason for their struggle.

Their house was just two miles north of Holly and Lois's on a road overlooking Lake Champlain in South Burlington. Nina, 44, and Stacy, 41, arrived home at about 1:30 that afternoon in a cheerful mood, unaware that for two hours television and radio news all across the country had been reporting the outcome of their case. At home, they found that Langrock's office had left four messages on their answering machine. Get to the Ramada, they were told. The press conference will start at 2 P.M. The result was positive, but it was complicated. Get to the Ramada. We'll fill you in.

They headed off for the press conference with Seth in his car seat and Noah's memory riding with them. This was the moment they had been waiting for.

STAN BAKER, 53, was at work that morning at the Counseling Service of Addison County in Middlebury. He was a psychotherapist with curly silver hair who spoke in evenly modulated and reassuring tones. Even the features of his face were soft and reassuring.

It was his name that had been attached to the case, now widely known as the *Baker* case. Baker knew that as the only male couple among the plaintiffs, he and his partner, Peter Harrigan, would be the focus of the most severe hostility. Male homosexuality was more threatening to the culture than lesbianism, and the idea of two men who wished to marry each other was something many people could not grasp. But for Stan and Peter, theirs was a commitment as important and fulfilling as that of their parents'.

It was plain to Stan Baker that marriage between men who loved each other promoted virtues of commitment, stability, and family solidarity—the opposite of the fear-inspired picture drawn by those who opposed gay marriage. Stan's marriage to his wife, Priscilla, had ended after a long struggle on Stan's part to recognize and accept that he was a gay man. Now he believed his relationship with Peter was just as deserving of legal recognition from the state as his marriage to Priscilla had been.

He got a call that morning from Beth Robinson. Get up to Langrock's Burlington office ASAP, she had said. They would have to get their act together before the press conference.

Meanwhile, Peter heard the news on the car radio as he did some Christmas shopping in Burlington that morning. For weeks he and Stan had stayed in touch every Friday in case a decision came down. After hearing the news on the radio, Peter, a thirty-eight-year-old professor of theater, headed home to shave and put on a suit. The curtain was going up on the biggest drama of his life. Stan and Peter both knew that the hopes of gay and lesbian couples all across America were riding on the struggle they had initiated. They did not yet know that in Vermont the struggle was just beginning.

ROBINSON AND Murray had made their phone calls, including a call to Mary Bonauto, a lawyer in Boston who had been instrumental in putting together the case with them. Finally they managed to download a copy of the thirty-page ruling. It was time to go to Burlington.

As they headed north on Route 7, Robinson drove while Murray flipped through the pages of the ruling, which was written by Chief Justice Jeffrey L. Amestoy. She saw quickly that the court's response was complicated: The five-member court had been unanimous in support of Amestoy's ruling, but there was a concurring opinion by Justice John A. Dooley and from Justice Denise R. Johnson there was an opinion that concurred in part and dissented in part.

They traveled through the rolling hills of the Champlain Valley, one of the rare places in Vermont that affords open vistas of long distances. Yet this was not a picture-postcard day. By December 20 the browns and grays of winter dominated the landscape: the mud, the stubble on the brown cornfields, the bare woods, the unpainted barns. Snow was late in coming this year, leaving the landscape forlorn and bleak.

Murray searched the ruling for meaning, reading out sections of Amestoy's words. In the first paragraph she found an important statement:

> The issue before the Court . . . does not turn on the religious or moral debate over intimate same-sex relationships, but rather on the statutory and constitutional basis of the exclusion of same-sex couples from the secular benefits and protections offered married couples.

It was significant that the court was willing to view marriage as a secular institution and remained unswayed by the religious arguments of the opposition.

Amestoy quoted that portion of the Vermont Constitution that formed the basis for his opinion. It is called the Common Benefits Clause. Government was meant to serve the "common benefit," rather than the "particular emolument or advantage" of any person, family, or group.

Robinson had argued that denying gay and lesbian couples the benefits of marriage violated this provision of the Vermont Constitution. *Amestoy got it,* Robinson thought. *So where was the hitch?*

Murray saw in the second paragraph what Amestoy had done. He had found that the state was "constitutionally required to extend to same-sex couples the common benefits and protections that flow from marriage under Vermont law." Then came the part that made this ruling unique. "Whether this ultimately takes the form of inclusion within the marriage laws themselves or a parallel 'domestic partnership' system or some equivalent statutory alternative, rests with the Legislature."

To Robinson the decision was both extraordinary and infuriating. How could Amestoy do this? He had copped out. He had handed the resolution of the case to the Legislature. After all these years, their struggle to win the case on the basis of the law now would become embroiled in the uncertainties and passions of politics.

Murray was more hopeful. The court had retained jurisdiction. If the Legislature failed to provide equal rights, the court would do so.

As they headed down a long slope toward the small city of Vergennes, the view opened up to the west, and they could see the Adirondack Mountains of New York, rank upon rank of mountains, gray in the grim gray light. Robinson lived in Ferrisburgh, the next town north of Vergennes, and they had to stop there so she could change into the electric blue suit she had planned on wearing for so long.

But what kind of victory had she won? If the issue of gay marriage was going to the Legislature, Robinson knew it would unleash the full wrath of Vermont's fundamentalist Christians. Biblical phrases from Romans and Leviticus would be marshaled to condemn the perversity of homosexuals and their "degrading passions." The strategy of opponents, honed in legal battles in Florida, California, and elsewhere by antigay activists twenty years before, would place special emphasis on protecting children. That argument was outrageous to Robinson, who had been particularly touched by the life and death of little Noah.

Robinson and Murray had an additional reason for their commitment to the issue. They were both lesbians, in longterm relationships with their partners. Their own orientation had not entered into the story to any great extent, but they understood better than most the struggle for dignity, respect, and equality that was the compelling motivation behind the case.

Beth Robinson knew she had to contain her emotions, but as they headed north, she felt more and more angry at what she saw as a betrayal of the law. As she listened to Murray reading sections of Amestoy's ruling, she tried to understand what he had done. Amestoy noted that the Common Benefits Clause reflected Vermont's commitment to equal rights, which "was the product of the successful effort to create an independent republic and a fundamental charter of government, the Constitution of 1777, both of which preceded the adoption of the 14th Amendment by nearly a century."

Vermont was one of only three states where settlers had established republics independent of the United States. When the thirteen colonies had declared independence in 1776, Vermont was not among them because it was not a colony. It was a rugged jumble of mountains and valleys wedged between New Hampshire and New York, claimed by both but unwilling to be subsumed by either colony. Vermonters had established their own republic in 1777 and remained independent until the state's admission as the fourteenth state in 1791. This history left Vermont with a sense of its own exceptionalism similar to the exceptionalism that characterized the history of Texas and California.

Now Amestoy was using the Vermont Constitution both to grant and to refrain from granting full rights to gay and lesbian Vermonters. Justice Denise Johnson's dissent contained language urging the kind of action Robinson and Murray had sought.

> I concur with the majority's holding, but I respectfully dissent from its novel and truncated remedy, which in my view abdicates this Court's constitutional duty to redress violations of constitutional rights.

A few minutes later Robinson and Murray were on the strip of highway leading into Burlington, where they would have to explain to their clients what had happened and what they should say when they went before the reporters and the television cameras at the Ramada. They had always planned their public statements with care, making sure everyone clearly understood how to explain the meaning of the case. The politics of gay rights were always volatile, and for four years now they had been engaged in a public relations campaign designed to educate the public and to keep the political waters calm.

As they drove down College Street toward the handsome brick house where Langrock Sperry & Wool had its Burlington offices, Robinson didn't know yet that the politics of the case were already getting ahead of her. Indeed, the political waters ahead were stormier than she could have imagined, and soon she would find herself in the middle of the storm.

2.

FOR WEEKS the office of Governor Howard Dean had been trying to get an inkling of how the court would rule in the *Baker* case. Dean, a Democrat in office for eight years by that time, had approached the issue with caution, refusing to say what ought to be done on the issue of gay marriage. The issue was in the hands of the court. That was his standard response.

Dean had fashioned a reputation in Vermont as a moderate willing to stand up against the liberal wing of his party. He came from a wealthy Long Island family and had moved along the well-traveled route of privilege from prep school to Yale and then to medical school. He had become a physician, and he had married a physician. But his restless energy and his ambition had carried him into politics as a member of the Vermont House and as lieutenant governor. Then on an August morning in 1991 he was treating a patient at his office in Shelburne when word came that Governor Richard Snelling had died. That day Dean was sworn in as governor, and he left his medical practice behind.

He did not want to be blindsided by the issue of gay marriage. He was entertaining thoughts of a run for president, and he wanted to be ready when the court issued its ruling in the *Baker* case. He had been cagey enough not to get too far out in front of the issue, but whatever his larger ambitions, he had no intention of abandoning his commitment to equal rights.

On Monday, Dean was in Burlington, conducting interviews with prospective candidates for state education commissioner. The call came into his Montpelier office at about 10 A.M., informing his staff of the court's decision, and the staff immediately called Dean in Burlington. The court had ruled in favor of the plaintiffs but had left it up to the Legislature to approve gay marriage or what it called a *parallel* institution equivalent to marriage. *Domestic partnership* was the term being used at the time.

Dean was enormously relieved. He knew there would have been far-reaching resentment and protest if the court had imposed gay marriage on Vermont. Even securing domestic partnership legislation would not be easy. But it would allow room for supporters of gay rights to compromise, which might appease some opponents and would steer clear of the word *marriage,* a highly charged term fraught with religious significance.

By 11 A.M., Dean had convened an impromptu press conference where he told the press that the court's decision was "a very elegant solution." He quickly staked out a position against gay marriage and for the alternative. "It's in the best interest of all Vermonters, gay and straight, to go forward with the domestic partnership act and not the gay marriage act. And that's what I intend to do."

He was glad the court hadn't ventured into what he called "uncharted territory."

"I don't think this will be nearly the problem that might have occurred if the court made a more radical decision," he said. And he predicted that the Legislature would never be able to muster the votes for any alternative other than domestic partnership.

Dean was famous in Vermont for his frank manner, which had sometimes gotten him into trouble. On the issue of gay marriage, he made a statement in Burlington that people would remember. "It makes me uncomfortable," he said, "the same as anyone else."

This admission, admirable in its candor, irritated supporters of gay rights, but Dean was touching on an important truth. The fact was a lot of Vermonters were uncomfortable with gay marriage, as they were with the whole idea of homosexuality, which most people were not accustomed to talking about. Members of the Vermont Legislature, who now were required by the court to take up the topic, would be no more comfortable than their constituents, and Dean knew it.

A SHORT TIME later Robinson and Murray reached their offices in Burlington, and they were joined by most of their clients. The clients managed to wolf down some sandwiches as their lawyers bustled in and out of the conference room, making phone calls, trying to clarify their thoughts. Stan Baker, the therapist, remembered later that there was grief to process and there were decisions to make. They needed to hide their disappointment and show their happiness.

None of the couples or their lawyers was prepared for the battle to persuade Vermonters that gays and lesbians deserved the right to marry. Now the court had allowed Vermonters the opportunity to give less than marriage. The phrase that came to Robinson's mind was *separate but equal,* the legal justification used for decades to legitimize school segregation.

But now was not the time to complain or criticize. This was a first step and, although they were disappointed, they all understood they had won a great victory.

Robinson handed a camera to Kimberly Farnham. It would be Kimberly's job to make a photographic record of the day.

As they walked into the Ramada's meeting room, the handful of supporters who had gathered broke into cheers, and news photographers began to snap pictures. Nina Beck and Stacy Jolles arrived as the press conference was starting, and the news photos included baby Seth cradled in Stacy's arms. Lois Farnham remembered thinking, "It's just like on television." In fact, it was television. TV news crews were there as well as reporters from the major Vermont papers and the wire service.

Mary Bonauto, who had made a quick flight up from Boston, told the press:

> This is the first time that any state Supreme Court in this country has not only recognized that same-sex families exist, but for the first time has recognized that they have the same needs and deserve the same protections and rights all other couples and families have. That's a first. That's a legal and cultural milestone.

Beth Robinson wanted to put a positive spin on the decision, but she was not yet willing to allow that anything short of marriage would be satisfactory. She spoke with a sense of urgency.

> It's quite clear that the only remedy that would comply with the court mandate is to allow these folks to marry, because the court made it very clear that the constitution requires that same-sex couples and different-sex couples be treated the same under the law, and the only way that can be done is by granting them marriage licenses.

Robinson was in no way ready to talk about domestic partnership. Separate but equal would not be equal enough for her. She said:

> The court reserved jurisdiction. The court said the Legislature ought to take the first crack at this. But it's got to be constitutional, and that means you've got to treat same-sex couples the same. You've got to provide them with the same array of legal protections.

Then she touched on the political prospects.

> I'm quite sure that the Legislature will look at all sorts of models, but if it studies the court's opinion and it studies what it is the court's trying to accomplish and what the constitution requires, I don't think there's going to be any alternative to full equality short of full equality.

For the plaintiffs, concern over the legalities of the case could not dampen their joy. With Peter's arm resting around his shoulders, Stan Baker addressed the issue of whether gay marriage would weaken the institution of marriage.

> We bring to marriage, all of us, passion, commitment, equality, and love. And that's something that will only strengthen marriage. It's just incredible to have this day come. The reason we're involved in this suit is because we would like that love to be realized in marriage the same way it is for opposite-gender couples.

Holly Puterbaugh was on the verge of tears.

> We wished and prayed that each of us would have a Christmas filled with joy and love. Mine will be. I'm thrilled that the Vermont Supreme Court understands that same-gender couples have relationships that have the

depth and meaning that deserve the rights and protections of marriage. And I can't wait to marry Lois.

Later in the afternoon, gay rights activists and their friends filled the First Unitarian Universalist Society Church at the top of Church Street in Burlington to celebrate the court victory. There were more than one hundred people there that evening as freezing rain began to lash the pavements. The church was decorated with rainbow flags and colorful balloons for a rally that had been planned long before.

The six plaintiffs and their lawyers appeared amid cheers and songs. Stan Baker stood before the crowd with his partner, Peter. "The train has left the station," he exulted. "We may need one stop to get there, but we're going to get there. There's no stopping us now."

There were speeches by numerous supporters. Roddy O'Neill Cleary, an affiliate minister at the church, told the gathering that change strengthens an institution like marriage. Without change, social institutions wither up and die, she said.

Meanwhile, the plaintiffs' true feelings began to find expression in interviews to reporters. Stacy Jolles was furious with the court's unwillingness to go the whole way on gay marriage. "We began this lawsuit because it was about family," she said to a reporter. "Through biological motherhood and second-parent adoption, we were legally connected to [Noah], but we couldn't be legally connected to each other, and that didn't make sense. Anything other than the status of marriage isn't equal," she said, with Seth in her arms. "It's clear we won, and they just need to work out the logistics." Then she said, in reference to Seth, "It's clear that he's going to be better protected."

Lois Farnham, too, was disappointed. "It's a great first step," she said, "but I was hoping we would have a decision, and we could go get our marriage license."

Holly Puterbaugh agreed. "It would be wonderful to be able to set a date and plan it. But you don't always get it exactly the way you want."

Lois Farnham, the only one of the six plaintiffs who was born in Vermont, was optimistic. "Vermonters are ready for doing what's right for people. We always have been, and we always will be." She noted that Vermont was the first state to outlaw slavery. "Now we'll be the first to have same-sex marriage," she said.

3.

THROUGHOUT the day on Monday, word of the court's decision filtered out to legislators at their jobs and homes. Bill Lippert, a Democratic House member from the town of Hinesburg, was at his desk in the small Burlington office occupied by the Samara Foundation, which he had established in 1992. Lippert was the only openly gay member of the Legislature, and the Samara Foundation was dedicated to defending the interests of gay, lesbian, and transgendered Vermonters. He sublet the office from lawyer Eileen Blackwood, and that morning Blackwood came running down the hallway of the office. "They've done it! They've done it!" Blackwood shouted.

But they hadn't done it, Lippert found, as he scanned the court's ruling on his computer screen. It became clear to him immediately that what the court had done was thrust a historic task squarely onto the shoulders of Bill Lippert.

He had purposely taken a position five years before on the House Judiciary Committee, and now he was vice chairman. In that position, he had expected he would have the job of blocking antigay legislation or pushing a domestic partnership bill in the event the court rejected the plaintiffs' claims in the *Baker* case.

But now he had another, more important, role to play. As the only openly gay member, he knew the gay constituency would be looking to him to champion their cause. At the same time, he understood that members of the Legislature were looking to him as well. Thus, Lippert would be a pivotal figure, able to help the gay community understand political realities and able to represent the gay community in the eyes of legislators. How he approached the issue would have crucial influence on House members who were afraid of voter backlash and who were unfamiliar with the reality of homosexuality in Vermont.

Lippert was tall and balding, with a warm smile and a deeply resonant voice. He had short gray hair and a clipped gray beard. In conversation he took pains to search himself for the truth of his feelings. While in the Legislature, he had won the respect of fellow House members, and it was important for him to maintain that respect. He could not be seen as a captive of a special interest group, even one whose cause he believed in.

He knew that Beth Robinson and other advocates would face an excruciating inner struggle about the question of whether to settle for domestic partnership rather than gay marriage. "But it wasn't immediately evident to me that supporting gay marriage was the best thing to do."

Lippert understood that members of the Legislature were terrified of the issue of gay marriage and they would be hardly less terrified of domestic partnership. He had spoken privately with some members, hoping that if there were ever a bill to make gay marriage illegal, they would vote against it. Fellow members of the Judiciary Committee had agreed they would oppose such a bill, but some wanted Lippert to promise they would never have to vote on a bill that would legalize gay marriage. Lippert assured them they wouldn't have to do that. That was being taken care of through the courts. Or so he had hoped.

During the rest of that Monday, Lippert was on the phone with friends around the country, trying to assess his own feelings and weigh his political options. He immediately saw that the coming legislative session would be one of the most demanding experiences of his life. He knew the kind of hatred that would surface and the pressures fellow House members would be subject to. They would be pulled by numerous crosscurrents: their own religious beliefs, the anger of their constituents, the views of the court. Lippert would be able to add another factor: He could put a human face on what it meant to be gay in Vermont.

Before long, Lippert was in touch with Michael Obuchowski, the speaker of the Vermont House, and other House members who would meet within a few days to chart their course for the coming session. It was obvious this issue would dominate the session as no issue ever had before.

Over the past decade, gays in Vermont and elsewhere in the country had been making incremental gains. In the late 1980s and the 1990s, more than a dozen cities had established benefits for domestic partners that included gay partners. Massachusetts and California had approved domestic partnership benefits as had nearly eight hundred corporations. In Vermont, state employees won domestic partnership benefits from the state labor board. In these cases, the benefits available to partners were specific and limited and came nowhere near to matching the full array of benefits and responsibilities that accompanied marriage.

Yet the issue of gay marriage was about more than marriage. It was about how far a secular democracy would expand its arena of freedom.

Steadily, over fifty years, that arena had been widened. No one seriously argued anymore that restaurant owners had the right to deny service to African Americans or that employers had the right to discriminate against women. Even so, it was the late 1990s, and nowhere in the United States had it been established that the partner of a homosexual had rights with regard to probate, medical care, child custody, or property equivalent to the rights that marriage gave.

As it turned out, the struggle to secure the benefits of marriage for gay and lesbian Vermonters would become a lesson in democracy on a human scale; neighbors with fiercely clashing views were thrown into the political cauldron together without the interference of large-scale media politicking or the machinations of large interest groups.

It would become apparent that the issue of marriage touched a far more sensitive nerve than did the question of whether a few limited benefits might be shared by a domestic partner. Gay marriage forced the full reality of homosexuality squarely in front of the American public. Marriage was about sex and the most profound human passions. It was about how society organized itself. It touched on fundamental religious doctrines and constitutional principles. The Vermont Supreme Court had forced the people of Vermont to confront these issues more directly than anyone had before. As Lippert reflected later, "The world shifted on December 20, 1999."

TOM LITTLE took a call at his Burlington office informing him of the Supreme Court decision. Little, a Republican, was chairman of the House Judiciary Committee, which meant that any bill about gay marriage or domestic partnership would probably originate in his committee. Though most of the participants had expected that gay marriage would either win or lose in the court, Little had confided in some House members his suspicion that the court would seek to involve the Legislature in order to put a stamp of political legitimacy on the resolution of the case.

Little, 45, was low-key in manner and unrevealing in expression, with reserves of humor and intelligence in his eyes. He had a law practice with offices on St. Paul Street, overlooking City Hall Park in Burlington. On that gray December day he could look out from his second-floor windows onto the bare branches of the maples in the park.

He was a member in good standing of the Chittenden County Republican establishment. His father, George Little, had been a state senator, and during Tom Little's first term, they had served in the Legislature together. Tom Little represented Shelburne, the wealthiest town in Vermont.

December was the busiest time of the year for Little's law practice, and he had little time to devote to politics that day. He called his father and his wife, Susan, with the news, as well as members of the Judiciary Committee. He believed members of the Freedom to Marry Task Force would be bitterly disappointed by the ruling, but he believed the court had done the right thing. For society to accept the fact of gay marriage or domestic partnership, society would have to address the issue squarely, confronting and overcoming the prejudices that stood as obstacles to equal rights. "Leaving out the Legislature would have been a mistake," Little said.

In the next few days Little would have to get together with Lippert, Obuchowski, and others to develop a legislative strategy. They needed to decide whether a bill would originate in the House or Senate. If it were to originate in the House, it would be the work of Little's committee to write it. That would put him at the center of an issue with national implications, and it would be up to him to chart a steady course.

As he told a reporter that day, "The Legislature is going to need a lot of strong leadership in order to handle the issue professionally and fairly and expeditiously."

It would have been contrary to his self-effacing manner for him to carry that thought to its logical conclusion: that he would be the one to exercise that leadership.

DERBY, VERMONT, is a world away from Burlington. It is in the far northeast of the state on the Canadian border, which runs right through the middle of the Haskell Free Library and Opera House, a town landmark.

Nancy Sheltra, fifty-one years old at the time, was the Republican House member from Derby. During nine years in office, she had made a name for herself as one of the Legislature's most ardent opponents of legalized abortion and gay rights.

She heard the news of the *Baker* decision in the middle of the day, and she saw it as another sign of the drift of American society toward the kind of secular humanism she believed was ruining the nation. She was disappointed but not surprised by the ruling. Vermont had strayed so far to the left she had almost come to expect the continuing advance of causes that, in her view, ran counter to God's word.

God's word, not the ideals of liberal democracy, shaped Nancy Sheltra's politics. In conversation, religious certainties tumbled forth without apology. "If you want to be a nation that is blessed, we have to follow biblical teachings," she said. "There is no separation of church and state. That was originally put in place to protect the church."

On the day of the court decision, she talked to her pastor, Fred Barker of the United Church of Derby, and she talked with friends who were concerned about what the Legislature would do in response to the ruling.

Sheltra was not sanguine about the Legislature's willingness to oppose gay marriage. "I knew at that point it would pass the Legislature," she said later, "because the Supreme Court would not have done that unless they had the Legislature lined up." But as she and her fellow legislators would discover during a protracted three-month-long battle, the Legislature was far from lined up.

In a way, Sheltra saw herself as a voice in the wilderness. She knew she could never have been elected in Burlington or other liberal districts because she never could have voted the way the people would have wanted her to vote. As a representative from the Northeast Kingdom, a region of vast woodlands, small towns, and conservative politics, her efforts to bring the biblical word to the State House were viewed more favorably than they would have been in trendy Burlington. Her insistence that the Bible condemned homosexuality would make her one of the most outspoken opponents of the court's decision and the Legislature's effort to craft a law in response.

It was the early push for gay rights in the 1970s that had given impetus to the emergence of fundamentalist Christian movements such as the Moral Majority. And nothing energized the religious right more than the prospect of gay marriage, a threat that brought together diverse religious denominations, including Baptists, Roman Catholics, and Mormons. In the view of opponents, any effort by the state to recognize the legitimacy of homosexual relationships was a violation of God's word. That view would be heard in Vermont following the court's ruling in the *Baker* case, and Sheltra would become its most vocal exponent.

———

ABOUT 25 MILES to the south of Derby in the town of Craftsbury, Bob Kinsey was out stacking wood on December 20. Kinsey, 72, had the broad shoulders and thick hands of a man who had farmed all his life. In addition to his farmwork, he had served in the Legislature for twenty-nine years, including four years as assistant Republican leader and four years as Republican leader.

He still did all the work on the farm except the milking, which was handled by his son Jeffrey. By winter Bob had firewood piled high around the doorway of the small white farmhouse where he and his wife, Eunice, had raised seven children. He was an elder at the East Craftsbury Presbyterian Church, and he and Eunice had sung in the choir there for fifty-two years.

The dramatic events taking place in Montpelier and Burlington that day did not reach Bob Kinsey until evening when he leaned back in his recliner and heard the news on television.

It wasn't the end of the world for him. He expected he would vote against any kind of gay marriage or domestic partnership bill. He was not a conservative in the mold of Nancy Sheltra; he had supported abortion rights for women. But he was nervous about the prospect that Vermont might become a mecca for gays and lesbians. He didn't think that would be good for Vermont.

He had neighbors who were gay. For a time, there was a psychologist in town, a gay man, who had lived with another man, an artist. There were others he was acquainted with, and the question of sexual orientation didn't matter to Kinsey one way or the other.

The Legislature would convene in two weeks, and he would focus on the issue then. In the meantime, he had to make sure his wood supply was ready for the long winter. Already tonight, the freezing rain was pounding on the roof of the old farmhouse.

FROM THE windows of his corner chambers on the third floor of the Supreme Court building, Jeffrey L. Amestoy, who had been named chief justice in 1997, could look up a knoll to his right to the Vermont State House, its golden dome gleaming against the dark hillside behind it. If he turned to his left, he could see the Pavilion Office Building, where the governor's offices occupied the fifth floor. The three branches of government stood in a row, and in the center was the Supreme Court.

It had been a hard year for Amestoy. He had been born and raised in Rutland but in recent years his mother had been living in Sausalito, California. She was ill and in the final months of her life, and Amestoy had made several trips to be with her. At the same time, he was working on a ruling in a case with national implications that had the potential for tearing his state apart.

Amestoy's unassuming manner and his sense of humor had made him a popular figure around Montpelier during more than fourteen years as the Republican attorney general. In fact, he had served so long as attorney general he began to refer to himself as the "eternal general." There was usually a boyish twinkle in his eye, and more often than not he was as happy to talk about baseball as about the law. But he was fifty-three now, and his cheeks were lined by creases. The thick shock of hair that shot up from his head as if drawn by a cartoonist was now white.

Amestoy had pushed to have the *Baker* decision finished before Christmas and the start of the legislative session in the first week of January. The court staff had put in long hours over the weekend copying and collating the decision, and the court had taken the unusual step of announcing a decision on Monday.

Amestoy had been determined to craft a ruling that would win the unanimous support of the court, but he had been unwilling to adopt the approach favored by Justice Denise Johnson, granting gays and lesbians the immediate right to marry.

In the end Johnson had concurred in part and dissented in part. Johnson had a history of writing sharply worded dissents, and she had written one in the *Baker* case. She had referred to Amestoy's decision to turn the matter over to the Legislature as a "truncated remedy." She had accused the majority of an "abdication" of its constitutional duty.

Amestoy had responded by writing that Johnson "greatly underestimates what we decide today and greatly overestimates the simplicity and effectiveness of her proposed mandate."

Amestoy wrote that his opinion "provides greater recognition of—and protection for—same-sex relationships than has been recognized by any court of final jurisdiction in this country with the instructive exception of the Hawaii Supreme Court."

Hawaii was instructive because in 1993 the Supreme Court there had ruled in favor of same-sex marriage, leaving the legislature out of the process. The people of Hawaii responded with a referendum amending the constitution and allowing the legislature to ban same-sex marriage, which the legislature had done. By involving the Vermont Legislature in the resolution of this case, Amestoy hoped to reach an outcome that would have firmer political support.

In his ruling, Amestoy quoted a *Harvard Law Review* article by Cass R. Sunstein, titled "Foreword: Leaving Things Undecided":

> When a democracy is in moral flux, courts may not have the best or the final answers. Judicial answers may be

wrong. They may be counterproductive even if they are right. Courts do best by proceeding in a way that is catalytic rather than preclusive and that is closely attuned to the fact that courts are participants in the system of democratic deliberation.

The system of democratic deliberation would now begin with a vengeance in Vermont. But Amestoy could breathe a sigh of relief. His work was done.

AS DARKNESS fell on Montpelier that afternoon, the national media picked up on the *Baker* decision. Dr. Laura Schlessinger, a talk-radio host, gave out Governor Dean's phone number over the air, and soon Dean's office was flooded with calls.

Pro- and anti-gay rights groups chimed in. Gary Bauer, the conservative Republican presidential candidate, denounced the ruling. In some ways, he said, it was "worse than terrorism."

Robert Knight of the Family Research Council said of the Vermont court, "They did something very wrong, which was to impose marital-type benefits on non-marital relationships. That undermines the authority of marriage. It undermines its importance in society."

Evan Wolfson, a lawyer for the Lambda Legal Defense and Education Fund, was one of the nation's leading advocates for the freedom to marry, and he had consulted with the lawyers in the *Baker* case. He told CBS News: "It's a substantive, important legal victory that says that gay people and our families are entitled to full and legal protections under the law."

National news organizations immediately picked up on the story. John Roberts of CBS News told viewers: "In Vermont the state Supreme Court broke new ground on the front lines of gay rights."

Connie Chung on ABC reported: "The ruling makes Vermont the only state that's on the road to recognizing gay unions."

Tom Brokaw of NBC reported that gay activists had praised the ruling as "a major breakthrough since it could affect everything from adoption to inheritance to health care."

AT THE *Rutland Herald,* the story moved on the AP wire in the late morning, and I knew immediately that we would have to respond decisively. I read Amestoy's ruling, I struggled through Dooley's concurring opinion, and I read Johnson's concurrence and dissent. I was not acquainted at the time with the parties to the case, and I knew little more about the freedom-to-marry movement than what I had read in the paper. Like perhaps a majority of the heterosexual population, I was aware of and sympathetic to the gay rights struggle, but until that day I was largely removed from it.

After December 20 no one could be removed. The language of the Supreme Court described the issue with compelling moral force. The court's frequent reference to the nation's landmark civil rights cases made clear the issue of marriage for gays and lesbians represented an important new chapter in the broader movement for civil rights in America.

It was plain to me that the state of Vermont had reached a crossroads, and I believed the newspaper could serve as an example, showing it was possible to take a stand even as a hurricane of controversy was beginning to blow. That day I wrote an editorial praising the Supreme Court. The headline over the editorial said, A BRAVE RULING.

AMESTOY HAD based his ruling on the Vermont Constitution, and his opinion had included a historical analysis of the egalitarian principles underlying that 1777 document.

In a sense, those advocating gay marriage were refighting

the fight of Thomas Jefferson, seeking to protect the secular sphere from the overweening authority of religion. The fundamentalists who opposed gay marriage may have wished they could have that fight over again, combating the natural-rights philosophy and the deism of Jefferson, which they might today denounce as secular humanism. But in the American system, the moral worth of the individual is a value that trumps the moral judgments of any particular sect, allowing previously marginalized groups the legal basis for asserting their dignity.

In confronting the issue of gay marriage, the nation confronts a paradox of liberal democracy. The dignity of the individual was a moral value that rested on religious and philosophical traditions prevailing in eighteenth-century Britain and its colonies. Yet liberal democracy lifts that value into the secular realm, where it serves as the premise for equality and justice before the law.

Religious teachings used to justify unequal treatment of African Americans, women, or homosexuals run counter to that premise. But the methods of secular democracy require that the religious argument supporting unequal treatment be countered by a secular argument about the fairness of the law.

It is well-known that Christian teaching served as the headwaters of the American civil rights movement, but the civil rights movement achieved its gains because when Martin Luther King, Jr., talked about "all God's children," his understanding of individual dignity was easily translated into the secular language of the U.S. Constitution.

It has been the struggle of the gay rights movement, including the freedom-to-marry movement in Vermont, to establish that homosexuals are also God's children and to show that our system of secular laws demands respect for their inherent worth. Gays and lesbians face an additional challenge because, for many people, it is not apparent that homosexuality is anything other than a lifestyle choice. And, if it is a life-style choice, it may be subject to moral condemnation in the way that adultery and promiscuity are condemned. And certainly it need not be sanctioned by the state.

The debate over gay marriage, therefore, involves more than a question of constitutional rights. It requires people to engage in a searching discussion of sexuality and the nature and importance of sexual attachment. In Vermont gay rights activists had to win not only the constitutional argument, they also had to confront the visceral repugnance that, for whatever reason, homosexuality inspired in many people.

For many Vermonters the issue of gay marriage made its appearance with shocking suddenness on the day of the *Baker* decision. Could it be true that Vermont was preparing to legalize gay marriage? How could this have happened? In fact, the *Baker* decision was a shock only because most people preferred to avert their eyes from issues involving homosexuality. December 20 was one passing moment. The movement that brought the *Baker* case into view was a river flowing in plain sight from the fundamental fissures within society relating to civil rights, sexual autonomy, the changing family, and religious sectarianism. The river ran deep, and it went all the way back to the first stirrings of the gay rights movement thirty years before, through legal and political turbulence over issues such as hate crimes, discrimination, and adoption. The case itself had been in the works for four years. Many citizens didn't see this history. Instead, they saw themselves confronted by a moral question that was unfamiliar and threatening to them.

Thus, the debate about gay marriage fractured the state in a way it had never experienced. For many Vermonters, the demand by gays and lesbians for the rights and benefits of marriage was another step on the slope toward moral degradation. A grassroots movement calling on Vermonters to "take back

Vermont" from liberals, flatlanders, gays, environmentalists, and other presumed non-Vermonters would lead a furious backlash. Unlike antigay movements in other parts of the country, the take-back-Vermont movement was as much nativist as it was religious in inspiration. In response to that nativist appeal, however, the demand for respect and understanding became just as strong. Defenders of gay rights looked to another native tradition, Vermont's long history as an opponent of slavery and a place of tolerance. They also took comfort in the final sentence of Amestoy's ruling, which was one of its most frequently quoted passages:

> The extension of the Common Benefits Clause to acknowledge plaintiffs as Vermonters who seek nothing more, nor less, than legal protection and security for their avowed commitment to an intimate and lasting human relationship is simply, when all is said and done, a recognition of our common humanity.

AFTER THE cheering stopped at the Unitarian Church, it was finally time to go home. Robinson, Murray, and their six clients had ridden an emotional roller coaster that day, none more so than Robinson.

When she made it home to Ferrisburgh, she finally broke down and wept. She told her partner, Kim Boyman, that she would not take any calls. All her hopes had come crashing down even as the greatest victory of her career was being hailed across the country.

Robinson had never expected she would have to take her battle to the people of Vermont. How much faith could she put in the people? It had been a long struggle just to gain a measure of acceptance and respectability among the many friendly and well-disposed Vermonters she had met during the past four years. It was going to be an altogether more serious struggle when she would be forced to confront the determined opposition of opportunistic politicians, impassioned religious zealots, and outright homophobes.

She had believed in the law and the law's power to shine a clear light on the constitutional requirements of equality and justice. But the law had let her down. Now Vermont would have to make new law, and the battle to do that would begin the very next day.

CHAPTER TWO

BEGINNINGS

I.

A YOUNG Bill Lippert dug into the pocket of his jeans for coins. There was an old-fashioned phone booth, with a folding door, in the back of Calvi's, a soda fountain and newsstand on Main Street in Middlebury. The phone booth would allow him the privacy he needed for the important and frightening phone call he was about to make.

It was the fall of 1972, a turbulent time, and a whole generation of people Lippert's age was on the move. He was twenty-two years old, and he had graduated from college that June. Passersby on Main Street could not help but notice the tall young man with the full brown beard and the long ponytail braided down his back. Ordinary Vermonters, still absorbing the changes brought about by the younger generation, might have labeled him a hippie. They would have little notion that one day he would become an important member of the Vermont Legislature and a central figure in the most controversial issue of the time.

He was born in Port Trevorton, a tiny town in central Pennsylvania where his father was minister for two churches, the United Brethren and the Evangelical Church. Bill was the oldest of four children, and it was expected he would grow up to be a minister, too. He was active in the church as a young man; in 1968 he was a youth representative to a United Brethren gathering in Dallas.

The Reverend William Lippert, Sr., served churches all up and down the Susquehanna River in central Pennsylvania, and by the time Bill Jr. was in high school, they were living in Williamsport. Late in high school, Bill was becoming aware of something about himself that was the cause of much private agony and searching introspection. It was dawning on him that he was gay, which he believed would prevent him from following his father into the ministry.

After high school, he attended Earlham College, a Quaker institution in Richmond, Indiana, where he studied Western European history. It wasn't until late in his years at Earlham that he got up the nerve to go to a college counselor to talk about his sexual orientation.

In some colleges, such an admission would have been grounds for immediate dismissal. Lippert was wracked by confusion, guilt, and fear as he sat down with the counselor. He didn't want anyone to know that he was gay. He had never known a gay person, or to put it more precisely, he was not *aware* of knowing anyone gay. He was petrified that his parents would find out. But it was something he had to admit, to himself and, at least for now, to the counselor.

Years later he remembered the one piece of advice the counselor had for him. "You will probably have to go to a large city," he said.

THOUSANDS of gay Americans were reaching the same conclusion during those years, thronging to gay communities in New York, San Francisco, and other cities. It was during the summer of 1972 that Harvey Milk moved from New York to San Francisco, where he established a photo shop and became one of the most influential people in the emerging gay rights movement.

Three years before, riots at the Stonewall Inn, a dingy, Mafia-controlled dive in Greenwich Village, had brought the gay rights movement out into the open. The riots began on a Friday night, June 27, when the New York City police came under siege during a routine raid of the Stonewall.

The Sheridan Square neighborhood was teeming with young people that evening, and they were ready to believe the worst about the police. The antiwar and civil rights movements had already acquainted many in the milling crowd with the brutal methods the police employed to harass protesters or minorities. So when a drag queen decided to resist arrest, the crowd joined in. They threw trash cans and ripped up parking meters and eventually forced the police to retreat into the inn until they were rescued by reinforcements.

The riots at the Stonewall lasted for three nights and touched off a wave of activism among gays comparable to the activism that had swept up antiwar protesters, blacks, and other groups.

By 1972 gay activists were working in all the large cities, commemorating the Stonewall riots in many places each June with gay pride parades, struggling to gain political power, and proclaiming more openly than ever before their right to a free and open sexual life.

At the time, the issue of gay marriage was far from the top of the agenda for the gay rights movement. But it was an issue of importance for some gay activists, including two young men in Minneapolis who had brought the issue into the open in 1970 when they announced their plans to marry.

Jack Baker was the leader of a gay student group at the University of Minnesota, and Mike McConnell had been hired by the university to work as a cataloguer at the university library. Their application for a marriage license had two results: The clerk of court rejected the application, and the University of Minnesota withdrew the job it had offered to McConnell.

The McConnell-Baker case became an early test of the marriage issue, though the gay activists who belonged to Baker's group were more interested in gay liberation than in gay marriage. Baker's group was called Fight Repression of Erotic Expression, and the freedom to be sexual without harassment or punishment was a more important goal than the freedom to marry.

Eventually, the Minnesota Supreme Court rejected the idea of same-sex marriage, and the U.S. Supreme Court let the Minnesota court's ruling stand. A federal appeals court also upheld the position of the University of Minnesota, denying McConnell a job. Similar lawsuits in Wisconsin and Kentucky seeking to establish the right to same-sex marriage also went down to defeat in those years.

In the summer of 1972, these events were far removed from the life of Bill Lippert. He had graduated that spring, and he took his college counselor's advice and moved to Philadelphia for the summer. In June he went to a meeting of the Gay Activists Alliance, and he became swept up in a social life like none he had never imagined. There were dances, movies, baseball games. He had never heard of the gay pride parades that had been held in June for the past three years, but after he became enamored with one of the leaders of the Alliance, he was invited to attend the march in New York City. It turned his world upside down.

Even so Lippert was not sure about life in the city. He had grown up in small towns, and he had observed the intimate settings within which his father was able to practice his ministry. So

Lippert leaped at the chance to join his parents and his brother Tim later that summer for a hike in the hills of Vermont.

He had applied for a job at a bookstore in Philadelphia, and he decided if he got that job, he would head back. Otherwise, he decided he would stay in Vermont for a while. His summer in Philadelphia had shown him, in his words, that he was "a small-town guy." And the advice of the college counselor, though well-intentioned, had overlooked the fact that there were gays and lesbians on farms and in small towns all across the country. They did not enjoy the protection of large numbers or anonymity that gays and lesbians enjoyed in the cities. But Lippert knew they were there. He had been one of them.

As it turned out, he didn't get the job in the bookstore. He ended up renting a room on Seminary Street in Middlebury and taking a night job with a company in East Middlebury that manufactured small wooden toys. For a time, he spent his nights spray painting wooden trains and rocking horses.

WHAT MAKES someone like Bill Lippert a small-town guy? What was it about Middlebury that drew him away from the excitement and camaraderie of gay Philadelphia?

The appeal of small-town America is lodged in the American consciousness as firmly as the contrary appeal of the city. During the 1970s a renewed interest in country life arose as an antidote to the growing violence and decay of urban America. In this period, Wendell Berry, the writer from Kentucky, wrote *The Unsettling of America,* in which he promoted the value of a respectful and restrained relationship with the land. He also promoted a view of the family and of marriage in which each person had a constructive role to play in fashioning a life on the land and where the family itself thrived on its common dedication to enduring values.

Berry's was not the only voice celebrating rural life and the value of the natural environment. But he gave insightful expression to a view that was conservative in a radical way. Out of his social critique of modern America came a view that found value in traditional things, including marriage.

Even if they didn't want to work on the land, many of the new Vermonters of that time came to the state with the belief that living in the countryside or in the small towns and cities of Vermont would allow them to adhere to the simple, wholesome values that Berry celebrated. It was a good place to raise a family. That some of these newcomers were gay should not be surprising. Nor should it be surprising that family was important to them as well.

During the 1960s and 1970s, Vermont enjoyed a population gain unprecedented since the 1820s. Newcomers came from all parts of the country, and journalists wrote of a "rural renaissance." The new Vermonters learned how to plant gardens, can tomatoes, and split wood. There were a few well-known communal experiments, following a tradition of experimental living that went back to the early nineteenth century. But more lasting and important was the arrival of young men and women like Bill Lippert who were hoping not to live apart but to become a part of life in Vermont.

My wife, Kathy Clarke, and I arrived in Vermont one sultry day in July 1975. We had been married the previous April at our apartment in San Francisco and shortly thereafter packed our belongings into a Volkswagen van and drove across the country. We did not fashion ourselves part of a social movement. Kathy had attended college in Vermont, and back in San Francisco, we had examined a map showing the many small towns tucked within the state's hilly landscape. Many of those towns had their own small newspapers, she told me. Surely I could find a job there. By 1977 I was the managing editor of a weekly paper in Middlebury, the *Valley Voice,* and we owned a small white-clapboard house across from a picturesque church in the village of Salisbury. At the schoolyard down the road, our three children played baseball and soccer, and in the winter they sledded down the steep embankment above the baseball field.

For the generation of our parents, the iconography of small-town life had been fixed in the American consciousness through the work of artist Norman Rockwell, who did much of his most popular work while living in Arlington, Vermont. The appeal of Rockwell in the '30s, '40s, and '50s had to do partly with the nostalgia felt by millions of Americans whom events had transported to cities and suburbs far from the small towns where they had grown up. By the 1970s young refugees from urban areas were streaming back to the small towns their parents' generation had left behind.

Bill Lippert could experience this small-town ideal if he walked down South Street on a Saturday afternoon, maple leaves brilliant overhead, fine old houses—mostly white—on either side of the street. He would have heard the cheering crowds at the high school football games just across the river. The autumn afternoons would be bracing and clear, and as homeowners raked the leaves in their tidy yards, Lippert would have had an intimation of the home he had left behind.

But he was looking for more than a Norman Rockwell image of small-town life. His awakening as a gay man had alerted him to another reality that remained hidden from view. In Middlebury there was no trace of gay life. There were no social events, no organizations, no gay bars, no means by which gay people could safely identify one another. Gays and lesbians in the cities may have enjoyed the solidarity of their increased visibility, but in rural America it remained highly risky to be identified as a gay man.

So when Middlebury College organized a symposium on sexuality that fall, Lippert went. One session had to do with homosexuality, a topic still so delicate in Vermont that the organizers of the symposium had to invite gay people from Boston to come up and talk about being gay. During that session, Lippert was aware of a bristling tension in the room. He knew the room was full of gay and lesbian students, but no one would admit it.

In Philadelphia Lippert had seen and felt the joy that could follow from a willingness to be open about one's sexual orientation. If he was going to stay in Vermont, he was not going to allow himself to live in isolation. So he searched out the organizer of the symposium. He said he was gay and that he didn't know any other gay people in Vermont. Wasn't there anyone who was out? Weren't there at least the beginnings of gay consciousness in Vermont?

It turned out there was someone. The college administrator told Lippert about a man named Donald Poole, who lived by himself in a trailer in the mountain town of Lincoln. Lippert might want to give Donald Poole a call.

So Bill Lippert stood on the sidewalk in front of Calvi's digging for the change needed to make the call from that old-fashioned phone booth. What would he say to Donald Poole? How do you call up someone out of the blue and ask him if he is gay?

He slid the door of the phone booth shut and sat on the little seat. He tried to formulate the words he would say. Finally, he dialed the number.

"Hello?"

"Hello. Is this Donald Poole?"

"Yes."

"My name is Bill Lippert. I understand that you're interested in gay liberation."

He had said it. He didn't know it at the time, but this phone call was a first step in the struggle for gay rights in Vermont.

Donald Poole was about thirty years old, a gay man who supported himself by making candles and who was as flamboyant and out as a gay man was likely to be in Vermont. He wore an ostentatious leather coat and maintained a defiant attitude that, as Lippert remembered it, drew verbal taunts on the street. Lippert recalled that Poole did not fit the stereotype of what a man was supposed to look like, and it made Lippert nervous to walk down the street with him. But Poole had gay friends, and Lippert said he was interested in getting together. There were six or seven of them, and eventually they began to meet each week at a different person's house, forming a support group for gay men that would continue for years to come.

Lippert still had some unfinished business, however. He still had not told his parents he was gay.

In the winter of 1973, he came down with a case of mononucleosis, and he had to return to Pennsylvania for several months to convalesce. Finally, one evening at dinner he worked up his courage to tell them.

His mother, Joanna Wentz Lippert, said something that remained with him for years. She was upset but not for the reason he had expected. "How could you have imagined," she said, "that I could do anything but love you?"

His father, who had a degree in psychology and whose ministry involved much personal counseling, was also supportive. It was an enormous relief for Bill, and he was able to move back to Vermont with the feeling that he could continue to communicate with his parents about the reality of his life. The acceptance he had from them contrasted starkly with the experience of some of his gay friends.

Lippert's brother Jonathan later shone a different light on his parents' reactions. "You don't know what it was like to them when you weren't there," he said to Bill. Jonathan, who was also gay, saw how his parents had to wrestle with Bill's revelation, and he vowed he would never come out to his parents. It was a vow he would break six months later.

Back in Vermont, Bill began a life that would lead to a career as a therapist, taking his father's spiritual ministry into the secular world. He also became a leader in the nascent gay rights movement of Vermont, a respected public figure, unapologetic about who he was and a model for other gay people struggling to accept their identity.

Lippert's story was of a young gay man finding a home in a new place and seeking to enlarge the space of comfort for gays and lesbians in his corner of the nation. That corner of the nation had slumbered for a hundred years as a poor, rural backwater, dominated by the politics of thrifty Republicans. They used to say that when the Depression hit Vermonters didn't notice. During the latter part of the twentieth century, Republican control of state politics had weakened. Even so, the anti-slavery origins of the state's Republican Party had shaped the state's political heritage, and political figures leading the way on gay marriage included Republicans and Democrats who understood that gay marriage was fundamentally a question of civil rights. Two members of the Vermont House, one from the country, one from the city, would demonstrate how the evolving politics of Vermont had grown increasingly hospitable to claims of equal rights. Bob Kinsey, farmer, legislator, father, husband, was a sort of Vermont Everyman, emblematic of how ordinary Vermonters were willing to confront the issue. Tom Little, a lawyer from the city, provided the leadership necessary for Vermont to weather its most turbulent conflict while adhering to the fundamental principles of secular democracy.

2.

IT WAS EARLY February 1947, and Bob Kinsey hoisted himself into the bus that would take him from the little town of Barton to Montpelier. Kinsey was a slugging outfielder on the Barton town team and one of the top baseball prospects in all Vermont. One day he received a letter from Carl Hubbell, the great New York Giants left-hander who in the '40s was the team's chief scout. In the letter Hubbell told Kinsey to report to Palatka, Florida, for spring training. Kinsey would be playing outfield for the New Orleans Pelicans, a minor-league team in the Giants' farm system.

Kinsey was only nineteen, a brawny farm boy who had worked hard all of his life on the farm where the family milked thirty-five cows and delivered milk to customers every day. When the snow got deep in the winter, Kinsey hitched a team of horses to the front of the family pickup truck and stood on the front bumper with a hand on the rear end of each horse. His mother drove, the horses pulled, and they managed to get through the snow on their quarter-mile driveway.

Although he was heading to an exotic and unfamiliar place, Bob Kinsey was worried mainly about whether he could hit professional pitching. The bus from Barton took him to the train depot in Montpelier, and he had to wait there for five hours to catch the train. During those five hours, his doubts about leaving home—and about leaving a young woman named Eunice— grew. If the train had been there when he got to the depot, he probably would have gotten aboard and headed south. But after spending five hours considering his future, he decided to return home, walking all night in the midwinter cold.

Soon he and Eunice were married, and Bob was working on a farm in East Craftsbury when an old bachelor farmer, Ora

Anderson, told Bob he would lend him some money so he and Eunice could buy a farm on the road between East Craftsbury and South Albany. The farm with its 347 acres had been up for sale for seven or eight years, and it was in poor shape, but the Kinseys were able to buy it for $6,300.

It was 1948, and the road to South Albany consisted of two tracks in the grass, lined on both sides by high trees and stone walls. But as remote as it was, Kinsey figured an enterprising farmer could make a go of it. Kinsey began with twenty-three cows, using electric milking machines and an electric cooler for the milk.

The kind of life the Kinseys led resonates with the persistent and cherished myth of the self-sufficient rural household, in which man and woman share the duties of husbandry and domesticity, with children working along beside them. It was Wendell Berry without the poetry. Mostly, it was a lot of work.

When people talked about the real Vermont, this was it. If the outsider viewed it as the embodiment of a rural mythology, those who lived it experienced it as a round of endless labor—stacking hay bales on sweltering afternoons or repairing broken machinery at twenty degrees below. What made the hard work worth it was the family itself; studio portraits of all seven children covered one wall of the Kinsey living room, and in conversation Kinsey was quick to mention the accomplishments of each of his children.

The round of constant labor did not keep Bob Kinsey from involving himself in his community. In 1971 he took the oath of office as the House member from the district that included Craftsbury and three nearby towns. He was among a coterie of conservative Republicans, many of them wearing sport jackets that fit too tightly and haircuts that were less than fashionable. Kinsey distinguished himself as a member of the House Appropriations Committee where he was able to apply his fiscal acumen to the state budget. By 1980 he was Republican leader.

But if Bob Kinsey was a conservative, he was a conservative with a long memory and a strong sense of what it meant to live among neighbors in a small town. He remembered an incident on Halloween in the mid-1930s when he was nine or ten years old. His family lived about a mile away from Barton village, and that year for the first time he and his brother went into town to join the Halloween fun.

There was a group of fifty to sixty kids roaming the streets that evening. "Some of the kids were older than kids," Kinsey recalled, "and they should have known better."

At the time, there were three or four Jewish families in Barton, including the family of Sam Schneider, who made his living buying and selling junk. "They lived beside the Congo church in Barton," Kinsey said, using the familiar term for Congregational. "We had no reason to hate them at all. We peddled milk to them on our milk route."

Many of the sidewalks in town back then were made of planks, and the kids were grabbing any loose planks they could find and heaping them in front of the schoolhouse door. Eventually, they began to help themselves to pieces of junk from the Schneiders' yard.

"Then some of the big boys found an old milk pail," Kinsey remembered, "and they stepped into the river and filled it with muddy water." With their pail of muddy water, they returned to the Schneiders' house and knocked on the door.

"Sam had the choice of not opening the door," Kinsey said. "But Sam knew the crowd would get rowdier if he didn't open the door and take that pail of muddy water in the face. And he did. He never said a word, and the kids had a big laugh and went up the street to look for other trouble."

Kinsey was just a kid, a bystander, but he always remembered the night that Sam Schneider took a pail of water in the face.

"They had to take it," he said. "They wouldn't fight back because the police never thought it was serious enough to do anything about it."

Years later, as Kinsey heard about the insults and prejudice silently endured by gay Americans, he remembered Sam Schneider. He hated being part of the crowd that cheered when someone threw a pail of water in Sam Schneider's face. That Halloween he learned what bigotry was, and he never forgot it.

BIGOTRY wears many guises, and in Burlington, Vermont, it wore blackface.

For decades the high point of Winter Carnival at the University of Vermont had been Kake Walk, a boisterous dance competition popular among the university's fraternity brothers. Contestants in Kake Walk put on blackface, wore kinky wigs and gaudy uniforms, and competed in a high-kicking dance routine judged for agility and style. The competition itself was called "Walkin' Fo' de Cake," and it took place to a tune called "Cotton Babes" that had been composed years before by a University of Vermont alumnus.

By 1969 Kake Walk was becoming an indefensible vestige of a racist tradition. There had been agitation throughout the 1960s about Kake Walk, and the students had eliminated the most outrageously racist elements of the competition. Some students tried green or purple faces instead of black. Even so, black students continued to point out that the entire event had its origins in America's minstrel show tradition. To white Americans, Kake Walk may have seemed like harmless fun. But African Americans, whose voice had gained in strength and authority throughout the 1960s, made clear that Kake Walk was degrading and offensive. And in the fall of 1969, the school finally decided to abandon its tradition.

Tom Little was a high school student in 1969 when the Kake Walk controversy reached its culmination. He was a child of the establishment, the son of a Republican state legislator who ran a successful printing business. His mother had been a member of the city's Planning Commission. His family lived in a comfortable home on the hill near the university campus in Burlington.

As a white, middle-class teenager in a small New England city, Tom Little was safely removed from the violence that had seared America's urban landscape during the 1960s. But Vermont was not untouched by the era's racial struggles, and Little, growing up in a politically aware household, took in the lessons taught by the events of the day. These included the notorious Irasburg affair of 1968 when someone fired a shotgun through the window of a house where a black minister lived. The police had focused their attention not on the shooter, who faced minimal charges, but on the black minister, whom they cited on a bogus charge of adultery. The incident shook Vermont's political establishment, reminding Vermonters that racism could thrive even in a state that prided itself on its tradition of tolerance.

Tom Little, future chairman of the House Judiciary Committee, recognized the essential feature of bigotry: blindness to the humanity of the victim. It was during these years of social ferment, when the nation was especially attuned to issues of racism, that the gay rights movement stirred to life. And as straight America began to confront the civil rights claims of gays and lesbians, the nation's experience with race offered important lessons about the nature of discrimination and the meaning of equality.

Vermont's own experience with race was distinguished both by the small number of African Americans who have lived there and by the fierce abolitionism that characterized the state's early history. Vermont had declared itself a "free and independent state" when it adopted its constitution of 1777. Article One of the constitution states that no adult "ought to be beholden by law, to serve any person, as a servant, slave or apprentice." This declaration made Vermont the first state in America to outlaw slavery. Nine years later the Vermont Legislature declared that "the idea of slavery is totally exploded from our free government."

In the 1820s and 1830s Vermont became fertile ground for abolitionism. William Lloyd Garrison, the abolitionist crusader, spent six months early in his career in Bennington where he began agitating for immediate emancipation of the slaves. Over time the state was aflame with the demands of those preaching "immediatism" rather than "gradualism." (Vermonters debating the question of marriage vs. civil union more than a century-and-a-half later would echo that debate.)

New England was never hospitable to slavery. "An area of small farms, little capital, and hard winters, it could fit none but freemen into its economy," wrote historian David M. Ludlum. The religious fervor that propelled moralistic crusades against liquor and Masonry in the 1830s also fueled the crusade against slavery.

Nor was Vermont's hostility to slavery forgotten in later years. Rowland Robinson, a Quaker from Ferrisburgh who wrote short stories and novels in the 1880s and '90s, was the author of a collection of stories called *Out of Bondage and Other Stories*. Drawing from the experience of his own family, which had a secret room for hiding runaways in the back of their house, he wrote stories of Vermonters protecting runaways from slave catchers. Visitors to the Robinson home, now known as the Rokeby Museum, can see the secret chamber used for hiding slaves.

Tom Little remembered the lesson of Kake Walk when he went on to Bowdoin College in Brunswick, Maine. He majored in philosophy, and his education acquainted him with the theory and practice of liberal democracy. He had grown up attending the Episcopal church, where he had been an acolyte during junior high and high school, and he continued to be active in the church as an adult, serving as chancellor of his diocese. But from his education he gained an appreciation for the way the separation of church and state protected one from the other. He also understood the need to allow scope for social pluralism. The liberal theorist John Rawls, whom Little read as an undergraduate, promoted an idea of democracy as a system of cooperation in which people with differing religious viewpoints could find common ground, in part, by refusing to impose their viewpoints on others.

Years later the issue of gay marriage would test the ability of those on opposite sides of the question to find this common ground.

Following his undergraduate years at Bowdoin, Little attended law school at Cornell University. It was after his first year at Cornell that he met Susan Keelty, whom he married in December 1977. They moved to Ithaca, New York, as he finished law school, then they moved back to Burlington, where Little served a clerkship with U.S. District Judge Albert Coffrin.

As a young lawyer whose father was a state senator and whose family had always been involved in the life of the community, it was only a matter of time before Little, too, became involved. He was a Republican, but in 1991 the new Democratic governor, Howard Dean, appointed him to fill a vacancy in the Vermont House.

It is possible, therefore, to view Little as the model of an establishment politician, a lawyer with a photo of Calvin Coolidge on the wall of his office and someone who played a role in both his church and his state. He understood the difference between the two, and when the time came to defend the wall that separated them, he was ready.

3.

STAN BAKER began the odyssey that led to the *Baker* case a long way from Vermont. He was born in Manhattan, Kansas, in 1946, and he moved to Long Beach, California, when he was three months old. He grew up there, a golden-haired California boy, active, happy, and engaged in the life around him. He played cello in a high school orchestra of national renown. He ran cross-country and track, and he was involved in student government. He was able to fit in well with enough groups that he felt no incongruity between the heterosexual world that was visible to him and the stirrings inside him that drew him to other boys.

His mother was a Quaker from Onawa, Iowa, and Baker remembered walking down the streets of her hometown with his uncle. "Everyone knew him," he said. One of his uncle's morning rituals was to raise the American flag, and he had a piece of advice for his nephew. "He would say, 'Don't let them steal your flag,'" Baker remembered. To Baker that meant it was important to keep in your heart the real meaning of what you do. Years later, Baker applied that lesson to his quest for the right to marry. "One of the most radical things to do is to go into a culture, right into the heart of the culture, and say I belong here," he said.

Baker grew up as a Quaker, and in 1964 he enrolled at Swarthmore College, a Quaker school in Pennsylvania. Opposition to the Vietnam War was strong at Swarthmore, and Baker remembered that the class of 1968 became depleted by the departure of men who were drafted or who fled to Canada to avoid the draft. Baker became involved in the antiwar movement and determined that when the draft became an issue for him, he would declare himself a conscientious objector.

But there was additional turmoil for him. He had dated women, but he was also aware of his attraction to men. He had long told himself that his interest in men was only a phase, but at Swarthmore, he said, "the phase theory began to crumble." He had no model to help him understand what was happening to him. He fell in love with a male student, and they became roommates, but he found it difficult to carry on with the relationship. A dean at the school told him not to worry, that no one would ever know about it, as if his paramount concern should be to hide the reality of who he was.

After college he worked in Los Angeles at an alternative school for young children in order to fulfill the community service requirement of his status as a conscientious objector. It was there that he met Priscilla, and he fell in love with her. Despite what he had learned about himself at college, he was still holding on to the phase theory, he said.

By 1971 Stan and Priscilla were married, and they did what many of their generation did. They threw their belongings into a Dodge van, and they headed across country. With memories of Onawa, Iowa, in mind, Stan wanted to find a place small enough in scale that he could feel he was part of a community where everyone would know him. They drove across

Wisconsin and upstate Michigan, looking for a setting that fit the idea of the small town that they carried in their heads. When they reached New England, they traveled across Vermont, New Hampshire, and Maine, deciding they would settle where they found work.

So it was that in 1971 Stan became director of a Head Start day-care center in Winooski, Vermont, and Priscilla became a teacher in a private elementary school in nearby Underhill.

Vermonters, who are not averse to their own brand of chauvinism, often say the only real Vermonters are those whose families go back five generations. They say it partly in jest, knowing that few would qualify. The bearded, long-haired Californian who arrived to teach young Vermonters would seem to be far from qualified as a Vermonter.

But Stan Baker brought with him a Vermont pedigree that the most curmudgeonly native would have to credit. His Baker connection went back eight generations to one of the leading Green Mountain Boys, a cousin of Ethan Allen by the name of Remember Baker. If Stan Baker was eventually to take part in a civil rights revolution, there was precedent in his family history. Even so it would be another decade before the gay rights movement emerged to take a visible role in Vermont. Elsewhere in the nation, gays and lesbians had begun to speak out more insistently for equality and respect, and quickly the furies of bigotry struck back.

CHAPTER THREE

FREEDOM

I.

ON THE NIGHT of November 27, 1978, forty thousand people gathered in front of the lofty dome of City Hall in San Francisco, many of them holding candles, creating a flickering sea of flame that filled Civic Center Plaza. Much of the grief-stricken crowd had marched from Castro Street, the neighborhood that provided a safe haven for thousands of gay San Franciscans. The crowd was mourning the murders of Mayor George Moscone and City Supervisor Harvey Milk, the first openly gay city official in America, who had urged gay people all across America to declare themselves openly, to be out and proud.

While Moscone's death was awful in its own right, the killing of Harvey Milk brought home to a newly emboldened population of gay and lesbian Americans the reality that violence would continue to shadow their struggle for dignity and equal rights.

In the months that followed, tensions increased between the city's gay population and the police. Then in May 1979 the accused killer's trial ended with two verdicts of voluntary manslaughter, and a night of rioting and fire ensued. Dan White's defense portrayed him as an all-American family man who must have been out of his mind to kill Moscone and Milk. He had been depressed, and his depression had been worsened by the high-sugar junk food he had been eating. This was the notorious Twinkie defense. The subtext of the trial was that the aggressive behavior of homosexuals, represented by Harvey Milk, constituted a provocation that made violence understandable, if not acceptable. That White had purposely holstered his pistol that morning, snuck into City Hall through a window, and coolly put two bullets into the heads of each of his victims did not persuade the jury that White had acted with premeditation. In consequence, many in the gay community interpreted the verdict the way Cleve Jones did. As reported in Randy Shilts's book, *The Mayor of Castro Street*, Jones was a gay activist and a friend of Milk's. When asked for his response to the verdict, he said, "This means in America it's all right to kill faggots."

That night thousands gathered at City Hall, storming the building and torching police cars. The murder of Harvey Milk and the verdict in White's trial became a blazing example of all that gay Americans had to fight against.

THE GAY RIGHTS movement represented only one current within the flood of turbulent politics that characterized the 1970s. Racial politics, the women's movement, the environmental movement, all gained momentum during a period shaped also by the Vietnam War, the corruption of Watergate, and the resignation of President Nixon. But the gay rights movement was unsettling to many people in ways that other political and social movements were not. One consequence was the newly aggressive political activism of religious fundamentalists, who nurtured a fear of sexual deviance and whose strength grew in perverse symbiosis with the rise of the gay rights movement.

The first significant instance of antigay activism occurred

in Dade County, Florida, in the year before the murders of Milk and Moscone. In January 1977 the Dade County Metro Commission approved an ordinance barring discrimination against people because of their "affectional or sexual preference." The Dade County ordinance brought out Anita Bryant, the popular singer and patriotic icon. She joined forces with Christian fundamentalists such as the Reverend Jerry Falwell, founder of the Moral Majority, to take her antigay rights campaign nationwide. Their rhetoric was vicious, and they were able to tap into a deep vein of fear, overturning the gay rights ordinance in Dade County and checking the advance of gay rights in political battlegrounds across the nation.

The arguments that characterized the battles of the 1970s would resurface in Vermont more than twenty years later. In the meantime, people like Bill Lippert were struggling to fashion a life for themselves. They were not unaware of the struggles in San Francisco, Miami, and elsewhere, but they needed to be careful.

2.

DURING THOSE years gay Vermonters had no formal organizations and no place to gather other than a few bars—the High Hat and the Taj Mahal in Burlington, the Andrews Inn in Bellows Falls. Bill Lippert, who continued to lead his gay men's support group each week, recalled that even in the gay bars he knew of in Burlington, the owners maintained rules forbidding gay men from touching each other as they danced.

It was in the Taj Mahal one night that Lippert met a young man who had grown up on the family farm in the town of

Hinesburg. Howard Russell—known to his friends as Howdy—
was one of six children, and he loved life on the farm. The
Russell farmhouse sat on a knoll in the center of Hinesburg village, two doors down from the IGA market and across Route
116 from the Hinesburg town office.

Russell joined Lippert's support group, and for a time the
two became romantic partners. Both had a measure of cautious reserve in their manner, and they shared a deeply felt
sense of indignation that drove them eventually to help launch
a homegrown gay rights movement in Vermont. It was during
those years that Lippert, Russell, and a small nucleus of gay
men began to meet for volleyball each week at the playground
of Christ the King School in Burlington. Those weekly volleyball games became instrumental in bringing gay men together
and fostering their burgeoning political awareness.

But it wasn't until 1983 that the gays and lesbians of Vermont were ready to stage the kind of gay pride parade that had
become a common event in many cities. At the time, the lesbians of the Burlington area were better organized and more
assertive than the gay men. The women's movement had provided a foundation for lesbian activism, and a group of women
in Burlington had founded a magazine called *Commonwoman*
or, at times, *Commonwomon*. In 1983 the women of *Commonwoman* received a small grant from the Haymarket Foundation
to organize a gay pride parade in Burlington; Howdy Russell
and his brother Harry, who was also gay, were invited to join
the march committee.

Russell remembered how afraid he was at the prospect of
marching down Church Street for all the world to see. Organizers had no idea how many people would show up. Would
they be there by themselves, a band of twenty or so lonely,
frightened people with their placards and their defiance? Police
had received threats that there might be crowds at the top of

Burlington's parking garage throwing things at the marchers. The night before the march, Russell's brother Harry asked him, "Are you actually going to march in this parade?"

Howdy said he was.

Harry took a deep breath. "If you are going to," he said, "then I have to."

That first year three hundred people turned out for the Gay Pride Parade. There was a rally first in City Hall Park, and Howdy Russell was among the speakers. "I'm really scared being here," he told the crowd, "but I'm angry that I'm scared."

The parade brought with it a feeling of exhilaration and newly discovered power. "It's hard to imagine what a turning point that was," Russell said. People in Vermont were not anonymous in the way they might be in San Francisco or New York. Someone walking down the street in Burlington was likely to be seen by someone he knew, an employer, perhaps, or a neighbor. "A whole lot of people faced their ultimate fear and did it anyway," Russell said. "And those people who weren't ready to do it saw other people doing it."

Russell, Lippert, and their friends knew they could easily move away from Vermont to gay communities in the larger cities. But Russell's family had lived in their Hinesburg farmhouse for more than a century and a half. It was insulting to him that his safety could be assured only by moving away. "This is my home," he told himself. "I'm not going anywhere else."

The parade in 1983 was a catalyst for the formation of a group called Vermonters for Lesbian and Gay Rights, an organization based in the Burlington area that would become active on behalf of a variety of gay rights issues. Vermont was changing, and the gay and lesbian activists of Vermont would become an important minority voice, increasingly insistent that it would be heard.

FOR BILL Lippert, the second Gay Pride Parade, held in June 1984, became a personal and professional test. Public visibility had the potential to create serious problems for his promising career as a mental health professional.

In 1973 Lippert had gone to work for the Counseling Service of Addison County, the principal mental health agency in the Middlebury area, and by 1984 he was in line to become director of the agency. He had come to the mental health field just as the profession was abandoning its designation of homosexuality as a mental illness, and over the years he worked to develop new therapies for gay men and women. He knew that alcohol and drug abuse and the risk of suicide were high among gays because of the isolation and confusion they often suffered. He recognized that during his own college years he probably would have been considered clinically depressed because of the intense isolation he felt.

"When you work in a mental health center," he said, "you have a window into the community." He knew the struggles gay Vermonters were facing, and when a young man committed suicide, it was common for therapists to wonder if the man were gay.

By 1984 Lippert had earned a master's in counseling psychology, and when the director of the Counseling Service resigned, Lippert became one of three finalists for the job. His final interview was scheduled for a Tuesday in June, three days after the second Gay Pride Parade in Burlington. "My friends told me don't go to Gay Pride," he said. "At least, if you go, don't be visible." He decided he would attend the parade but take no active role, and he marched with three women, including one who was carrying a sign that said PROUD IN MIDDLE-BURY. Surely, he had nothing to be afraid of.

The next morning he opened the *Burlington Free Press* to check out coverage of the parade and saw himself emblazoned on the front page in a large color photograph. Out and proud? He was both. But now he wondered if he had ruined his chances to become director of the Counseling Service. Distraught, he went for a long walk that afternoon in the fields and woods behind his house. He gave a lot of thought to what his public identification as a marcher in the Gay Pride Parade might mean to his public appointment as director of a large mental health organization. As he hiked, the familiar peak of Camel's Hump rising up to the east, he came to a decision. "OK," he said to himself, "they get all of me or they get none of me."

Thinking back to that afternoon, he said that this moment of self-acceptance, of self-affirmation, had an extraordinary calming effect on him. He sailed through his interview the next Tuesday, and no one mentioned the photo. That he was appointed director became a point of immense pride to him. As leader of a mental health institution, he said, he was "working in the heart of the beast."

"I talk about the three pillars of oppression. There is the law, the church, and mental health or psychiatry. You're illegal, you're immoral, or you're sick." By becoming director of the Counseling Service he was bringing down one of those pillars.

EVEN AS GAYS in Vermont were becoming more visible, the politics of reaction was gaining strength across the nation. President Ronald Reagan, elected in 1980 and reelected in 1984, was a popular spokesman for what conservative Christian groups called traditional values. But Vermont did not participate in the conservative backlash that propelled Reagan to power. Gay and lesbian Vermonters had barely begun to assert their legal claims in the 1980s, but as they were taking their first tentative steps, the political atmosphere was growing more hospitable for them. And by the end of the decade they could no longer be ignored.

One of the important changes in Vermont was the election of Madeleine Kunin as governor in 1984. She was a former House member and lieutenant governor. Her inauguration in January 1985 was accompanied by a sense of jubilation among those who saw in her rise to power a validation of America's promise of equality. She had arrived in America as a girl with her mother and brother, Jewish refugees fleeing Switzerland in the days before World War II. As an immigrant and a woman, she had worked her way into the Vermont political establishment, facing the need to prove that she could be as tough and as competent as a man.

At the time Kunin took office, the issue of gay rights was simmering beneath the surface of Vermont political life. She was sympathetic to the demands of the gay rights movement, but the state Equal Rights Amendment of 1986 showed how volatile and politically divisive the reality of homosexuality could be.

Two consecutive Vermont legislatures had already approved an amendment to the Vermont Constitution barring discrimination on account of sex. The impetus behind the bill was to protect the rights of women, but the word *sex* set off alarm bells within the religious right. The state ERA would be on the ballot in November 1986, and it became the focus of a divisive campaign involving national leaders from both the feminist and the family values movements.

The wording of the amendment said only this:

Equality of rights under the law shall not be denied or abridged by the State of Vermont or any of its political subdivisions on account of the sex of the individual.

But those few words drew forth the direst of warnings. Phyllis Schlafly, leader of the conservative Eagle Forum, came to Vermont to argue that the ERA was "antifamily." She knew that bias against gays was a well that went deep, and she drew from it. An amendment that outlawed discrimination based on sex would lead to gay marriage, she argued, and it would encourage the spread of AIDS.

These were proven tactics. With them, Schlafly had helped defeat an equal rights amendment in Maine two years earlier. By equating women's rights with gay rights, opponents of the ERA were wielding a powerful weapon, and the accusations of bigotry quickly followed.

At the same time, supporters of the ERA were divided on how to respond on the question of gay rights and gay marriage. A law professor at the Vermont Law School, Heather Wishik, wrote an article saying that the ERA might well provide a legal basis for gay marriage. "Rules which say that a man only can be sexual with a woman are rules which are based on the man's biological gender," she said.

That was not an argument that supporters of the ERA wanted to hear—though Wishik's arguments would form an important part of the argument by the plaintiffs before the Vermont Supreme Court twelve years later. In 1986 supporters of the ERA felt compelled to distance themselves from the idea of gay marriage. Jonathan Chase, dean of the Vermont Law School, countered Wishik's argument, saying that laws barring gay marriage would not be counter to the Equal Rights Amendment because they would not discriminate on account of sex. "It's discrimination against a certain kind of relationship," he said.

Chase's appraisal of the gay marriage issue was quoted by the *Rutland Herald:* "The law is very seldom ahead of the enlightenment of the people. And we're just not ready as a society to sanction same-sex marriage."

As late as June 1986 the ERA enjoyed support among two-thirds of Vermonters responding to polls, but the insistent warnings about the possibility that gay marriage would be the result began to erode support. When the ballots were counted in November, the amendment had lost, 51 percent to 49 percent. Voters responding to an informal exit poll in Rutland County told a reporter from the *Rutland Herald* that the issue of gay marriage had been decisive.

The reaction of the gay community in Vermont was swift and strong. Shortly after the election, the Vermont Lesbian and Gay Network issued a statement denouncing liberal supporters of the ERA for failing to stand up to the attack on gays:

> We feel certain that if the bigotry being expressed had been against a racial minority or a religious sect, Vermont's pro-ERA organizations would have been quick to condemn such sentiments. But in this ERA campaign all we heard from the state's pro-ERA groups was "The ERA has nothing to do with sexual orientation."

Opponents of the ERA had argued that the ERA was a way for gay activists to bring their agenda in through the back door. After the defeat of the ERA, Howdy Russell and fellow activists decided they would let fellow Vermonters know they were "coming through the front door." They would pull their movement off the shoulders of the women's movement and stand up for themselves.

3.

ROGER MACOMBER, 27, had gone to a gay bar called Pearl's in Burlington one night in April 1990. There, witnesses reported that sometime around midnight they saw Macomber leave the bar with a man wearing a baseball cap and work boots. Witnesses said the man, his arms draped around Ma-

comber's shoulders, went into a nearby alleyway where he performed oral sex on Macomber.

Some minutes later police found Macomber in a pool of
blood, his pants around his feet, with multiple skull fractures,
brain damage, and partial blindness. It was one of the most vicious beatings Burlington police had ever encountered. Later
that night police picked up a man in a baseball cap and work
boots whose clothes were stained with blood. According to a
police affidavit, Kevin Murray, the alleged assailant, said, "You
want to know the truth? I went looking for it, went to Pearl's,
found a fag, and kicked the shit out of him." That he also had
oral sex with his victim suggests a pathological combination of
attraction and self-loathing.

At the time of the assault on Roger Macomber, a hate
crimes bill had already passed the Vermont House, but it was
lodged in the Senate Judiciary Committee, where the chairman, Senator John Bloomer of Rutland, had little use for it.
The beating of Roger Macomber changed everything.

The hate crimes bill became a significant early step in the
political struggle by gays seeking to secure their safety and
their rights. It had already set off the kind of furious debate
that would occur repeatedly over the next ten years whenever
the issue of gay rights surfaced.

Passage of the bill by the House, a month before the beating of Roger Macomber, had been far from easy. During a
committee hearing on the bill, Representative John Murphy, a
Democrat from Ludlow, had shown what kind of opposition
gay rights legislation would encounter again and again. Murphy, a stocky, garrulous man who fashioned himself a champion of the working class, was in his twenty-second year in the
Legislature. In committee he ranted against the bill: "You're
doing all this for the lezzies and the queers. This bill puts
homosexual people on a golden pedestal."

When the bill reached the House floor, passage was by no means assured. Francis Brooks, one of two black House members, sought to awaken the sensitivities of fellow members to what it meant to live as one of a minority. He gave a moving speech on the floor of the House about the sense of vulnerability he felt even among his colleagues. "Sometimes I am seen not as Francis Brooks as himself, but as Francis Brooks appears," he told House members. He was a hardworking, soft-spoken high school teacher, and he was well-liked in the Legislature. His words had their effect. But that effect went beyond what anyone had expected.

"Mr. Speaker!" The voice was that of John Murphy. As he stood, his colleagues groaned. They could only imagine what he might say. As he stood at his desk following the speech by Francis Brooks, his colleagues braced themselves.

But instead of inveighing against the bill, Murphy announced he had experienced "an unexpected change of heart."

"As I listen today, I have searched my soul and said that I guess I've been wrong," he said, according to the *Rutland Herald* account. "When I listened this afternoon to the real reason for this legislation, I have to take the same stand as I do on labor. In the past I've been on the wrong side. Mr. Speaker, I've changed my mind. Today I hope to do what is right. I'm going to support this bill."

Murphy's change of heart created a sensation in the House. After the vote, Murphy told a reporter, "This bill isn't any different from the other bills I've killed in the past. It's Murphy who's different."

The hate crimes bill passed the House, 80–51, but in the Senate it languished in the Judiciary Committee. Then the beating of Roger Macomber provoked an outcry not even the conservative chairman of the committee, John Bloomer, could withstand. Jeffrey Amestoy, the Republican attorney general and future chief justice, declared the beating was "the most graphic example that I can imagine of the need for a hate crimes bill. Passage of the bill is critical."

Denise Johnson, another future Supreme Court justice, was then chairwoman of the newly established state Human Rights Commission, which provided information about the attacks suffered by minorities in Vermont. In fact, most of the testimony heard in the Legislature concerned assaults and harassment against homosexuals; the assault on Roger Macomber was merely the most brutal example. It was the achievement of the hate crimes bill to establish that crimes motivated by hatred against gays were equivalent to crimes motivated by hatred against blacks or other minorities. Simply to include gays in the list of minorities worthy of protection was an accomplishment.

Senator David Wolk, a Democrat from Rutland, was sponsor of the hate crimes bill in the Senate, and he finally managed to persuade Bloomer to hold a hearing on it.

The hate crimes bill brought Governor Kunin to the State House to testify. As governor, she had never testified on pending legislation, but following the beating of Roger Macomber, her Holocaust experience compelled her to speak out.

> When there is violence against any person in society, because he or she is different, it threatens us all. Only by speaking out are any of us safe. We cannot tolerate the abuse of homosexual and gay Vermonters under any circumstances. This law, while not perfect, allows us to make a statement of conscience, to reaffirm our values, and to counter the evil that surfaced in a dark alley. I urge its passage.

When the bill reached the full Senate, Wolk took the floor to say why he thought the bill was important.

When criminal acts are clearly motivated by racism, by homophobia, by anti-Semitism, or by some other minority status of a victim, then it is incumbent upon us as leaders to indicate through our words as well as our deeds that Vermont will not tolerate criminal expressions of prejudice and that this conduct will be more severely punished.

In the end, the momentum in support of the hate crimes law proved irresistible. The Senate passed the bill 24–6. The battle for the bill had engaged the attention of several people who would become important in the struggle for gay rights, including Jeffrey Amestoy and Denise Johnson. David Wolk continued to champion the issue of gay rights, but like many politicians willing to take up that cause, he would pay the price.

4.

ONCE THE GAY rights struggle moved from the streets to the halls of government, gay rights advocates had engaged all of society. Their claims were no longer the claims of an ignored minority, clinging together in their own groups, publishing their own newspapers, gathering in the streets with banners and placards. Now their claims would have to become the claims of people who were not gay, who were unfamiliar with what it meant to be gay. Specific claims of a minority would have to transcend particular grievances to become a question of equal rights that mattered to all Americans, an overarching issue of principle. For progress to occur, a historically persecuted minority had to win over not only people like Francis Brooks, who could be expected to understand their difficulties, but also people like John Murphy. And yet there was a cost for the mainstream politician who promoted the cause of gay rights.

David Wolk was a popular elementary school principal who had served in the state senate for six years. He was the son of a beloved Rutland pediatrician, and he had an amiable, relaxed friendliness well-suited to his political ambitions.

His experience as a teacher and principal had opened his eyes to the prejudice children sometimes suffered. "I had seen too many kids in the schools where I worked who were discriminated against because of their sexual orientation," he said. His work in 1990 on behalf of the hate crimes bill had also acquainted him with the vicious treatment gays and lesbians sometimes faced. So in 1992 he sponsored an antidiscrimination bill that placed him at the center of a political maelstrom.

The purpose of the antidiscrimination bill was to add "sexual orientation" to the list of categories, along with race, gender, and religion, that could not be the basis of discrimination. In many ways Vermont's experience in passing that bill, and the resistance it provoked, offered a preview of the battle over civil unions that would follow eight years later.

But the antidiscrimination bill, like the hate crimes bill two years before, faced a formidable obstacle in Senator Bloomer, who refused to bring it before the Judiciary Committee. David Wolk, however, was able to make a deal: Bloomer would allow the committee to vote on the antidiscrimination bill if Wolk helped advance a constitutional amendment in which Bloomer had an interest.

The public outcry against the antidiscrimination bill was harsh. The Senate Judiciary Committee held a public hearing in February 1992, drawing four hundred people to the State House in Montpelier. Lin Christian expressed the attitude of

many. "We'll have half the city of San Francisco moving to the
state of Vermont," she said, according to the account in the
Rutland Herald. "To burn with lust for a person of the same sex
is not right."

But the bill had its defenders. Peter Cooper of Rutland told
the committee his stepson had died of AIDS and that everyone
should be given full rights. The Reverend Mitchell Hay of the
United Methodist Church in Danville said, "I was worried that
the only Christian voice tonight would be that of the radical
right." Then he told the committee: "I would now like to read
to you every word that Jesus said in Scripture condemning
homosexuality."

He leaned back in his chair and said nothing.

Bloomer continued to oppose the bill, but on March 25
he brought the bill before the committee for a vote, and it
passed 4–2.

When the bill reached the Senate floor, Wolk was its principal defender. He described how the attorney general's office
had received numerous complaints over the years alleging
discrimination on the basis of sexual orientation. But nothing
could be done because discrimination against gays and lesbians
was not illegal. Wolk also pointed out that even though Vermont had passed a hate crimes bill two years before, a gay Vermonter who filed a complaint about a hate crime risked losing
his job by revealing his sexual orientation.

The bill passed the Senate on March 31, 1992, by a vote of
20–9, but it still faced an uncertain fate in the House, where
debate on the bill would grow increasingly intense. House
Speaker Ralph Wright was pushing the bill, but rounding up
the seventy-six votes needed for passage would not be easy.
The House Republican leader, Sara Gear, supported the bill,
but she was not working to secure its passage.

The House Judiciary Committee became the focus of bitter debate. Lin Christian, who had testified before the Senate Judiciary Committee, made an appearance before the House committee as well. "If this law is passed," she said, "thousands of unsuspecting people will be drawn into sodomy. Sodomy is a crime against nature."

Another witness, John Pratt of Montpelier, used one of the most frequently heard terms to condemn homosexuality, calling it "an abomination against the Lord."

But the bill had equally determined supporters, such as Howdy Russell, who had become a leading figure in the gay rights movement. Two years before, Russell had come close to winning a seat in the state senate, running as an openly gay man. His campaign gave an enormous boost to the visibility of gay rights in Vermont, even if he had to face voters willing to curse and threaten him.

He appeared before the committee that year, talking about his family, their farm in Hinesburg, and his roots as a Vermonter. But he had another message for the committee members: "If you want to know about why this bill is important, don't listen to me. Listen to the opponents." He asked them to imagine they had a gay son or daughter. After hearing the denunciations and anger from the bill's opponents, did they believe their son or daughter could do without protection against bias?

Russell was correct in judging that the language of the opponents would push some House members toward supporting the bill. Representative Megan Price of Fair Haven described herself as a staunch Republican who had voted against similar measures in the past. But she was repelled by the zealous lobbying of the bill's opponents.

"The misinformation and fear and heavy lobbying by religious fundamentalists has convinced me of the need for the bill. This bill is a matter of fairness," she said.

The Judiciary Committee approved the bill 7–4 on April 9,

and the full House quickly took it up. Bill Lippert went to the State House that day. Because of his position with the Counseling Service, he was acquainted with some House members. One of them was Roger Kayhart, a farmer from the tiny town of Waltham and a conservative Republican. Lippert encountered Kayhart in a corridor before the bill came to a vote, and Kayhart was uncertain about whether to vote in favor of civil rights protection for "those people," as he called them.

Lippert did not generally talk about his sexual orientation, and he had never talked about gay rights with Kayhart before. But on that Friday it was time.

"Roger," he said, speaking warmly and with conviction, "I'm one of those people."

Kayhart looked at Lippert, startled. He had no idea that Lippert was gay. Lippert knew that putting a face on the idea of homosexuality could have a powerful effect, but he had no idea what effect his revelation would have on Kayhart. The bill passed, 78–51, that day, and he was gratified when Kayhart voted for it.

But procedures in the Vermont Legislature would require another vote, and no one could predict the outcome. Bills in the Legislature had to pass through three readings. The first reading came when the bill was introduced. The second reading occurred when a bill came to a vote, as the antidiscrimination bill had that Friday. Bills that won approval then required a third reading where they had to pass again. The third reading was usually no more than a formality, but supporters of the antidiscrimination bill were worried that pressure at home over the weekend might persuade some members to reverse their votes. That is what worried Lippert about Kayhart. But when Lippert approached Kayhart in the corridor on Monday, there was a look of astonishment and outrage on Kayhart's face.

"I was preached against in my own church," Kayhart sputtered. In fact, preachers throughout his district had attacked him that Sunday. "I get it now," Kayhart said. "That's what they're talking about."

On April 13 the bill came to a final vote in the House, and opponents would have their last chance to stop it. Representative Nancy Sheltra, the outspoken conservative from Derby, expressed her disapproval. "I don't think the state of Vermont should put its seal of approval on conduct that is unnatural."

Representative Megan Price held firm in support of the bill. "I have heard men say, 'If I hire these men, what if they make a pass at me?' Well, welcome to the world of women. You can be the sickest heterosexual on the block, but you've got all the rights."

The bill passed on April 13 by a vote of 73–67.

But the campaign of vilification and harassment against supporters of the bill would continue long after its passage.

BY 1992 David Wolk had higher political ambitions. His good friend Howard Dean had won election as lieutenant governor in 1986 and then had become governor in 1991. So in the election of 1992, the post of lieutenant governor was open, and Wolk decided he would run for it.

It had been a difficult year for Wolk. During the antidiscrimination debate in the spring, Wolk had received hundreds of messages of hate in the mail and death threats over the phone. "Watch yourself. The roads are dangerous," one caller said. He was the father of four, and his children had heard callers tell them, "Your father's a fucking pervert," and "Your father's going to rot in hell."

Voters did not forget Wolk's vote when the election campaign began. That spring Wolk came face-to-face with the anger of the opposition when he attended a parade in the

Franklin County city of St. Albans. Franklin County borders Quebec in northwestern Vermont and is home to a large French-Canadian population. Wolk was preparing to march in the parade with his twelve-year-old son, Adam, when a burly man with a full beard and a red-and-black checked shirt approached him. Wolk braced himself.

"Hey, Wolk," the man said. "You take your fucking faggot friends and put them on a boat and sail them out to sea and you go with them because that's where you all belong."

Wolk was shaking. He didn't know what to say to the man, who stood over him, face glaring, fists clenched.

After a moment, Adam spoke up. "Hey, Dad," he said. "What an idiot."

Wolk whisked his son away, leaving the bearded man gaping at the two of them. "We're just starting this," he told his son, "and you're just going to have to take it."

Adam countered, "I'm really sorry, Dad, but I don't think he was going to vote for you anyway."

Adam's good humor helped them through the day. But they would face other incidents during the campaign. At a parade in the small city of Vergennes, Wolk encountered people with signs that said, NO RIGHTS FOR SODOMITES and WOLK WILL ROT IN HELL.

Despite the abuse he received during the campaign, Wolk was convinced he would win the election. In November when it turned out he had lost, he retreated to his Burlington hotel room with his wife, Diane, and broke down weeping. His hopes had been high, but the punishment he had endured on the trail had been severe. In the end, he came away with only 44 percent of the vote. The vicious treatment he experienced was a sign of how even modest steps toward gay rights could ignite hatred of shocking virulence.

The day after the election, feeling broken and exhausted, the Wolks headed to their home near Rutland. They stopped for breakfast at Rosie's, a roadside restaurant in Middlebury, hoping they could get away without talking to anyone. But as they sat at their table, a man approached them. Wolk dreaded what the man might say. He couldn't stand another attack.

"I know who you are," the man said to him. Wolk's heart fell. "I want you to know you did the right thing. You changed my life."

Wolk broke into tears, quickly placed money on the table, and left the restaurant without eating his breakfast. Years later, after he had become president of Castleton State College, he ruefully recalled that morning: "The low point became the high point," he said.

5.

IT WAS A sunny Sunday morning, June 13, 1993, and about two dozen people had gathered for the weekly Quaker meeting at the Middlebury Parent-Child Center. Every Sunday at 10 A.M. Quakers and visitors sat in a circle in the commodious room where large framed photographs of smiling children hung from the walls. They sat in silence, listening to their own breath. It was a time of meditation, a time simply to be. It was Quaker practice to sit for an hour. Sometimes the whole hour passed without a word. But anyone was free to speak, to bear witness to the truth of what was in his or her heart. Those who spoke knew their words would find an accepting audience.

I happened to be there that Sunday morning. It was my first visit to a Quaker meeting, and I didn't know what it would be like. My wife and I had recently been divorced, and I thought the spiritual companionship of the Quaker meeting would be a comfort.

The silence continued. People sat with their eyes shut or looking around at others. There was only the sound of breathing, an occasional cough, the shuffling of feet, the sound of birds outside.

"I have something I want to say." The circle was attentive. Some people opened their eyes and looked; others kept their eyes closed. The speaker was Stan Baker. He and his wife, Priscilla, were close friends with many of the regulars at the Sunday meetings. But Priscilla was not there this morning.

"It's very hard," Baker said. "But I want to tell you that I am coming out as a gay man, and my marriage with Priscilla is ending."

Someone gasped. Someone burst into tears. Priscilla and Stan were a much-loved couple, active with the Middlebury Quaker meeting for many years. No one at the meeting that day would condemn Baker's homosexuality; acceptance was a cardinal principle of the Quaker way. But they would mourn the loss of what had been.

At the end of the hour-long meeting, people rose from their chairs to engage in the usual greetings and small talk. Stan Baker did not wait around to chat. For him this announcement had been a wrenching and difficult experience. It signaled a watershed in his life. After years of struggle he had given up on the phase theory of sexuality and finally had admitted to himself that he was gay. It was not something he could stand around, cup of coffee in hand, making small talk about.

BILL LIPPERT'S activism on behalf of the gay community continued into the 1990s. By then his long ponytail was gone, and his beard was trimmed. As director of the Counseling Service he was able to make sure that mental health services in the region were appropriate for and available to gay and lesbian Vermonters. But he also saw a need for the gay community to help itself, and he began to talk of establishing a foundation for that purpose.

Ultimately, it was the toll of AIDS that helped get Lippert's foundation off the ground. A friend named Robert Mundstock had helped Lippert in the establishment of Vermont CARES, an organization dedicated to assisting people with HIV and AIDS. Yet Mundstock himself had contracted AIDS, and by 1992 his health was failing. Lippert went to visit him that year in Montpelier at a time when Mundstock had begun giving away his belongings. Mundstock was an artist, and he gave Lippert an elegant, blue-and-white stained-glass snowflake that years later was still hanging in the window of Lippert's living room.

Mundstock had heard Lippert talking about the foundation he hoped to establish, which Lippert then was calling the Human Rights Foundation of Vermont.

"Lippert, have you started that foundation yet?" Mundstock asked him that day in Montpelier.

"No, I haven't," Lippert said.

Mundstock told him he had better hurry. "Because if you don't have the foundation, I can't leave you any money."

Within a week, Lippert had established the foundation, but Mundstock had another request. He told Lippert there was a word—samara—that had special meaning to him.

Samara is the word that describes the winged seedpod of the maple, elm, or ash tree. Children in Vermont fling samaras and call them helicopters. Author May Sarton had written in one of her works about death, saying she did not believe when she died she would go away. Rather, she would be like a samara, a seed spread by the wind and growing up again from

the ground. Mundstock wanted Lippert to use the word
samara in the name of his foundation.

Soon Lippert rechristened his organization as the Samara
Foundation, in part because it was meant to disperse grants
and other support for the gay, lesbian, bisexual, and transgendered communities the way the winged seedpod of the maple
disperses itself over the landscape.

Before he died, Mundstock asked Lippert to place a stone
in the wall at his Hinesburg home in Mundstock's memory.
"I'd like to see Camel's Hump," Mundstock said, referring to
the peak that rose up within view of Lippert's yard.

Years later the stone rested in Lippert's garden with these
words chiseled into its surface:

ROBERT MUNDSTOCK

APRIL 13, 1947

OCTOBER 11, 1992

Upon his death, Mundstock left the fledgling Samara Foundation $4,000, which, combined with other bequests, got the
organization on its feet.

Lippert got into politics in 1994 when a vacancy opened up
in the Vermont House. It was assumed among Democrats in
the Hinesburg district that Howdy Russell, who had twice
come close to election as state senator, would be the favored
candidate for appointment by Governor Dean. But Russell had
taken a new job with the Middlebury Parent-Child Center, and
he said the duties of legislator would be too much for him. Lippert was among four candidates Dean interviewed, and by the
time Lippert had arrived home, Dean had left a message on his
answering machine. Lippert was to be a member of the Vermont House.

So Lippert was in place for a new chapter in the struggle
for gay rights. During the 1980s the gay and lesbian commu-

nity had been fighting mainly for negative freedom—freedom from violence and discrimination. During the 1990s the community would begin fighting for positive freedom—freedom to live a life of their choosing, to form families, to raise children, to marry. Politically, the players were lining up to carry that fight forward. But outside the State House, the movement for the right to marry was also taking shape, led by a team of dedicated lawyers and their six clients and propelled forward by a grassroots movement that would bring the issue of gay marriage to the doorstep of the Vermont State House.

CHAPTER FOUR

FAMILY

I.

ON MAY 15, 1989, Susan Bellemare and Susan Hamilton left Bennington, heading north toward their home in the central Vermont town of Duxbury. Their fourteen-month-old son, Collin, was in the backseat of their blue Toyota Camry. The past fourteen months had been hectic and difficult ones for the two women, and this weekend they had decided to give themselves a break. They dropped Collin off at the home of Susan Hamilton's parents in New Jersey and went on by themselves for the weekend at Long Beach Island on the New Jersey shore.

Now the weekend was over, and they were heading home, a drive of about two hours from Bennington. The highway rose above Rutland into the town of Mendon. Bellemare remembered that Hamilton was turned slightly in the passenger seat, her leg tucked up in front of her, so she could pay attention to Collin in the backseat. As they approached a bend in the highway, Susan Hamilton looked up ahead of them, then she shouted, "Watch out!" Bellemare looked up. For a brief moment, she saw a pickup truck careening into her lane. That was the last thing she remembered.

BY THE LATE 1980s an increasing number of lesbian couples around the country were having babies. Figures were hard to come by, but in 1989 the *New York Times* was reporting a baby boom among lesbian couples who were prevented by law from adopting children or serving as foster parents. It was new legal territory, and lawyers were searching for ways to establish custody rights for lesbian parents.

By 1987 Susan Bellemare and Susan Hamilton had been partners for eight years, and they were giving a lot of thought to the question of whether to have a child. During walks on the beach in Fort Lauderdale, they had discussed the potential repercussions of having a child, wondering how it would change their lives and considering the social and psychological pressures a child brought up by two lesbian parents would face.

Still, Susan Hamilton felt a strong maternal drive and the desire to bear a child. Susan Bellemare wanted to be a mother also, but she did not feel the need to bear the child herself.

Collin Hamilton was born at 12:24 A.M. on February 24, 1988, after a long and difficult labor. Susan Bellemare held him first, then she gave him to Susan Hamilton to hold. After Hamilton and the baby returned to Hamilton's room, Susan Bellemare walked into the waiting room to give her father and brother the news.

"It felt weird," she remembered. "Usually, it's the proud papa. I walked into the waiting room and said, 'It's a boy!'"

ON THAT Monday morning in May 1989, Douglas J. Bickford, a thirty-four-year-old resident of Belmont, was driving west in his pickup truck on Route 4 with his three-year-old son, Carlos. He was feeling the strain of a life in turmoil. His marriage was falling apart, and he had become embroiled in a custody dispute with his wife over the future of his son. Witnesses said Bickford was driving as fast as seventy-five miles per hour as he came around a curve on the highway. That is when his truck crashed head-on into the blue Toyota.

When Susan Bellemare regained consciousness, she was trapped in the wreckage of her car. She looked over at Hamilton, who was unconscious, her neck resting on the dashboard.

"Susan," she said, "talk to me."

It seemed like forever before rescue workers arrived at the scene of the crash. Bellemare shouted at them, pleading with them to get the baby out of the car.

Shortly an ambulance took Hamilton away. "Is she alive?" Bellemare asked.

One of the rescue workers held her face in his hands. "Look at my eyes," he said, trying to calm her down.

A second ambulance took Susan Bellemare and Collin Hamilton to the hospital. Collin had suffered only a broken rib; Bellemare was more seriously injured. At the hospital she still had no word on Susan Hamilton's condition.

Finally, a nurse came into her hospital room. "I'm sorry, Susan, your friend died."

Bellemare was in shock. She didn't know what was happening to her. Then her father, Bernard Bellemare, walked into the room, holding Collin. Bernard was crying.

"Dad, Susan died," Bellemare said.

"I know," he said.

Bernard Bellemare couldn't bring himself to come to his daughter's side or to comfort her directly. Susan saw her father's emotion was directed toward his fourteen-month-old grandson, whom he held in his arms.

Susan Bellemare had suffered a fractured hip, a fractured patella, and bruises to the heart and lungs. It would take her months to recover.

Within days she had additional bad news. Philip and Elsa

Hamilton, Susan's parents, had quickly gone to court and received an order that gave them custody of Collin. Collin was already with them in New Jersey. Susan Bellemare knew immediately that she would fight to have her son back.

SUSAN MURRAY picked up the *Rutland Herald* one day in May 1989 and saw on the front page a color photo showing a hideous car crash. A pickup truck on its side was engulfed in flames. Next to it was a blue sedan, its front end crushed. There was a second photo showing Rutland firefighter Tom Dipalma carrying a small boy with blond hair and blue sneakers away from the wreckage.

The story made an impression on Murray, then a thirty-one-year-old lawyer with Langrock Sperry & Wool in Middlebury. She had an interest in family law and handled many divorce, adoption, parentage, and custody cases. She understood all too well the difficulties that gay and lesbian couples had in asserting their rights in family matters. Gay marriage was not yet on the radar screen of activists in Vermont, but the case of Susan Bellemare was on Susan Murray's radar screen. Murray quickly won Bellemare's trust and took up her case.

SOON AFTER the crash Susan Bellemare had surgery during which a plate was implanted in her hip, and for six weeks she underwent intensive physical therapy. She had to get back on her feet if she was going to show a judge that she was a fit mother.

On June 30 there was a probate court hearing in Montpelier, and Bellemare was sitting in the courtroom when Philip and Elsa Hamilton walked in. Collin, in blue denim overalls, was in his grandmother's arms. It was the first time Bellemare had seen Collin since the day of the crash. Quickly, a bailiff took Collin away from his grandparents and carried him to a back room.

Susan Bellemare felt that Philip Hamilton had never been happy about his daughter's relationship with her. His wife, Elsa, seemed more accepting, frequently visiting them in the cities where they had been posted as nurses. Elsa had come to Collin's birth. Philip had not. Susan Hamilton had been the oldest of four children, and Philip Hamilton had probably hoped she would have a "typical nuclear family," Susan Bellemare said. Now that Susan was gone they wanted to hold on to the grandson she had given them.

Lawyers for the Hamiltons sought to have the hearing closed because it would involve information of a "sensitive and personal nature," but Judge L. John Cain refused. He needed to settle the matter of immediate custody, so he called Bellemare to the stand.

He asked her how she was feeling.

"I'm back at work," Bellemare told him. "I'm driving. I'm back at home and able to provide for the child."

She told Cain she was the child's other parent. She had made a commitment to Susan Hamilton to love and parent him. It was in their will.

Cain made a quick decision. There appeared to be nothing wrong with the will. Collin would go home with Bellemare.

Patrick J. Monaghan, one of the Hamiltons' lawyers, was outraged. He said giving Collin to Bellemare would cause "irreparable harm to the child," and he insisted the boy's "blood relatives" be given unrestricted visitation rights.

The only evidence of harm was the fact that Bellemare was lesbian, but often in the past that had been evidence enough. It wasn't enough evidence for Judge Cain, who gave custody to Susan Bellemare, allowing reasonable preplanned visits for Collin's grandparents.

Her case was a potent mixture of grief, anger, love, and confusion. It was also a test of definitions. The Hamiltons' emphasis on their blood relationship with Collin relied on the biological interpretation of family. For Bellemare to assert that she was Collin's parent was to extend the definition of parent beyond the biological. Of course, there are instances in law and custom when the term *parent* refers to someone other than a biological one. Adoption is the obvious example. But during the 1980s and 1990s, gay and lesbian couples struggled to enlarge the definition of parent even further, and gradually the courts had begun to comply.

Those weeks in the summer of 1989 when custody was still at issue were a time of enormous tension for Bellemare. She understood her every action would be scrutinized to determine if she was a fit mother. There were hearings ahead during which the Hamiltons continued to challenge the will, charging that Bellemare had exerted undue influence over their daughter. Susan Murray continued to assert that there was no basis for their challenge other than the fact that the Hamiltons did not like what their daughter had written into her will. "But that's too bad," Murray argued. "That's not the legal standard."

After several years of appeals, the Hamiltons gave up the fight. Bellemare knew that the Hamiltons wanted to hold on to Collin as a way of holding on to the memory of their daughter. And over the years, they established a routine of regular contact. Collin continued to visit his grandparents in New Jersey and attend a camp in New Hampshire each summer with his grandmother.

Finally, in the summer of 2002 something seemed to change for Philip Hamilton. He came to visit Susan Bellemare, her new partner, Pamela Brown, and his fourteen-year-old grandson at their new home in rural Fletcher, Vermont. All had experienced enormous grief, resentment, anger. What had

survived was a family, newly defined. By that time Collin
Hamilton was a handsome teenage boy, familiar with the story
of his mother's death and his other mother's struggle to continue to care for him.

For Susan Murray the Bellemare case was a good example
of how the law placed gay and lesbian couples at a disadvan-
tage. In cases of adoption or step-parenthood, a heterosexual
couple does not work under the presumption that the partner
of the biological parent is unfit. And with the option to marry,
a heterosexual couple could establish plainly the nature of
their relationship and their relationship to their children. Without changes in the law, gay and lesbian couples would have to
engage in an ad hoc struggle each time they had to confront
the legal system. Murray said the struggle Bellemare faced was
an "outrage," demonstrating to her that the state needed to
take important new steps to provide gay and lesbian couples
with the same protections enjoyed by everyone else.

2.

SUMMERS ON the California coast can be cool and, as the sun
was sinking into the Pacific one afternoon, two women who
would play important roles later in Vermont were snuggling
under a blanket on the beach.

It was 1991, and Nina Beck was thirty-five years old. She
was a physical therapist who had met Stacy Jolles two years before when she joined a class in kung fu that Stacy was teaching
in Oakland. Quickly, they fell in love, and soon Nina had
moved into Stacy's house on Peralta Street in Berkeley.

It turned out that both women had a parent from Vienna

who was a Holocaust survivor. Evylyn Torton Beck, who became a professor of women's studies at the University of Wisconsin, lost much of her family at Dachau and Buchenwald. Anthony Jolles, an engineer who worked in the semiconductor industry in California, lost his mother at Auschwitz. Both managed to escape to the United States before they could be sent to the camps. For their two daughters, the legacy of the Holocaust, combined with their identity as lesbians, inspired in them a willingness to stand up for what they believed.

It was a glorious day on the beach in Ventura. The ocean glowed pale blue as the sun sank toward the horizon. It was on that afternoon that Nina asked Stacy to marry her.

They knew the law did not provide the rights and benefits of marriage, though they also knew just a few months before, in March 1991, three gay couples in Hawaii had filed a suit seeking the right to marry. *Baehr v. Lewin* would be a landmark in the freedom-to-marry movement, though it would not end in success for the plaintiffs.

In its initial stages, the case in Hawaii lacked the backing of national gay rights organizations because of the fear that the lawsuit was premature and would provoke a backlash. Despite those fears, however, a variety of circumstances had combined to force marriage higher on the agenda for gay activists.

AIDS had swept through the gay community like a scythe, and committed, long-term relationships seemed increasingly to offer physical as well as spiritual safety. Moreover, the lesbian baby boom of the late 1980s had shown that same-sex couples were ready to assert their right to nurture families. Nina and Stacy believed that legal victory in Hawaii was a remote possibility, and they were not willing to wait for events to unfold in the courtrooms there. It was not up to Hawaii, California, or any other jurisdiction to define for them the nature of their relationship. There was no doubt in their minds that the refusal of the states to offer them the rights and benefits of marriage was a form of illegal discrimination. But until the states brought their laws into line with the rights guaranteed by the Constitution, they would define marriage in accordance with the law of their hearts.

On March 22, 1992, about fifty people gathered at a park in the redwood forests that cloaked the Oakland hills. It would be a traditional Jewish wedding, conducted by a lay rabbi inside a park building during a driving rain. There was no sense in anyone's mind that they were not witnessing a marriage, even if the state of California did not agree. "It was as much of a wedding as we thought we'd be able to have," Stacy said. At the same time, they figured that if Hawaii went ahead and legalized gay marriage, they would be eager to take the final step.

EVAN WOLFSON, cherubic and bald, was working out of the New York City office of the Lambda Legal Defense and Education Fund. As coordinator of the fund's Marriage Project, he had become one of the nation's leading advocates for the freedom to marry. He had sought to persuade his colleagues at Lambda to join the legal team arguing the *Baehr* case in Hawaii, but they were wary. It wasn't until the Hawaii Supreme Court's initial ruling in favor of the plaintiffs that Lambda decided Wolfson should join the case as co-counsel.

Wolfson has described the Hawaii case as a "tectonic shift" in the legal landscape of the gay rights movement. But Wolfson was more than a legal strategist. For him gay rights were civil rights, and he took inspiration from what he called the "methodologies of social change" advocated by the Reverend Martin Luther King, Jr.

In an article he wrote for the *New York University Review of Law and Social Change,* Wolfson quoted from King's book, *Why*

We Can't Wait: "It is an axiom of social change that no revolution can take place without a methodology suited to the circumstances of the period." King spoke of a "multiplicity" of methodologies, Wolfson said. Lawsuits alone would not be enough, though lawsuits would be an essential tool. Pressure on legislators would not be enough without public education to dispel the prejudice that held legislatures back. "A social movement that only moves people is merely a revolt," King wrote. "A movement that changes both people and institutions is a revolution."

Wolfson described the freedom-to-marry movement:

> As in any major civil rights effort, our struggle demands vision, strategy, courage, dedication, teamwork, patience, and luck. We are in this for the long haul, and ought to pace our efforts and choose our tactics accordingly . . . *Baehr v. Lewin* engendered a broad coalition and tremendous political activism that have truly begun a sea change throughout the social institutions of Hawaii.

Such a sea change would not occur without a struggle. Wolfson quoted King: "Freedom is never voluntarily given by the oppressor; it must be demanded by the oppressed."

The *Baehr* case in Hawaii offered a preview of the battles over marriage that would follow in Vermont and elsewhere. The plaintiffs based their claims on the Hawaii Constitution, rather than the United States Constitution. They knew that the United States Supreme Court had already ruled in *Bowers v. Hardwick* that states did not violate the constitutional right to privacy when they passed laws barring "homosexual sodomy." There was little likelihood the conservative Rehnquist court would overturn that precedent by requiring states to recognize gay marriage. Therefore, basing the case on Hawaiian law would protect it from an uncertain fate in the federal courts.

Even so, the United States Supreme Court had set down precedents that would be more useful than *Bowers*. In *Loving v. Virginia* the Supreme Court had established that laws barring interracial marriage were unconstitutional. In *Zablocki v. Rehail* the Supreme Court had expanded on its ruling in *Loving*, throwing out a law that prevented deadbeat dads from remarrying. In that case the court found that the right to marry was a fundamental freedom that could be restricted only by a narrowly crafted exception that had a compelling social purpose.

In a case involving the right of prisoners to marry, *Turner v. Safley*, the court found that there were many benefits to marriage apart from the potential for procreation. These included emotional, spiritual, and economic benefits. Opponents of same-sex marriage often relied on the argument that the purpose of marriage was procreation, and the court's ruling in *Turner* dealt a blow to that argument.

The thunderbolt from Hawaii came on May 5, 1993, when the Hawaii Supreme Court reversed the lower court's dismissal of the *Baehr* case. The Supreme Court sent the case back to the trial court so the court could determine whether there was a compelling reason for discrimination barring gay marriage.

The Hawaii ruling relied on a concept that would surface later in other cases. Justice Steven Levinson based his decision on that provision of the Hawaii Constitution that bars discrimination based on "race, religion, sex, or ancestry." It was not because homosexuals shared an equal right to marry that Levinson found in their favor. Rather, it was because the discrimination that prevented them from marrying was based on sex. In the *Loving* case, the United States Supreme Court found that to bar a black man from marrying a white woman was to deny the black man the right to make an important personal choice solely because he was black. In Hawaii the only reason

Ninia Baehr was barred from marrying Genora Dancel was
that she was a woman.

The freedom-to-marry movement in Vermont would
eventually employ the multiple methodologies advised by
Martin Luther King, including a well-organized campaign of
public education. But during the mid-1990s, Wolfson's work
was focused on Hawaii. In Vermont the freedom-to-marry
campaign was just beginning to take shape.

PERALTA STREET is on the quieter north end of Berkeley on
the other side of the University of California campus from the
countercultural mecca of Telegraph Avenue. The north side
was where students, faculty, and others lived on quiet, tree-
lined avenues at the foot of the Berkeley hills.

But it was not quiet enough. For more than twenty years
urban crime had been driving young people away from the
cities toward America's small towns. There were numerous
shootings in downtown Berkeley during those years, and when
a shooting occurred on Peralta Street, Nina Beck and Stacy
Jolles began to think seriously about moving away.

First, Nina conceived a child with sperm from a sperm
bank. The prospect of raising a child gave additional incentive
for them to look for safer surroundings, and they began to research places where they might move.

They settled on Asheville, North Carolina, a small city
with a reputation as a home for artists. They were looking for
a place where a lesbian Jewish couple raising a child on their
own would find acceptance. So with Nina seven months preg-
nant, they moved.

Two months later they were planning for the birth of their
child at their new home in Asheville. But after four days of
labor, they realized they would have to go to the hospital for
delivery. It was there that they had the kind of memorable en-

counter that has served gay and lesbian couples as ample justification for the struggle to win the right to marry.

Nina was on a gurney in the grip of labor, and the nurses were wheeling her toward the delivery room. She and Stacy were both exhausted, and Stacy was walking by her side as they headed toward what they hoped, finally, would be the birth of their child.

At that moment a nurse turned to Stacy and said to her, "Who are you?"

Stacy had been half expecting such a challenge, which she viewed not only as a challenge but as an insult.

"I am her partner," she said, and she showed the nurse legal papers they had signed in advance, giving Stacy permission to attend the birth. She was carrying them in her back pocket.

After delivery by Caesarean section on February 18, 1995, they had their son, Noah Jolles, and they had become a family of three. Quickly, however, Noah was shifted to the neonatal intensive care unit. It turned out Noah was suffering from a congenital heart defect that caused the thickening of the ventricle wall. His doctors did not expect him to live. Stacy and Nina were with him twenty-four hours a day during the first few days of his life. Finally, after a week Noah was doing well, and the family of three went home.

But the question "who are you?" had stung Stacy to her core. It is a question that shadows the lives of gay and lesbian couples, forcing them to justify what should need no justification. Years later Stacy remembered that question as a typical example of the attack that society makes as a matter of course on the dignity of gay and lesbian couples. It was a question, spoken or unspoken, that had turned them into fighters on behalf of their own dignity and the dignity of others. They didn't yet know what shape that fight would take in the years ahead.

3.

SUSAN MURRAY was gaining a reputation as a lawyer who understood the specific needs of gay couples seeking legal protection with regard to wills, health care, child custody, and other matters where the law left them vulnerable. The Susan Bellemare case was a dramatic example, but her work also involved ordinary legal questions that for gay couples were often far from ordinary.

By 1994 she was working with the Vermont Coalition for Lesbian and Gay Rights, which had become involved in the issue of adoption as it related to gay couples. Just as the Equal Rights Amendment had alarmed conservatives about the prospect of gay marriage, adoption reform alarmed them about the prospect of adoption by gays and lesbians.

In June 1993 the Vermont Supreme Court became the first supreme court in the nation to approve adoption by a homosexual partner. The case involved Jane Van Buren and Deborah Lashman of Burlington, who had lived in a monogamous relationship since 1986. They had met in Boston then moved to Washington, D.C. As their lawyer told the Supreme Court, they wanted to have the kind of close family that each had grown up with, and so they decided to have children. In order that their children would be full siblings, the two boys born to Van Buren were conceived by artificial insemination from the same anonymous donor.

When the first child was due, the pair moved to Burlington, where Van Buren's family lived. There the two of them raised their children. The boys called Van Buren "Mommy," and they called Deborah "Ima"—Hebrew for mother. But in order to establish her rights as a mother in the eyes of the state, Lashman had gone to probate court to adopt the children. The state Department of Social and Rehabilitation Services had de-

termined that allowing the adoptions was in the best interest
of the children, but Probate Judge George Belcher ruled that
state law did not allow a nonmarital partner to become a second adoptive parent. That is how the case that became known
as *In re: B.L.V.B.* came before the Vermont Supreme Court.

The Supreme Court justice who wrote the unanimous decision in *B.L.V.B.* was Denise Johnson. Governor Madeleine
Kunin had appointed Johnson to the bench in December 1990
in part because of her record as a civil rights lawyer who had
championed the rights of women. Johnson, the first woman to
sit on the Vermont Supreme Court, had played a role earlier
that year in pushing for passage of Vermont's hate crimes law.
Two and a half years later the case of *B.L.V.B.* came to her. She
could not know it at the time, but the ruling she wrote in that
case would be one of the crucial precedents paving the way for
the court's decision in the *Baker* case six years later.

In writing the court's decision in *B.L.V.B.*, Johnson said she
found the lower court's ruling to be illogical. "In interpreting
Vermont's adoption statutes, we are mindful that the state's
primary concern is to promote the welfare of children," Johnson wrote. Johnson acknowledged that Belcher's reading of
the adoption law was technically correct. But since the laws
had been passed, families had changed. "When social mores
change," Johnson wrote, "governing statutes must be interpreted to allow for those changes in a manner that does not
frustrate the purposes behind their enactment. To deny the
children of same-sex partners . . . the security of a legally recognized relationship with their second parent serves no legiti-
mate state interest." By employing the phrase *second parent,*
Johnson had enlarged the meaning of the word parent.

Soon the Vermont Legislature took the issue of gay adoption even further. The Legislature was working on an adoption reform bill that dealt with issues such as the right of

adoptees and birth parents to trace their biological parents or children. In an early indication of the trouble that would be caused by the issue of same-sex couples, the Senate Health and Welfare Committee voted in March 1995 to strip out language that would allow gay and unmarried couples to adopt. The committee's language, adopted by a 3–2 vote, would allow only single people or married couples to adopt.

That committee's vote was not the end of the matter, however. When the Senate Judiciary Committee took up the bill, Senator Richard Sears, a Democrat from Bennington, offered an amendment allowing gay and lesbian couples to adopt. Sears, who was himself an adoptee, acknowledged that gay adoption had become a "lightning rod," even though the question took up only a few paragraphs in a bill that was 110 pages long. His amendment failed on a 3–3 vote, but during the summer the Judiciary Committee continued to work on the bill, eventually changing its mind and opening up adoption to gay and lesbian couples. When the full Senate passed the adoption reform bill in January 1996, it rejected an amendment that would have barred gay adoption.

When the bill moved to the Vermont House, it became the focus of long hours of work by the House Judiciary Committee. Representatives Thomas Little of Shelburne and Bill Lippert were both members of the committee, and both mentioned later that the committee's protracted labors on the adoption bill forged a working relationship among members that would be essential to their success years later.

Eventually the House also passed the adoption reform bill, including provisions allowing for adoption by gays and lesbians. In working on this bill, important figures in the civil unions debate were taking their places. Tom Little and Bill Lippert in the House and Dick Sears in the Senate had seen how volatile the issue of gay rights could be, but they had not been spooked by the issue of gay relationships.

AS SUSAN Murray became more involved in the work of the Vermont Coalition for Lesbian and Gay Rights, she gained a new and important ally.

Beth Robinson had joined Langrock Sperry & Wool in February 1993, four years after graduating from the University of Chicago Law School. Those who have worked with Robinson invariably describe her as a brilliant lawyer with a rigorous intellect. Like many who have moved to Vermont over the years, she had gained an appreciation for small-town life during her childhood. She was born in Karachi, Pakistan, where her father was working as a physician for the United States Agency for International Development. But she remembered a childhood spent on a quiet dead-end road in Bloomington, Indiana, where she used to ride around with the milkman in his truck as he made deliveries. She took a 66 percent cut in pay, leaving her firm in Washington to move to Vermont, but at her home in Ferrisburgh, she had the garden that was essential to her idea of rural living. And she had a sense of community.

In the view of Peter Langrock, senior partner at Langrock Sperry & Wool, Beth Robinson and Susan Murray made an ideal team. At the outset, Langrock said, not all members of the firm were "up to speed on the gay issue." But as they learned more about the freedom-to-marry movement and the legal challenge that Robinson and Murray hoped to mount, members of the firm allowed the two lawyers wide latitude to pursue their case.

Marriage was not the first priority of the Vermont Coalition for Lesbian and Gay Rights, however. After all, there was no unanimity within the gay community about whether marriage was a good thing. Many people still believed marriage was the product of an oppressive patriarchal society, and they were happy to be free of it. But Susan Murray's work with Susan Bellemare and other gay clients had made it clear to her that for those gay and lesbian couples who wished to form committed, long-term relationships, the law was discriminatory.

Murray found another ally in 1994 when she attended a meeting of Gay and Lesbian Advocates and Defenders (GLAD) in Boston. Mary Bonauto, a lawyer working for GLAD, was already one of the leading gay rights advocates in New England. She had significant experience with the constitutional issues surrounding the right to marry, and she became part of the effort to pursue a marriage case in Vermont.

In 1995 Murray and Robinson joined with a handful of supporters to form the Vermont Freedom to Marry Task Force. It was an organization focused on a specific task with a long-range vision of what it would take to achieve real equality.

At the outset the task force had two goals: to reach out to the community in order to prepare the way for gay marriage and to find plaintiffs willing to pursue a case in court. It wouldn't be easy persuading Vermonters that gay and lesbian couples could be suitable, loving parents, and that difficulty became evident during the controversy over *Daddy's Roommate*.

4.

IT WAS A sweltering evening in June 1995, and 180 people had crowded into the Nella Grimm Fox Room upstairs at the Rutland Free Library. Outside, another 160 people waited on the sidewalk. They were hoping for a chance to join the crowd inside, where a bitterly divided community was debating whether the library should remove a book called *Daddy's Roommate* from the library shelves.

The book, with pictures and text by Michael Willhoite, describes the life of a family that includes a man and his young son and the man's gay partner. The story begins as Daddy loads his suitcase into the trunk of his car and the little boy is saying, "My Mommy and Daddy got a divorce last year." As the story unfolds, the boy learns that Daddy has a roommate named Frank. The two men "work together, eat together, sleep together, shave together." The book shows these commonplace events, and it shows how the boy and Frank become friends. The two men and the boy go to ball games, the zoo, the beach. They do what any family would do. Then toward the end of the book, when the boy is wondering what it means to be gay, the mother explains that being gay "is just one more kind of love."

The drawings are innocent but real. The boy says that sometimes the two men fight but that they "always make up." The drawing shows Frank reaching up to touch Daddy's shoulder. Daddy is wearing a tank top, and his shoulder is bare, so Frank's gesture is both tender and intimate.

Karol Raiche of Rutland, mother of three, discovered the book on the shelf of the children's section and was appalled by it. She complained to the library's board of trustees, prompting a public outcry, and the board decided to hold a public hearing.

The ceiling fans revolved slowly in the second-floor room. The library board sat at a table across the long side of the room, facing an emotionally charged crowd and the television cameras that had arrived to record the scene.

When Raiche stepped to the microphone, she made an impassioned plea on behalf of her sense of right and wrong. "Is it wrong to ask the library to protect the children, to teach them the normalcies of life?" She was near tears. "Do we teach them that homosexuality is normal and correct? Is there any-thing abnormal today?"

But the library had its defenders, including sixteen-year-old Erin Gluckman. "I've been living with my lesbian mother and her partner for six years, and I have not been corrupted," she said. "Let me set one thing straight. I like men. I did not choose to be straight, just as my mother did not choose to be a lesbian."

William Meub, a Rutland lawyer who later ran unsuccess-fully as a Republican candidate for governor and for Congress, told the board the real issue was one of fear. Parents fear they are losing control over their children, he said. But fear should not be allowed to govern our selection of books at the library. "Fear is the enemy of freedom," he said.

As the hearing extended into the evening, moderator Ted Corsones struggled to maintain a civil tone. The close atmo-sphere and the bristling emotions filled the room with tension.

FOR RELIGIOUS fundamentalists, fear of modernity has taken many forms. In the early part of the century, Christian fundamentalism received its impetus from fear of the way that history and science had begun to provide a view of human origins and biblical history that challenged the literal word of the Bible. Thus, in 1925, John Scopes, a high school biology teacher in Dayton, Tennessee, went on trial for teaching the theory of evolution.

In the latter part of the century, the fear of sexual freedom and new stresses on the family had put sex at the center of the battle between religious fundamentalists and the modern world. The argument in Rutland took a familiar form. On the one side there were those counseling tolerance and openness, arguing that new ideas were nothing to fear, that fear itself was the greatest threat to democracy. On the other side were those who defended what they saw as imperiled traditional values and who wanted to protect children from alien ideas in order to protect society from destruction.

And yet there was a paradoxical twist to the argument about *Daddy's Roommate,* as there was in the argument about gay adoption and, later, about civil unions. Many sitting in the overheated meeting room at the library in Rutland or milling impatiently on the sidewalk outside viewed homosexuality merely as the indulgence of perverted sexual desire. In their eyes, gay parenting, gay adoption, and gay marriage threatened the American family. The family, they argued, is fundamental to society; it is how we nurture our young and transmit our values to the next generation. In order to defend the family, children must be protected from books such as *Daddy's Roommate.*

But the case for strong families was also a case for *Daddy's Roommate* and for laws that allowed gay partners to adopt and to form stable unions. The implicit message of the book was that families exist in many forms. This was not something the author was making up. Two of the couples who became part of the *Baker* case were raising children. And as the testimony showed, there were those in the audience at the Rutland library who lived with gay or lesbian parents. Those defending *Daddy's Roommate* recognized that the traditional notion of the nuclear family did not encompass the fullness of reality and that the family as a social bulwark was not strengthened by attacking some families or forcing them to live in the shadows. As conservatives argued for the importance of families, gay and lesbian couples were nodding in agreement. "You're right," they were saying, "and that includes us."

The library board adjourned the meeting that night after hearing powerful testimony on both sides. Soon, the board decided *Daddy's Roommate* would stay on the shelf. It was the library's job to bring information to the community, including information about gay families.

NINA BECK, Stacy Jolles, and Noah were now a family of three, but Asheville did not prove to be the kind of home the two women had been hoping to find. They had found jobs and had bought a comfortable house on a wooded hillside in a residential neighborhood. But about a year after they had moved there, friends of theirs admitted they did not feel they had become part of the community even after living there for eight years. Nina and Stacy had the same feeling, and they decided that they did not want to wait eight years before trying to rectify it. Once again they began to research the question of where they could find a small city that might provide them with a feeling of community. They knew little about Vermont. They were from California, where sunshine, beaches, and radical politics were the stuff of everyday life. Nina had grown up in Wisconsin, so she knew that if they were to move to Vermont, Stacy ought to understand what winter was about. So they visited Burlington over a long weekend in February 1996. Shortly thereafter they sold their house in Asheville, and in May 1996 they made the move to Vermont.

The next month Nina and Stacy attended the annual Gay Pride Parade in Burlington, and that is where they came across a brochure from the Vermont Freedom to Marry Task Force. Susan Murray and Beth Robinson had begun their work in earnest, speaking to community groups, and spreading the word that they hoped to mount a lawsuit that would challenge the exclusion of gay and lesbian couples from marriage in Vermont.

Mary Bonauto had met with Robinson and Murray at Robinson's house in 1996, and that is when they decided to go ahead with a lawsuit. They considered Vermont to be a promising venue for a number of reasons. Vermont's hate crimes law, antidiscrimination law, and adoption reform law showed that Vermont was likely to be as sympathetic as anyplace to the cause of gay marriage. The fact that the Vermont Constitution was difficult to amend also meant that advances made in the courtroom would be difficult to reverse.

Nina and Stacy had thought that if they ever had the chance to become plaintiffs in such a case, they would give it serious thought. It was outrageous to them that they both could be connected to Noah legally but they couldn't be connected to each other. So they got in touch with Murray and Robinson and said they wanted to be a part of the suit.

It was at an annual conference of the Vermont Coalition for Lesbian and Gay Rights—an event called Queer Town Meeting—that Lois Farnham and Holly Puterbaugh heard about the Freedom to Marry Task Force. They had been together for more than twenty years, and they were becoming interested in involving themselves in the larger gay community. When the idea of joining the marriage lawsuit occurred to them, they decided they were well suited for the challenge. They were both professionals who were respected members of the community. "I think it was important for the heterosexual community to see that," Holly said later. So they signed on to the lawsuit, too.

Joseph Watson had been a member of the Freedom to Marry Task Force from its inception, and he had considered joining with his partner, Michael Warner, as plaintiffs in the case. But Murray and Robinson wanted plaintiffs from Chittenden County, which encompassed Burlington and surrounding towns and was the most urban and liberal county in the state. Watson, who was from Middlebury, had enlisted Stan Baker in the work of the task force by asking him to narrate a video Watson was making about the marriage issue. Watson knew Baker and his partner, Peter Harrigan, as an articulate and committed couple who were living in Shelburne, and he suggested to Robinson and Murray that they would be ideal plaintiffs for the lawsuit.

Robinson and Murray wanted plaintiffs who would be able to put a personal face on the cause. They would be speaking to community groups and the media, so they needed to be articulate and committed, strong enough not to become defensive when attacked. The lawyers also wanted a varied group. The three couples in the suit included one male couple, one pair of younger women, and one pair of older women. These three couples would have to remain steady under immense pressure, and they would have to show by the example of their lives the strength of their case.

By 1997 only five years had elapsed since Vermont had passed the antidiscrimination bill that had convulsed the Legislature and divided the state. As the furor in Rutland over *Daddy's Roommate* showed, fear and hostility were dry tinder ignited quickly by the issue of gay rights. But the controversy also showed that even in a conservative city such as Rutland the voices urging openness and tolerance were not unafraid to join the fray.

5.

WHERE THE Westford Road nears the Westford town line, the land flattens out, affording a magnificent view of Mount Mansfield, Vermont's highest peak. The folds of the mountainside catch the shadows as the sun makes its passage during the day, and the seasons transform the slopes from gleaming white to green to blazing orange during the course of a year. In April 1997 the pale green of spring had yet to touch the mountainside.

Lois Farnham and Holly Puterbaugh lived here on the Westford Road in the town of Milton. They had 150 acres and operated a small Christmas tree farm behind their ranch house and their three-car garage.

On April 25, 1997, they got into their car and headed into town. The road descended through woods, passing a tall weathered barn, a scattering of unremarkable houses, and the Milton Wood Products plant. As they entered the village of Milton, they passed a row of grand old houses, maple trees lined up in front of them. The Westford Road became Main Street as it passed through the village, and then Main Street ran up against Route 7. The village's Civil War statue with its listing of the dead from Milton stood in front of Cody's Irish Tavern.

They pulled up at the town clerk's office on Bombardier Road. They were nervous about the step they were taking. "It was, gulp, here goes," Holly said later. They had called the day before to say they were coming and what they wanted. The clerk, John Cushing, was someone they had known for many years. He was grateful for the warning. He would have time to prepare a letter telling them why it wasn't in his power to grant them a marriage license. He was a gentleman about the whole thing. Nobody wanted any hard feelings. It wasn't a surprise to him that Holly and Lois considered themselves a couple. But there was nothing he could do to help them.

That the legal and social revolution leading to the creation of civil unions in Vermont had its beginnings on an ordinary Thursday in this ordinary town should not be surprising. The movement toward civil unions was based on the premise that marriage for gays and lesbians ought to be as commonplace as it was for anyone else. Because the issue was about sex and love, it unleashed fear and confusion among many people, and the hatred on display was real. But hatred was countered by an instinct toward neighborliness and courtesy. John Cushing knew Holly and Lois. He didn't want to be unkind. The law was the law—at least for the time being. That was something they all understood.

By June Stacy Jolles, Nina Beck, Stan Baker, and Peter Harrigan had visited the town clerks in South Burlington and Shelburne. In order to pursue a court case, each couple had to seek a marriage license. Now all the plaintiffs had letters explaining that town clerks were not empowered by Vermont law to issue marriage licenses to same-sex couples. The stage was set for the historic case they hoped would end up changing the law.

ON JULY 22 Murray, Robinson, and Bonauto were ready to announce they had filed suit to secure for their six plaintiffs the right to marry under existing Vermont law. "We are challenging the notion that a couple in love can't marry each other simply because they made the mistake of falling in love with someone of the 'wrong' gender," Bonauto told a press conference.

Susan Murray told the press: "Finding a partner, finding a mate, and getting married, is a basic human right. The state of Vermont should not be allowed to step in and tell two consenting adults that they cannot marry one another."

Attorney General William Sorrell responded to the announcement of the lawsuit by saying the Legislature should resolve the issue, not the courts. Governor Howard Dean countered that he thought the Legislature should leave it alone and let the courts decide.

For the plaintiffs in the case, the July 22 press conference meant there was no turning back. "It was a major step in outing ourselves," said Holly Puterbaugh. "Anyone who had questions now knew for sure."

One of the three couples who brought the suit was missing from the July 22 press conference. A few days earlier, Noah Jolles, by then two-and-a-half years old, had fallen ill. Despite his heart condition, he had lived a nearly normal life, but on that day in July he began to experience a rapid heart rate, and Nina and Stacy raced him to the emergency room in Burlington. For the next three weeks, he was in and out of Dartmouth-Hitchcock Medical Center in New Hampshire for tests and medication. But he continued to have attacks of angina, and his condition worsened. Finally, Nina and Stacy took him to Boston Children's Hospital where he waited for a heart transplant. He was so heavily medicated that he did not regain consciousness. He died on August 29, 1997.

Seventy-five people came to a memorial service for Noah at a park in Burlington, where they planted a small maple tree in Noah's memory. Stacy said she didn't even know most of the people at the service. "He was an amazing human being," she said of her son.

The loss of Noah tested their relationship as such a loss would test any marriage. They went to hell and back, Stacy said, but each allowed the other to grieve in her own way.

At the same time, Stacy said, they felt "more compelled than ever" to remain part of the case. "I loved that Beth always kept Noah alive," she said. Noah, even in his absence, became emblematic of the importance of family, and they viewed their participation in the case as an opportunity. Not everyone was in a position to take a public role in so important a legal challenge. "We were perfect people to step out into the limelight—because we could," Nina said.

Now the action shifted to Murray and Robinson. The first step was to file a complaint in Superior Court. They knew lawyers for the state of Vermont would respond with a motion to dismiss their complaint. That meant that the arguments in the case would first be heard in response to the state's motion to dismiss. They also knew that whatever the outcome in the lower court, the case probably would be appealed to the state's only appeals court, the Vermont Supreme Court.

With the *Baker* case, the freedom-to-marry movement had moved to new terrain, and the outcome was now up to the lawyers who were preparing for the most important case of their lives. The great civil rights cases of the past provided inspiring precedent, but now the issue was not the color of one's skin. The issue was the most fundamental of human relationships. The bonds that held together the three couples in the *Baker* case had been tested by time and by tragedy. Many heterosexual couples would envy the strength of these relationships. But they were bonds that until now had existed outside the law.

The arguments that would be heard in the coming months would turn on the way words were defined and on the logic deployed by both sides. But beneath the battle of ideas, the case touched the deepest human passions. The lawyers in the case could describe the meaning of the marriage bond with the detachment of physicists describing the bonds holding the atom together. But they knew the power of that bond to be as explosive as any social force, and the passion that suffused the case gave a feeling of urgency and importance to the outcome. For Lois and Holly, Nina and Stacy, Stan and Peter, there would now be a long period of waiting. Eventually, as the case unfolded, America would get a lesson in the nature of freedom, the meaning of family, and the capacity of democracy to bend with the winds of change in order to accommodate the demands of human dignity.

CHAPTER FIVE

THE CASE

I.

ON NOVEMBER 18, 1998, Beth Robinson stepped onto the small platform behind the podium in the stately wood-paneled Supreme Court chamber in Montpelier. A deep green carpet created a richly dignified atmosphere within the chamber.

Robinson placed her notebook on the podium before her. "Thank you, Your Honors, and good morning," she said.

Behind her in the front row to her right, the six plaintiffs in the *Baker* case watched expectantly. Stacy, Nina, Peter, Stan, Lois, and Holly had been ushered to their places from a back room to avoid the crush of the press outside.

Robinson began:

Fifty years ago the California Supreme Court handed down its decision in the landmark case of *Perez v. Lippold*, striking down California's ban on interracial marriage. I'd like to take a few moments to talk about that case this morning because the parallels between that case and this case are striking.

It's easy to sit here in 1998 and look back and say that that decision was an easy one. Of course the ban on interracial marriage was unconstitutional. But at the time thirty of the forty-eight states in the country prohibited interracial marriage. In fact, six found it so odious that they prohibited it by constitutional provision. Nine out of ten Americans opposed interracial marriage.

Robinson spoke with a restrained urgency, gripping the podium with her left hand, gesturing with her right. The justices in their black robes looked down from their high-backed chairs, rocking occasionally. Chief Justice Amestoy sat in the center of the five. He was known for his sense of humor, but in the judicial setting the corners of his mouth turned down thoughtfully. To his right sat the Dickensian figure of Justice John Dooley, portly, double-chinned, with nineteenth-century-style sideburns, and half-glasses perched at the end of his nose. Justice Denise Johnson sat to Dooley's right. To Amestoy's left sat Justices James Morse and Marilyn Skoglund.

Robinson continued:

> No court in this country had ever concluded, despite numerous challenges, that an interracial couple might have a constitutionally protected right to marry. In fact the notion of a black person and a white person marrying was as antithetical to many people's concept of what a marriage was as the notion of a man marrying a man or a woman marrying a woman appears to be to the state of Vermont today.

It was a state supreme court that took the pioneering step against the ban on interracial marriage fifty years ago, and Robinson hoped the Vermont Supreme Court would take a similar role with regard to gay marriage.

> The California Supreme Court's decision at the time was controversial. It was courageous. And it was correct. Perhaps most striking for our purposes today are the argu-

ments which the California Supreme Court rejected in reaching its conclusion, arguments that resonate clearly with the state's arguments here today.

She summarized these arguments: Interracial couples did not have a right to marry because they had never previously enjoyed that right. The races were inherently different. The legislature might be compelled to legalize bigamy or incest. The ban flowed from the definition of things and was not discriminatory because whites and blacks were both barred from interracial marriage.

The California Supreme Court in 1948 rejected other arguments that were familiar from the state's arguments in the *Baker* case. It rejected the arguments that deference should be paid to the legislature and that interracial marriage was inherently unnatural and should be barred to protect children.

Vermont in 1998 was making all of the arguments made in 1948 by the dissent in the *Perez* case, Robinson said, and history had passed those arguments by. That left the state with only one contention on which to base its case: It was in the interest of the state to limit the definition of marriage because of the ability of heterosexual couples to beget children.

This was the procreation argument. Dismantling the procreation argument would be essential to Robinson's case.

2.

THE ARGUMENTS heard in the *Baker* case on November 18 were the culmination of a legal campaign that had gained surprisingly rapid momentum. It was only a few years before that Bill Lippert, Howdy Russell, and other gay rights activists were struggling against embedded homophobia to secure basic rights. No one imagined in 1992, during the furious debate about the antidiscrimination bill, that just six years later the state might be on the verge of legalizing gay marriage. But a variety of social forces, political changes, and legal decisions had flowed together to make the prospect of gay marriage a realistic possibility.

One of those favorable conditions was the Supreme Court itself. Jeffrey Amestoy had come to the court after a long career as Vermont's Republican attorney general. But in his earlier years, he had experienced a different kind of political education.

Amestoy had grown up in Rutland, where he was a diminutive shortstop and second baseman. Politically, the Amestoy family was not typical of the area. In earlier years William Amestoy, Jeffrey's father, had attracted the attention of the FBI because of his sympathies for the Spanish government during the Spanish Civil War. William Amestoy was from a Basque family in Los Angeles, and for a time he had considered joining the Abraham Lincoln Brigade, a contingent of Americans who had gone to Spain to fight the Spanish fascists. As a boy Jeffrey Amestoy was the only one he knew who supported Adlai Stevenson for president.

Eventually, the family moved to Connecticut, where Jeffrey Amestoy attended high school. Later, as a student at Hobart and William Smith Colleges in Geneva, New York, he became active in the antiwar movement, helping to organize a protest march in Washington, D.C., and campaigning in Indiana for Senator Eugene McCarthy in the Democratic primary of 1968. After law school in San Francisco, he returned to Vermont where he went to work for Vermont's Republican attorney general, James Jeffords. Amestoy decided he, too, was a Republican. Vermont was a place where the liberal wing of the Republican Party was still holding its own.

Other members of the court had backgrounds suggesting that even if it was hard to pigeonhole them as liberal, they certainly could not be defined as conservative. John Dooley had not served on the bench before he was appointed to the Supreme Court by Governor Madeleine Kunin in 1987. Observers of the court frequently said Dooley had great logical powers and a brilliant mind. He began in Vermont as a Legal Aid lawyer and then went to work in the administration of Governor Kunin. But if in politics he had worked for a liberal Democratic governor, his record on the court suggested that the logical imperatives of a case, rather than political bias, would generally guide his thinking.

James Morse had served as the state's defender general from 1976 to 1981, overseeing the state's system of public defenders. Morse served as a Superior Court judge from 1981 to 1988, when Governor Kunin appointed him to the high court.

Marilyn Skoglund was known for her boisterous sense of humor. She and a group of women friends in the Montpelier area had regular poker nights, and Skoglund was part of a country and western band. She was said to have a tattoo. She had never attended law school; instead she learned law as a clerk for Supreme Court Justice Louis Peck. She had been an assistant attorney general when Amestoy was attorney general, and in 1994 Dean had appointed her to the District Court and to the Supreme Court in 1997.

Denise Johnson's background as a civil rights lawyer made her well disposed toward the cause of gays and lesbians. She had shown she was willing to dissent from the majority if she thought the court had not been sufficiently deferential to the rights of Vermonters.

The court had already shown it was willing to provoke controversy. In 1997 the court, then under Chief Justice Frederic Allen, had declared Vermont's education funding system to be unconstitutional and, foreshadowing the remedy in the *Baker* case, had turned the matter over to the Legislature to solve. In a case brought on behalf of schoolgirl Amanda Brigham from the small farming town of Whiting, the court ruled that a system allowing wide disparities in revenue for education arbitrarily favored some towns over others. Significantly, the court relied on the Common Benefits Clause of the Vermont Constitution, holding that the state had no right to favor one group over another.

AS EXPECTED, the state's initial response to the plaintiffs' complaint in the *Baker* case was a motion in Superior Court for the judge to dismiss the case. And it was in crafting briefs to support or oppose this motion that both sides shaped their arguments. The state's lawyers made several points in arguing for dismissal.

The state argued that limiting marriage to heterosexuals was "rationally related" to the purposes of marriage and so deference must be paid to the intentions of the Legislature. "Vast societal changes should not be wrought at the honed point of a judicial ruling," said the state's brief.

Further, the state argued that the "plain meaning" of the word *marriage* indicated that the Legislature meant to restrict marriage to a man and a woman. The state quoted Webster's dictionary and *Black's Law Dictionary,* and it searched through Vermont statutes to show that marriage as a heterosexual union was woven into the scheme of Vermont's laws.

The state also argued that the purpose of begetting offspring was fundamental to marriage; indeed, inability to procreate may be grounds for ending a marriage. "Plaintiffs' true quarrel," the state wrote, "is with the definition of marriage, not its fair application between the sexes."

Gays and lesbians were not subject to gender discrimination, the state argued. Men and women alike were barred from marrying someone of the same gender and that was because of the definition of marriage.

The state argued also that it had an interest in protecting children by furthering the link between procreation and child rearing. And the state celebrated the worth of marriage as an institution that promoted the integration of the two genders. "Marriage venerates the diversity between men and women," the state wrote.

In opposing the state's motion to dismiss, Robinson, Murray, and their colleague in Boston, Mary Bonauto, sought to show that in the 1990s there was nothing unusual about gay couples raising children. They estimated that there were twenty million gay and lesbian people in America in 1989 and that anywhere from six million to fourteen million were raising children. And their parenting skills "are essentially the same as their heterosexual counterparts," the lawyers wrote.

One of the lawyers' important goals was to counter the argument about the "plain meaning" of the word *marriage,* and she did so by pointing to the "underlying purpose" of the marriage statute, which was to protect, encourage, and support the union of committed couples.

In looking to the underlying purpose, Robinson, Murray, and Bonauto made ample use of the Vermont Supreme Court's 1993 ruling *In re: B.L.V.B.* "The court in *B.L.V.B.* . . . found that the underlying purpose of the adoption law was not to prohibit certain combinations of individuals (such as lesbian couples) from adopting, but rather to provide legal security for children," the lawyers wrote. Thus, despite the literal words of the statute, the court found that a coparenting woman who was the lesbian partner of the biological mother should be allowed to adopt.

Robinson, Murray, and Bonauto quoted the words of Supreme Court Justice Denise Johnson in *B.L.V.B.*: "When social mores change, governing statutes must be interpreted to allow for those changes in a manner that does not frustrate the purposes behind their enactment."

In that case, Johnson recognized the ways that attitudes about family had changed. "This is not a matter which arises in a vacuum," she wrote. "Social fragmentation and the myriad configurations of modern families have presented us with new problems and complexities that cannot be solved by idealizing the past."

Robinson, Murray, and Bonauto also relied on the Vermont Supreme Court's recent *Brigham* decision, in which the court threw out Vermont's education funding system. "Equal protection of the laws cannot be limited by eighteenth-century standards," the court wrote in *Brigham*. "While history must inform our constitutional analysis, it cannot bind it."

There was also a line of cases outside of Vermont to support their argument. In *Griswold v. Connecticut*, the United States Supreme Court had found that laws banning the use of contraceptives were an unwarranted invasion of privacy. Though the state of Vermont was arguing that marriage must be limited to heterosexual couples because of their ability to procreate, Robinson, Murray, and Bonauto pointed out that in the *Griswold* case the court established that married couples had the right not to procreate.

In *Turner v. Safley*, the United States Supreme Court found that prisoners had the right to marry even when denied the opportunity to procreate. This case established the importance of the "unitive" value of marriage, which had emotional goals that were fundamental to its purpose.

In another important case, *United States v. Virginia et al.*, the United States Supreme Court found the Virginia Military Institute was not permitted to bar women on the basis of gender stereotypes. Broad generalizations about the sexes could not serve as the basis for the denial of rights, and those generalizations might also apply to the role of men and women in marriage.

Then there were the cases involving interracial marriage, both the *Perez* case in California and the *Loving* case, which was decided by the United States Supreme Court. Barring a man from marrying a man was like barring a white from marrying a black.

Robinson, Murray, and Bonauto also examined how the family had evolved over time from an institution important for survival in an agrarian society to an institution with "a multiplicity of purposes," including emotional fulfillment. And they pointed out that if protecting children was the goal of marriage laws, then the right to marry should be extended to same-sex couples. After all, two of the three couples who had brought the suit were raising children and would benefit if the protections and benefits of the marriage laws were extended to them.

Vermont's history, according to the plaintiffs, suggested the state had no right to deny those benefits.

> Vermont's deep commitment to protecting every Vermonter's equality in the eyes of the law, and every citizen's liberty from excessive state interference with individual choices, is reflected in Chapter 1, Article 7, of the Vermont Constitution.

Chapter 1, Article 7, was the Common Benefits Clause.

3.

ROBINSON, Murray, and Bonauto never had the chance to appear in Superior Court to present their case. In December 1997 Judge Linda Levitt dismissed the case, agreeing with Attorney General William Sorrell that there was no basis in Vermont law for the claims made by the plaintiffs.

But Levitt's opinion in dismissing the case gave the plaintiffs reason for hope because Levitt rejected six out of seven of the justifications offered by the state for excluding gay and lesbian couples from marriage.

Yet Levitt dealt a blow to the plaintiffs in refusing to consider the case under the higher standard of scrutiny that would be justified if Levitt had determined that the plaintiffs' "fundamental rights" had been violated.

Much of the argument in the *Baker* case would center on the question of whether the case would require "heightened scrutiny." A case that demanded heightened scrutiny would place a heavy burden on the state, requiring the state to show a compelling reason for the denial of marriage rights. If a case did not merit heightened scrutiny, the state would have to show only that there was a "rational basis" for the denial of that right.

Heightened scrutiny would be required if the plaintiffs could show that the state had violated a fundamental right. But as Levitt observed, the Vermont Supreme Court had taken "a cautious approach in finding fundamental rights under our State Constitution." The court had said those rights must be "so rooted in the traditions and conscience of our people to be ranked as fundamental" and are "implicit in the concept of ordered liberty." She found that same-sex marriage was not rooted in the traditions and conscience of the people, and she refused to declare it to be a fundamental right.

Another reason for giving a case heightened scrutiny is if those seeking redress are part of a "suspect class." To be considered a suspect class, a group must be able to show that it has suffered historical discrimination, that it can be distinguished clearly as a group, and that it is politically powerless.

The plaintiffs argued that gays and lesbians were a suspect class, but Levitt rejected that argument, saying the federal courts had consistently refused to grant homosexuals suspect-class status.

Levitt even refused to grant that the underlying purpose of the marriage law ought to make room for gays and lesbians, saying it appeared from the language of the law that the purpose of the Legislature was to unite men and women in marriage.

But even if the case did not merit heightened scrutiny, could the state show that there was a rational basis for excluding gays and lesbians from the marriage statute? Surprisingly, Levitt came close to saying no. Many of the state's arguments, she found, made no sense at all. In Levitt's view, there was no rational basis for denying the six plaintiffs the right to marry, except for the state's interest "in furthering the link between procreation and child rearing." She found this justification to be reasonable, and she dismissed the case.

But for the plaintiffs there was reason to hope. Did it make sense to argue that marriage was meant to support a couple's role in child rearing and yet deny to the parents of Noah Jolles the right to marry?

"I love appealing on that issue," Mary Bonauto told the Associated Press. "We have a couple in this case who are parents, or were parents until the death of their son this summer. So the reasoning is a little ironic."

The procreation argument, therefore, was the slender reed upon which the state of Vermont had won its case in Superior Court. But for Robinson, Murray, and Bonauto, there was no way to tell whether that argument was a slender reed or a stout oak or whether the Supreme Court would have an entirely different view of the question of heightened scrutiny. It was up to them over the next eleven months to prepare a case that argued all of these points.

4.

ROBINSON, Murray, and Bonauto appealed their case to the Vermont Supreme Court and immediately went to work preparing briefs that would contain the substance of their arguments. It was during this period, before oral arguments were heard, that a vicious crime occurred on a cold night out on the plains of Wyoming. The murder of Matthew Shepard in October 1998 touched the nation's conscience and revealed how much had changed—and what had not changed—in attitudes about homosexuality.

It was at the Fireside Bar in Laramie that Shepard met Russell Henderson and Aaron McKinney. Police said Henderson and McKinney told Shepard they were gay, and he agreed to leave the bar with them. Their motive, according to their lawyers, was robbery.

Eighteen hours later a college student, Aaron Kreifels, was riding his bicycle on a remote road outside Laramie when he saw a human form dangling from a barbed wire fence. At first he thought it was a scarecrow, but on closer inspection, he found it to be the battered, burned, nearly lifeless body of Matthew Shepard, who had been beaten with the butt of a pistol and strung up in the cold Wyoming night.

Kreifels summoned help, but Shepard died five days later.

News of his death resounded across the nation. His murder would not be just another gay bashing, excused, covered up, or ignored. In response to the crime, President Clinton urged passage of federal hate crimes legislation, and renewed discussion began in many places about violence against gays. Rebecca Isaacs, political director of the National Gay and Lesbian Task Force in Washington, D.C., told a reporter for the *New York Times*, "There is incredible symbolism about being tied to a fence. People have likened it to a scarecrow. But it sounded more like a crucifixion."

Demonstrations occurred in Denver, San Francisco, and Brattleboro, Vermont, where sixty people stood in a silent vigil outside the post office. In Montpelier there was talk about strengthening Vermont's hate crimes law.

Thirty years before, Shepard's death might have been dismissed as a robbery and nothing more. But his murder became a symbol of what gays had been saying for years about the violence they faced every day of their lives. Public revulsion at the crime was so extreme that defense lawyers in the case felt compelled to urge jurors not to punish the defendants as a way of salvaging the image of their town. Nor did the judge in the case show sympathy for the defendants. McKinney's lawyers had sought to use a so-called gay panic defense, arguing that McKinney had flown into an uncontrollable rage because he had been propositioned by Shepard. But the judge refused. Shepard's murder would not be seen as Shepard's fault. Much had changed since the murder of Harvey Milk twenty years before. There would be no manslaughter conviction for McKinney and Henderson; the gay panic defense would not protect them as the Twinkie defense had protected Dan White. After sentencing Henderson to two consecutive life terms, according to the *New York Times* report, District Judge Jeffrey

Donnell told the defendant, "You are not a victim here, Mr. Henderson. You are a perpetrator."

So did these changes in attitude mean that social mores had changed?

Justice Denise Johnson had argued in the *B.L.V.B.* adoption case that the court's interpretation of the law must reflect social changes. The Vermont Supreme Court was to hear oral arguments in the *Baker* case one month after Matthew Shepard's murder. To what extent was the court operating in a changed world?

In her book *All the Rage: The Story of Gay Visibility in America,* Suzanna Danuta Walters described the vast difference between the 1990s and the 1970s. In the 1970s, she wrote, "there were no out gay politicians, no gay studies programs in universities, no advertisements that featured gays, no gay TV stars, few out gay actors, little anti-discrimination legislation, no glossy gay magazines, no gay cruises, and few gay festivals." Teenagers coming out had no gay support groups, and parents of gay children had no parents' support groups. It was unheard of publicly for gays or lesbians to raise children. "Lesbian mother seemed like an oxymoron," Walters wrote.

During the 1990s gay themes became common in the mainstream media, as in the movie *Philadelphia,* for which Tom Hanks won an Oscar for best actor. *Philadelphia* came in for criticism from the gay press because of the way it "desexualized" the gay hero, going to great lengths not to threaten the heterosexual audience. But the fact that major movie stars were appearing as gay characters in major motion pictures was a sign of the increased visibility of homosexuality in the culture.

The coming out of Ellen DeGeneres on her television series *Ellen* was another milestone, in Walters's view. It wasn't just that the DeGeneres character (and DeGeneres herself) had revealed that she was lesbian. The widespread and respectful attention caused by the event—DeGeneres appeared on the cover of *Time* magazine—showed that even if acceptance of homosexuality was far from universal, public attitudes were far different than twenty years before.

But had social mores changed sufficiently to justify a change in the laws about marriage?

During the past two decades cities and states throughout the country had adopted a variety of civil rights protections for gays and lesbians, despite the opposition of traditionalists. At the time of Matthew Shepard's murder twenty-one states and the District of Columbia had passed hate crimes legislation that included crimes targeting people because of their sexual orientation. These actions were a sign that at the political level attitudes had changed. Now when gays and lesbians demanded equal treatment before the law, it became harder and harder to find reasons beyond an appeal to tradition to deny them their rights. By 1998 fear and hatred of homosexuality existed still, but they were no longer a uniform or prevailing social attitude.

THIS WAS THE world in which the Vermont Supreme Court would take up the issue of gay marriage. During 1998 the court became familiar with the case by studying the briefs submitted by both sides. It was in the duel of legal briefs that the case would likely be won or lost.

Eve Jacobs-Carnahan and Tim Tomasi were the lawyers in charge of the case for the Vermont attorney general; it would be up to them to carry to the Supreme Court the arguments that had won them a dismissal in the lower court.

Within the office of Attorney General William Sorrell the case had already been the occasion of considerable debate. It was the role of the attorney general to defend Vermont statutes when they were challenged in court. But there were a number of staff attorneys in Sorrell's office, including some who were gay, who wanted no part of the *Baker* case. "If we had taken a poll in the office," Sorrell said later, "there was probably a majority sentiment in favor of granting gay marriage or at least civil unions."

Sorrell himself was a close friend and political associate of Governor Dean. He was the son of a former state senator and longtime Democratic stalwart, Esther Sorrell, who had been Dean's political mentor. Presented with the job of defending the exclusion of gays and lesbians from the marriage statute, Sorrell considered his ethical obligations. Was it his duty to defend a statute even if he believed the statute to be unconstitutional? He concluded that the attorney general should not lightly reach a judgment that any law was unconstitutional. For him to do so would be a "huge usurpation of power," he said.

Even before Robinson, Murray, and Bonauto had filed their lawsuit, they had met with Sorrell to determine how he would respond. Sorrell could have bowed out, leaving it up to the attorneys for the three towns named in the case to defend the law. But there was always the potential that lawyers for the towns would decide to grandstand or mount an ideological crusade. Sorrell decided he would litigate the case, but he would not turn it into a political cause. "This was not my ticket to *Larry King Live*," he said later. He would mount a credible, professional defense of the law. "I avoided speaking about my personal thinking," he said. Given an opportunity to talk about his personal thinking four years later, he paused, thought for a moment, and said, "I don't think the sky would fall if we had gay marriage."

Meanwhile, at their offices on South Pleasant Street in Middlebury, Robinson and Murray, with guidance from Mary Bonauto in Boston, now dived into the preparation of their case. Bonauto and Robinson were the principal drafters of the briefs. They had many three-hour conference calls and the FedEx bill "went through the roof," Bonauto said. Peter Langrock said the firm sacrificed as much as $1 million in income because of the pro bono work Robinson and Murray were doing in the *Baker* case. But the partners in Langrock Sperry & Wool recognized *Baker* as a potential landmark.

In their briefs Robinson, Murray, and Bonauto described the social changes of the past few years. They cited an extensive trove of academic and legal writings, most from the last decade, showing that gay relationships were common, healthy, and worthy of respect. It was important for them also to establish that gay parenting was common and that academic studies had shown gay and lesbian parents to be as capable and loving as anyone else.

Robinson, Murray, and Bonauto filed amicus briefs from a variety of legal, professional, and religious groups supporting their case, indicating that in important sectors of society the idea of gay marriage was no longer anathema. These briefs showed that, even if unanimity did not prevail on behalf of gay marriage, it could no longer be said to prevail in opposition. And where there is difference, enforced compliance with one group's moral code was contrary to the tenets of secular democracy.

The religious groups that filed amicus briefs on behalf of the plaintiffs expressed dismay at the moral claims of the state. They included Unitarians, Quakers, Congregationalists, Jews, and Presbyterians. These groups were particularly concerned that, in their motion to dismiss, the state's lawyers had appealed to "canon law" as the basis of the common-law prohibition against gay marriage. They expressed alarm that by appealing to canon law the state was favoring one religious tradition over another. Whatever the state meant by canon law, it did not represent the beliefs of these religious groups, and they didn't like being subjected to someone else's dogma.

Robinson, Murray, and Bonauto also presented a brief prepared by a group of social workers, psychiatrists, and other mental health workers saying that "committed, loving relationships between two people of the same sex are comparable to committed, loving relationships between two people of different sexes." They pointed out that the mental health profession had long ago rejected the idea that homosexuality was a mental disorder.

The brief cited studies that evaluated heterosexual and homosexual couples, finding similar levels of satisfaction in the relationships of both. "Plaintiffs are not anomalous," they wrote.

They also cited literature showing that gay and lesbian couples made good parents as often as heterosexual couples did. They quoted the American Psychological Association from 1995: "Not a single study has found children of gay or lesbian parents to be disadvantaged in any significant respect relative to children of heterosexual parents. Indeed, the evidence suggests that home environments provided by gay and lesbian parents are as likely as those provided by heterosexual parents to support and enable children's psychosocial growth."

The state of Vermont had its own briefs with which to counter the arguments of the appellants. A brief prepared on behalf of the Roman Catholic diocese of Burlington and the Burlington stake of the Church of Jesus Christ of Latter-day Saints warned that the appellants in the case were urging the court "to fundamentally alter the legal nature of marriage, the most basic institution in our society . . . This is no small matter. At stake in this debate is the very foundation of our social order."

But marriage also had intrinsic value that went beyond its social utility, they wrote. "Rather than a semantical technicality, the heterosexual dimension of marriage is indispensable to its intrinsic worth. The physical, intellectual, and emotional blending of the male and female produces a bond and a union different from all others."

They called the traditional definition of marriage an "immutable reality." And they said that heterosexual relationships provided a "full human context" for children, that "marriage generates families," and that traditional families are "the best situated to teach public virtue."

The brief went on to attack the idea of homosexual marriage, saying it would create a "radically different vision of sexual relationships, rejecting the interdependency and indispensability of both sexes to marriage. Homosexual marriage would teach that fundamentally the sexes do not need each other and can—perhaps ought—to live separately."

The parenthetical phrase *perhaps ought* revealed inadvertently the difference between what the two sides were seeking to do. In fact, the plaintiffs in the case had no interest in telling heterosexuals what they ought to do or whom they ought to marry. It was the state that was seeking to define how homosexuals ought, or ought not, to live.

Another brief offered by the state acknowledged that, while social mores may have changed, those changes were a grave threat to democracy. It was up to the Supreme Court to resist. The brief written for a citizens' group called Take It to the People claimed that the appellants had couched their case "in the familiar language of our Western liberal tradition," but that the analytical framework of their case "has extraordinarily drastic and dangerous implications for our constitutional democracy."

Hal Goldman, the lawyer who drew up the brief, said the term *same-sex marriage* represented a "radical incoherence" that corrupted the language. And a corrupted language "is deeply subversive to the organizing principles of our government."

"This is not democracy," he wrote, "it is despotism."

5.

BETH ROBINSON was well into her arguments before the Supreme Court on November 18.

> Once we recognize that the ninety-year-old widow and the ninety-year-old widower in the nursing home who meet and decide to marry and spend their final days together have a valued marriage, a valuable marriage, and a constitutionally protected marriage in its own right, then we can't point to the fact that these folks [motioning to the six plaintiffs sitting to her right] can't biologically procreate to carve them out of the definition of marriage or to carve them off from the fundamental right to marry or to justify gender restriction in marriage.

In that one sentence Robinson had touched on the three theories underpinning her case: the theory based on the definition of marriage and a rational understanding of its underlying purpose, the theory that marriage was a fundamental right, and the theory that the ban on marriage was an impermissible gender restriction.

Robinson was already nine minutes into her arguments, and Justice Denise Johnson was ready for her to narrow her focus.

Ms. Robinson, you are giving me the impression that maybe we should have let the state go first so we could hear what their arguments were. You're the plaintiffs here, and if the court is going to reverse the lower court, we have to know what your theories are that entitle you to relief. You have a number of theories that you have alleged in your brief, and I can't tell from the way they are listed or phrased which you think is the most important, and I would like to know from you what you think your most reliable theory of relief is.

Robinson shifted gears in order to meet the give-and-take that would follow.

Your Honor, I would hesitate to pick one because we believe that all of them are strong and that these couples are entitled to marry on the basis of all of them. In the cases so far in this country involving couples seeking the right to marry, the action has been around the question of level of scrutiny.

Robinson went on to insist that the gender discrimination implicit in the state's position required heightened scrutiny of the state's claims.

Johnson asked: "To get to heightened scrutiny, do we have to find that homosexuals are a suspect class?"

Robinson said no. Because the right to marry is a fundamental right, then heightened scrutiny was appropriate without getting into the question of whether homosexuals were a suspect class.

Now Justice Dooley jumped in. "Why are you not raising a federal constitutional argument since you are using a federal construct?" he asked.

Vermont's Common Benefits Clause paralleled the Equal

Protection Clause of the 14th Amendment of the United States Constitution. But Robinson was not making an argument under the federal Constitution, and Dooley wanted to know why.

"A federal claim would add nothing," Robinson answered. The Vermont Constitution would provide protections as least as strong as the protections under the United States Constitution.

Unspoken was the possibility that if the case were based on a federal claim, it could be appealed to the federal court, where its success would be dubious. In fact, since the United States Supreme Court had taken a conservative turn under Chief Justice Warren Burger in the 1970s, lawyers in some states, including Vermont, had increasingly begun to rely on state constitutions to provide protections more expansive than the protections that might be expected under the federal Constitution.

Moments later, Chief Justice Amestoy entered the discussion. He pointed to the case of *Loving v. Virginia,* in which the United States Supreme Court had rejected Virginia's ban on interracial marriage. In that case Virginia had claimed that blacks and whites were treated equally because both were barred from interracial marriage. But the court had found the state's claim actually served to mask an impermissible motivation: white supremacy. What was the impermissible motivation behind Vermont's marriage statutes?

Robinson couldn't say what the state's motives were. But she said the state's justification for barring gay marriage was a "sham."

"When you peel away all the justifications that don't make sense, all you're left with is a bare preference for a part only of the community," she said.

Amestoy wanted to know if the state could retreat from the whole business of marriage for everyone or whether the state was required to recognize marriage, whether homosexual or heterosexual. Was marriage a fundamental right that the state was required to recognize?

"We don't have to go that far," Robinson said.

Dooley asked, "What if it gave them all of the individual bundle of rights but was unwilling to call it marriage? Would that be sufficient in your view?"

Robinson was loathe to agree that something other than marriage might be permissible.

No, Your Honor, the status of marriage is in and of itself a value, a benefit. . . . The state of Vermont can't impose a separate but equal regime in marriage here, anymore than the California Supreme Court could have said in 1948 that interracial couples can have all the benefits that accompany marriage, but we're not going to let them call it a marriage because it's a mixed race thing and it's a different thing.

Justice Morse sought to press the point.

"So the label is everything," he said. "If the Legislature just said we are just changing the label and calling marriage domestic partnership instead of marriage, but you get all the bundle of rights that marriage has, then it couldn't do that?"

"Probably not," Robinson said. "All we need to show is that the constitution requires that the Legislature provide marriage on an equal basis for everyone."

Later Robinson said it was impossible to gauge a court's thinking on the basis of its questions, but it was clear the justices were not interested in challenging the fundamental premises of Robinson's case. Rather, they were more interested in the analysis underpinning her arguments. They were ready to side with her. They just wanted to be clear about how they would do so.

Now the lawyers for the state faced the court. First was Eve Jacobs-Carnahan, who focused on whether there was a rational basis for the Legislature's action in forbidding same-sex marriage. If there was and the court refused to grant the case heightened scrutiny, then the law would be constitutional.

> The question in this case is not whether we in this room as individuals approve of a policy that permits same-sex couples to marry. The question in this case is rather whether the Legislature, having adopted a marriage statute that permits only opposite-sex couples to marry, has acted constitutionally.

Robinson had spoken with confidence and the passion of someone defending a cause to which she was committed. Jacobs-Carnahan spoke haltingly, and she quickly moved into shaky territory. She distinguished the *Baker* case from the interracial marriage cases by pointing out that same-sex marriage had never been granted anywhere before.

For Justice Johnson that was not a convincing argument. "Well, someone had to be first even in the interracial marriage case, right? Is that any reason for us not to consider?" she said.

Jacobs-Carnahan said that the appellants were asking for a fundamental change in the common law. That made the interracial marriage cases inapplicable.

Dooley did not seem convinced. "So what does that show other than how long-standing the alleged discrimination was?"

"It shows the rationality of the Legislature's choice for one thing. It shows that the Legislature was not acting in an arbitrary and capricious manner when it chose to describe marriage as a status that's given to one man and one woman."

In fact, that is what Judge Levitt found in the lower court: that the link between procreation and marriage provided a rational basis for the Legislature's action and that was enough.

The justices continued to probe the state's position. Justice Johnson suggested that limiting marriage to heterosexual couples was a "radically underinclusive classification." What could justify it?

Jacobs-Carnahan said that under rational basis review, the classification did not have to be a tight fit. It was a line-drawing problem, and the Legislature deserved deference.

Justice Morse wanted to know about cloning. "I have been reading up somewhat about genetics, and where we are going with that is that probably some day in the future same-sex couples can biologically have children."

Nina Beck, in the front row, nodded. She had conceived Noah by other than conventional means.

"What would happen to your foundation for upholding this law then?" Morse asked.

Jacobs-Carnahan deferred. She would wait until that happened.

Later, Justice Johnson pressed Jacobs-Carnahan on the same question the justices had asked of Robinson. "Do you believe there is a fundamental right to marry?" she said.

"Yes, but it is a fundamental right between one man and one woman to marry," Jacobs-Carnahan said.

Tim Tomasi took Jacobs-Carnahan's place to insist that the *Baker* case did not merit heightened scrutiny. Justice Johnson pressed him on whether he believed there was a fundamental right to marry; and he said that, yes, there was, but in a man-woman context. Nothing in all of history suggested that there was a fundamental right for same-sex couples to marry, he said. And he sought to reinforce what he perceived may have been a doubt in the mind of Justice Dooley. He said the appellants

were not making a federal claim in their case because there was
no federal right to support their claim.

Tomasi spoke with greater ease and confidence than
Jacobs-Carnahan had, but neither he nor his colleague brought
the same passion to the case that Robinson did. Justice Johnson
wanted to know from Tomasi what he thought of the case as a
gender discrimination issue. Tomasi referred back to the battle
over the Equal Rights Amendment in 1986 when it was widely
held that equal rights on the basis of gender was no mandate
for same-sex marriage. Both genders were deprived of the
right equally.

But wasn't that the same concept rejected in *Loving,* the interracial marriage case? Johnson asked.

Tomasi persisted. The question was whether a benefit was
being given to one gender but not to another.

But why were people being excluded from gaining a marriage license in the present case, Johnson wanted to know.
Why wasn't that gender discrimination?

The racial discrimination was an overlay in the *Loving* case,
Tomasi said. The case was about race, not marriage.

Tomasi did not appear to be making headway by the time
his presentation was finished. Then it was time for Robinson's
rebuttal.

> We're dealing with a class of people that have been his-
> torically subjected to discrimination, and we're dealing
> with laws that flow from a prior era, from the eighteenth
> century, from a time that everyone concedes that gays
> and lesbians were not accepted openly and embraced in
> society. Justice Johnson is absolutely correct that in this
> case, just as in the interracial marriage case, the fact of
> equal application does not insulate the state's gender re-
> striction from heightened scrutiny.

Imagine for a second—the state relies very heavily on the fact that in the *Loving* case the interracial marriage ban prohibited people of color of all different races from marrying white people but didn't prohibit them from intermarrying with one another, and therefore the law was about white supremacy. Let's imagine for a second that that wasn't the case, that the Legislature enacted a law that said nobody may marry outside of their race. Can there be any doubt that, equal application notwithstanding, that law would violate the Vermont Constitution?

The power of Robinson's belief filled the room in a way that neither Eve Jacobs-Carnahan nor Tim Tomasi could hope to match. She also brought comprehensive knowledge of the issue to her arguments. She was not looking at notes. She looked from one justice to another as she spoke. Of course, neither her conviction nor her knowledge justified an outcome in her favor, but it was plain that the state had found itself on the defensive during this hour-long courtroom drama.

Now Robinson shifted into what seemed to be her final summation.

At the beginning of our argument, we talked about *Perez v. Lippold*. The result of that case seems obvious to us now fifty years later. But it's clear that in 1948, when the California Supreme Court distinguished itself by being the first state to reject the ban on interracial marriage, that decision required a measure of judicial integrity and a measure of judicial foresight. That court could easily have followed the course of many courts before it and retreated into the safe haven of deference to the legislature, and it could have barred Estelle Perez from marrying her chosen life partner.

In many ways this is an easier case. Courts in Hawaii and Alaska have already paved the way. Public support for recognition of marriage between partners of the same sex is substantially higher than public support for interracial marriage in 1948. Nations around the world are rapidly moving in the direction of full protections and rights for families formed by same-sex partners. Most members of our younger generation don't understand what the problem is, why it is that gays and lesbians in Vermont don't enjoy full rights of equal citizenship. And openly gay and lesbian Vermonters have formed families both with and without children in every community in this state.

Against this backdrop we're confident that fifty years from now our grandchildren will look back at this case and wonder what the big deal was. What were they so afraid of?

We urge this court to draw guidance from history but be mindful of the future as you fashion a decision that will affect, in the words of this court, "not only this generation of Vermonters but those who will come after us in the decades yet to be."

Thank you.

It was over. The justices rose, picked up their folders and their legal pads, and exited through a door to their left. After years of preparation, there was nothing left to say.

6.

THE FIVE justices retreated to a conference room nearby and arranged themselves around a table. It was their custom after oral arguments to take an immediate sounding about where each justice stood on the case. As they went around the table in the *Baker* case, minutes after Robinson's closing words, they saw immediately that they would be siding with Robinson. That was satisfying to Chief Justice Amestoy. Individual justices were assigned cases in rotation, and this case happened to fall to Amestoy. It would be up to him to write the court's opinion, and he was intent on issuing a unanimous ruling.

But there was no unanimity on how the court ought to reach its decision or what the remedy ought to be. Justice Johnson saw the case as a civil rights case, and she believed the remedy ought to be immediate. Amestoy had other ideas.

The dynamic of the drama surrounding the *Baker* case was different for the public than it was for the court. For the public there would be two high points. First, there were the oral arguments, which brought the lawyers face-to-face with the men and women who would decide the case. The arguments were followed by months of waiting before the court issued its ruling. Those were the months when Beth Robinson wore her electric blue suit to work on Friday. The climax of the drama came when the court at long last made public what it had decided.

The drama for the court was different. There was no doubt about the outcome. That was decided moments after the hearing. For months they had been reading briefs in the case, and they had entered the hearing tending toward the plaintiffs' view. A retrospective viewing of their questioning during the oral arguments suggests that Jacobs-Carnahan and Tomasi didn't have a chance.

The drama for the court involved the intellectual struggle carried out in memos and drafts circulated among all five justices exploring the best way to respond to the complex arguments before them.

The main fault line within the court fell between Jeffrey Amestoy and Denise Johnson. Amestoy had an easygoing

manner on a personal level, but, according to his fellow justices, he was stern about the need for the justices to maintain a
civil discourse. He and Johnson thrashed out their differences
by means of the drafts that went back and forth among the
justices.

The differences between Amestoy and Johnson were stark,
and each of them used sharp wording to answer the opinion of
the other. Johnson was alone in urging an immediate remedy to
the discrimination suffered by the plaintiffs. She began her opinion quoting a United States Supreme Court ruling suggesting
that the righting of wrongs was not something the court could
delay: "The basic guarantees of our Constitution are warrants
for the here and now and, unless there is an overwhelming
compelling reason, they are to be promptly fulfilled."

She pointed out that the majority on the court agreed that
the Common Benefits Clause of the Vermont Constitution entitled the plaintiffs to the benefits and protections of marriage.
But she believed the court should have done more than issue
"an exhortation to the Legislature to deal with the problem."

One of the differences between Johnson and Amestoy had
to do with Johnson's view of the role of the judiciary. "The judiciary's obligation to remedy constitutional violations is central to our form of government," she wrote.

Amestoy had served as an elected official, working in the
executive branch, and he did not believe it was necessary for
the judiciary to reach finality in the case. Johnson differed. It
was the court's responsibility to decide, not to defer.

Immediate relief was appropriate because, in Johnson's
view, the *Baker* case was "a straightforward case of sex discrimination." The quickest way to end that discrimination would
be to hold that Vermont's marriage statute required that marriage licenses be issued to same-sex couples as they were to
heterosexual couples.

Amestoy and the majority had a different view. If they had held, as Johnson did, that the case was a civil rights case comparable to those of the civil rights era, it would have been hard for Amestoy not to declare that gay and lesbian couples had an immediate right to marry.

But Amestoy took an approach to the case that allowed him to stay his hand, giving the Legislature the chance to determine the remedy. Amestoy viewed the case as something other than a straightforward civil rights case. That's because he insisted on viewing it as a question of economic balancing rather than a question of fundamental rights. Under Vermont's Common Benefits Clause, the courts routinely ruled on whether one group enjoyed an impermissible advantage over another. Thus, the court had ruled that a law requiring large stores to close on Sunday showed an unconstitutional preference for small stores.

This analysis allowed Amestoy to decide that, rather than redressing the violation of a fundamental right, the court merely had to let the Legislature find a way to provide equality of benefits. It was an economic question. The plaintiffs were not entitled to a marriage license; they were entitled to the benefits that went with a marriage license.

It is impossible to say he tailored his analysis in order to achieve the result he wanted. But it is true that the analytical framework he used allowed him to reach a conclusion permitting him to involve the Legislature. To what extent did his political judgment about the need for legislative participation determine the shape of his analysis? He won't say.

Justice Marilyn Skoglund, who signed onto Amestoy's ruling, commented later on the role of the judiciary in relation to the Legislature. "I am loathe to extend court rulings that impinge on the legislative process," she said. "I adjudicate the law." She called herself a "strict constructionist," by which she meant she did not believe it was the court's job to write the marriage statute. The court's ruling would affect numerous statutes, and the Legislature was better suited to modifying the statutes to reflect the court's mandate.

Amestoy's ruling answered Johnson's dissent.

> Our colleague asserts that granting the relief requested by plaintiffs—an injunction prohibiting defendants from withholding a marriage license—is our "constitutional duty." We believe the argument is predicated upon a fundamental misinterpretation of our opinion. It appears to assume that we hold plaintiffs are entitled to a marriage license. We do not. We hold that the State is constitutionally required to extend to same-sex couples the common benefits and protections that flow from marriage under Vermont law.

Amestoy was saying the label didn't matter as long as the rights and benefits were equal. Call it marriage; call it domestic partnership. That would be up to the Legislature. If the Legislature did nothing, the court would determine a remedy.

Amestoy had heeded the example of Hawaii where an outraged population passed a constitutional amendment allowing for a ban on gay marriage. That was a political consideration that Johnson was not willing to indulge.

Amestoy wrote that Johnson's opinion "confuses decisiveness with wisdom and judicial authority with finality." He said no court was ever more decisive than the court that ruled in the Dred Scott case—"nor more wrong."

Years later Johnson still felt the sting of that analogy: Amestoy was likening Johnson's insistence on decisiveness with one of the most ruinous civil rights decisions in the Supreme Court's history. For Johnson, a civil rights champion, that was hard to take.

But the majority sided with Amestoy, paving the way for the three branches of government to work together in crafting a solution to the vexing problem of gay marriage, which Amestoy hoped would give greater legitimacy to the ultimate solution. "The implementation by the Vermont Legislature of a constitutional right expounded by this Court pursuant to the Vermont Constitution for the common benefit and protection of the Vermont community is not an abdication of judicial duty," Amestoy wrote, "it is the fulfillment of constitutional responsibility."

Amestoy did not adopt the heightened scrutiny test that Robinson had sought, though he insisted his reasoning was more rigorous than the minimal standard of a rational basis analysis.

He said the state's classification about who could and couldn't marry had to bear "a reasonable and just relation to the governmental objective in light of contemporary conditions."

This language represented brand-new law created by Amestoy to achieve the end he desired. A high-ranking judge who was familiar with the case expressed admiration for what Amestoy had done. The judge, who did not want to be identified, said Amestoy had taken the extraordinary step of creating a new legal standard. It was not the heightened scrutiny test, which surely would have resulted in the outcome Justice Johnson sought. And it was not the rational basis test, which may well have resulted in a ruling favorable to the state. Amestoy's new standard—"a reasonable and just relation to the governmental objective in light of contemporary conditions"—represented judicial activism in the best sense of the term, according to the admiring judge.

Contemporary conditions were different than the conditions existing in 1777 when the Common Benefits Clause was adopted. Amestoy wrote:

Out of the shifting and complicated kaleidoscope of events, social forces, and ideas that culminated in the Vermont Constitution of 1777, our task is to distill the essence, the motivating ideal of the framers. The challenge is to remain faithful to that historical ideal, while addressing contemporary issues that the framers undoubtedly could never imagine. . . .

Viewed in the light of history, logic, and experience, we conclude that none of the interests asserted by the State provides a reasonable and just basis for the continued exclusion of same-sex couples from the benefits incident to a civil marriage license under Vermont law. Accordingly, in the faith that a case beyond the imagining of the framers of our Constitution may, nevertheless, be safely anchored in the values that infused it, we find a constitutional obligation to extend to plaintiffs the common benefit, protection, and security that Vermont law provides opposite-sex married couples. It remains only to determine the appropriate means and scope of relief compelled by this constitutional mandate.

Thus, even if she did not win her preferred remedy, Beth Robinson and her colleagues had won their case.

ALL OF THE justices understood the magnitude of this decision. "Everybody was waiting for it and watching for it," said Justice Skoglund. "We knew that."

On the morning of December 20, 1999, the day the ruling was made public, Skoglund called the principal of Montpelier High School to make sure her daughter, Kate Israel, had a safe place to go if there was trouble. She said her daughter was resilient enough to deal with comments about "faggots" when she heard them at school. But there was heightened security at the courthouse on December 20, and Skoglund wanted to protect her daughter from any untoward incidents at school.

"She was fine," Skoglund remembered. "I was a wreck."

Skoglund was happy with the ruling, however. "I didn't expect people to be pleased. But I was sure we were right, so I was pleased."

She said Amestoy had a saying: "We make decisions, not friends."

Denise Johnson was also pleased. The differences between her and Amestoy, sharply etched in the wording of the decision, were not personal (the sting of the Dred Scott analogy notwithstanding). And she later acknowledged that in the coming year, as the Legislature took up the issue and the public became embroiled in the debate, Amestoy got what he wanted. The political system as a whole, not just the judiciary, had to grapple with gay marriage in Vermont. And when the dust had settled, even those who didn't like the result knew they had not been excluded from the process.

CHAPTER SIX

THINK ANEW

MONTPELIER is the nation's smallest state capital, with a population of something over 8,000 and only two main streets in its downtown district. State Street runs parallel to the Winooski River for several blocks until it forms a T with Main Street. State office buildings line much of State Street, including the marble-sheathed cube that houses the Department of Motor Vehicles and, next to it, the picturesque red stone building containing the Agency of Agriculture. Gleaming above the entire city is the golden dome of the State House, which rests atop a small knoll and in front of a wooded hill. Wide granite steps lead up to its imposing portico, where six massive Doric columns hold up a pediment of classical simplicity. The building itself is smaller than one might conclude from the impression it makes. It is a simple, two-story building of light-gray granite, with eleven windows on each floor looking down on the street. In an article about the State House, author Archer Mayor described it as "outwardly almost severe, making its topknot as quaintly out of place as a silk derby on a farmer."

The building contains many signs of Vermont's history and its self-conception. Portraits of the two presidents from Vermont—Calvin Coolidge and Chester Arthur—hang in the hallway on the ground floor. Arthur is largely forgotten, but

Vermonters maintain an affectionate regard for Coolidge. At the end of the Hall of Inscriptions there is a bust of Lincoln, and on the walls there are inscriptions chiseled into stone tablets, including the following from a 1928 Coolidge speech:

> If the spirit of liberty should vanish in other parts of the Union and support of our institutions should languish, it could all be replenished from the generous store held by the people of this brave little state of Vermont.

Ordinarily, a visitor can wander freely about the State House. In the mornings when the Legislature is in session, members' voices drone behind the doors of committee rooms on either side of the long hallways that run down the center of the building on both floors. Curving staircases lead up to the second floor where visitors wander unsupervised into the vast House chamber that extends out the back of the building.

Visitors can also wander into the Senate chamber, an intimate and ornate room with four elegant green couches and deep-green draperies bound by golden cords. There are only thirty senators, and the small room is like a cozy clubhouse placed within a Fabergé egg.

WHEN HOUSE Speaker Michael Obuchowski returned to his office at the State House in January, he understood the difficulties before him. But he could not have foreseen the way the issue of gay marriage would transform the State House into a teeming battleground, suffused with tension and the fear of violence. The Supreme Court's ruling emanated from the quiet sanctum of the court building just down the hill, shaped by the reasoned analysis of judges responding to finely crafted arguments. Ideas were parried by other ideas, political conflict distilled into a kind of martial art. Marriage was a concept defined in legal terms rather than the lived experience of love, sex, passion, laughter, joy, fear, disappointment, hatred, and violence that constituted marriage in actual life. But with the release of the *Baker* decision, actual life—unseemly, impassioned, chaotic—quickly swirled up around Obuchowski and the rest of the Legislature.

Obuchowski had been speaker of the House for five years when the *Baker* decision came down in December 1999. He was a well-liked Democrat from the village of Bellows Falls in the southeastern part of the state, known for his thick, brush-like mustache and the steady monotone of his voice. He had first been elected to the House in 1972 when he was a twenty-year-old student at Harvard, and over the years he had developed an abiding respect for the process of lawmaking. He eschewed the Machiavellian stratagems of his predecessor, Ralph Wright, who had been an effective and powerful speaker but who had engendered much partisan bitterness. Obuchowski was known as straightforward and trustworthy, and he preferred to delegate power to his committee chairmen and women. Most of his colleagues knew him by the friendly and familiar nickname Obie.

Within a few days after the *Baker* decision, Bill Lippert came calling on Obuchowski at Basketville, the importer, retailer, and manufacturer where Obuchowski worked. There were many decisions to make, and Lippert wanted to know how Obuchowski intended to respond to the *Baker* decision. As Lippert remembered it, Obuchowski told him, "OK, Lippert, we're going to take your lead. Tell us what it makes sense to do."

Lippert said some legislators were suggesting that they do nothing, thereby letting them off the hook while achieving the result they wanted. Inaction would be the best way to secure the freedom to marry because it would more than likely produce a subsequent ruling from the Supreme Court opening up marriage to gays and lesbians.

But Obuchowski and Lippert believed the Legislature needed to act. "We would have damaged our credibility and integrity as a branch of government, as a legislative body, to say we're not going to take this up," Lippert said.

In those early days neither Obuchowski nor Lippert sensed that the marriage issue threatened the Democratic majority in the House and Obuchowski's continued speakership. Maybe they should have. A rising tide of grassroots anger had shrunk the Democratic majority even before marriage had become an issue. A group called Property Owners Standing Together—or POST—had begun to raise hell in the late '90s after the Legislature passed a bill regulating the clear-cutting of timber. During the 1998 legislative session, the clear-cutting bill, combined with the overhaul of state education funding, had prompted members of POST, mainly from the rural Northeast Kingdom, to make a show of their disgust on the steps of the State House. They had obtained a used car recently sold by Senator Cheryl Rivers, one of the most liberal members of the Legislature. They hauled it to the State House and allowed people to bash it with a sledgehammer. The car was emblazoned with the words CHERYL'S CAR, and the anger and alienation the protesters showed that day were menacing portents of the anger that would erupt over the marriage issue.

In this volatile atmosphere Michael Obuchowski, Bill Lippert, and Tom Little, chairman of the Judiciary Committee, concluded they needed to act in a decisive fashion. It was at a meeting in the office of Governor Howard Dean that the legislative leadership determined a course of action.

Dean had been quick to voice support for the domestic partnership alternative, and he expanded upon that view in a meeting with reporters on December 22. He disputed the idea that domestic partnership created a "separate but equal" status for gay and lesbian couples.

"I think it's not 'separate but equal.' It's 'different but equal,'" he said.

Freedom-to-marry advocates grimaced at the notion that different could be equal. Was there any justification for a different status other than prejudice? But it was plain to Dean that domestic partnership would be the path of least resistance following the Supreme Court ruling, and it was his judgment that it was the only option with a chance of passing the Legislature.

One of the first decisions the leadership had to make was whether a bill should begin in the House or the Senate. At Dean's spacious office on the fifth floor of the Pavilion Office Building, the governor met with Obuchowski; Little; the president pro tempore of the Senate, Peter Shumlin; and Senator Dick Sears, chairman of the Senate Judiciary Committee.

Shumlin had a reputation for his irreverent sense of humor and his political cunning. In 2002 when he ran unsuccessfully for lieutenant governor, he made a point of the fact that he was dyslexic and had always had to work extra hard to overcome that disability. He also went out of the way to mock the dimensions of his own sizable nose. He was an astute politician, and he was worried that supporting gay marriage instead of domestic partnership could cost the Democrats control of the Legislature and even the governor's office.

Thus, Shumlin was leary of what actions the House might take, though he couldn't tell where Little stood on the issue. Little was playing his cards close to his vest and would not reveal his position, even in private. When the leadership concluded that the bill should begin in the House, Shumlin was pleased, believing that if the House did anything too damaging to Democratic prospects, the Senate could fix it.

His fellow senator, Dick Sears, was happy to let his colleagues in the House take up the issue first. They would have to do the heavy lifting, Sears thought. In a few weeks, he would discover how wrong he was.

The decision to begin in the House struck fear into the hearts of some House members. John Edwards was in his sixth year as the House member from the town of Swanton near the Quebec border. It was a poor, conservative, rural region with many French-Canadian Catholics and the state's largest concentration of Abenaki Indians. Edwards was a retired state trooper and a Republican, and because of his experience in law enforcement, he had been appointed to the House Judiciary Committee. He had not prepared himself for the possibility that the House would have to take up the marriage issue, and when he heard about the *Baker* decision, he said he was "absolutely flabbergasted."

Within the next day or two he had read the decision, and he quickly got on the phone with Little, the Republican chairman of his committee. Couldn't the Legislature put off a decision on how to respond to *Baker*? Or barring delay, couldn't the House let the Senate take up the bill first? Edwards knew instantly that if he were forced to vote in favor of gay marriage or anything like it, his seat in the House would be in danger.

Little was on the phone with other members of his committee in those days after the December 20 ruling, including Representative Diane Carmolli from Rutland, who was the ranking Democrat on the committee. "We just got a Christmas gift," Little told her.

Carmolli was a friendly and nurturing woman, a fifty-nine-year-old gray-haired mother of seven and a devout Catholic who taught religious education classes at Immaculate Heart of Mary Church. She also served on the Liturgical Council for the diocese of Burlington. She understood her church's teaching on homosexuality, but as she said later, "Not everyone's Catholic. I'm not here to judge someone who hasn't had the same gift of faith."

She, Little, and Lippert would become the central players in the struggle to craft a bill and build support among fellow House members so that when the time came they would have the seventy-six votes they needed. That meant they needed to bring along people like John Edwards and other Republicans on the Judiciary Committee who wanted no part of a gay marriage bill.

In the days before and after Christmas, Little needed to formulate a plan. Justice Denise Johnson had warned against sending the plaintiffs in the *Baker* case to "an uncertain fate" within the "political cauldron" of the Legislature. Now the cauldron was heating to a boil. The conservative citizens' group Take It to the People held a press conference on the steps of the State House the day after the court's ruling was released, urging the Legislature to uphold the traditional definition of marriage.

Callers besieged the governor's office and the Supreme Court, including one call to the court from Oklahoma equating Vermont with Sodom and Gomorrah.

In a *Rutland Herald* story, Attorney General William Sorrell described the complex decisions before the Legislature as it considered changing the law to allow for same-sex unions.

> Do you go through a ceremony in front of a justice of the peace? Is it something you would do at the counter of the clerk's office? . . . What's the registry mechanism for this relationship? . . . What happens when you turn around and file your taxes? . . . What happens if two individuals decide they no longer want to be in the relationship?

One of the most important decisions before Little and his committee was the one the court had refused to resolve: Should gays and lesbians be allowed to marry or should the Legislature create a parallel institution, some kind of domestic partnership? Little, like Governor Dean, understood the difficulty of pushing through a marriage bill, but unlike Dean he refused to say at the outset what the Legislature should do.

Bill Lippert also understood the difficulty of pushing for marriage, but he felt additional pressure because the gay community was looking to him as their man in the Legislature. They saw him as the one who could make marriage happen. He knew otherwise. It was possible they could win support for marriage from a majority on a divided Judiciary Committee, but he believed it would be impossible to get a marriage bill through the full House. It was Tom Little's estimate that there were only thirty to thirty-five votes in the House for marriage. Lippert had many conversations with gay friends both in Vermont and elsewhere, and he understood that anything short of the right to marry would be a painful compromise. But he could not set aside his understanding of political realities. He supported the freedom to marry. There was no question in his mind. But he was a member of the Legislature, and he had a responsibility, not only to the gay community but also to the legislative process. He did not want the efforts of his fellow legislators to go down in a brilliant and glorious defeat. Even if the court eventually granted them victory, who would be helped by a defeat that put on display the familiar bias against homosexuals? Wouldn't it be better to do the hard work of winning popular understanding and acceptance of gay relationships, even if that meant accepting a compromise measure?

Lippert felt these conflicts deeply. He had devoted his life to serving the interests of those he called his "gay and lesbian brothers and sisters." Pressure was building quickly. Opponents were clamoring that he was an abomination, a destroyer of the American family, and friends were pleading for him to hold out for a bill he knew would not pass. It would be important, he knew, to maintain his composure, to represent his people with calm and dignity, even as emotions whirled wildly around and within him. The four months that loomed ahead of Bill Lippert would be the battle of his lifetime.

2.

WHEN THE House Judiciary Committee gathered on January 11, the members got a taste of the pressure they would be feeling for the next two months. It was the first day of testimony on the *Baker* case, and the small meeting room was packed full with reporters, photographers, and onlookers—all with an intense interest in every word that was spoken. For the next several weeks, the committee members would be within arm's reach of people seething with resentment or fearful of betrayal or both.

Little had already made one of his most important strategic decisions, which he had outlined in a memo to committee members. He wanted committee members to refrain from taking a position on the bill until they had devoted several weeks to taking testimony from numerous experts and citizens. The memorandum displayed the measured yet determined tone that Little would take throughout the proceedings.

To Bill Lippert this was one of the most important decisions Little made. It gave breathing room to members who might otherwise lock themselves into one position or another. At the outset, there was no unanimity on the committee. John Edwards was afraid he would lose his seat by voting for any kind of marriage bill. Representative Cathy Voyer, a Republican from Morrisville, thought gay and lesbian couples might be accorded some benefits, but she did not think granting them the full range of marriage benefits would be necessary. Other members continued to wrestle with the contending pressures of conscience and politics.

By refusing at the outset to declare a position, the committee also granted the public a chance to enter into the discussion. If the public had sensed that the committee's mind was already made up—for marriage, domestic partnership, or some other choice—the process of public education would have been short-circuited, and the gathering of testimony would have been seen as a sham.

Little made another important decision at the beginning of the session. He decided that, after a few days of housekeeping work, the committee would devote its entire calendar to the marriage bill. It was an extraordinary decision, but it was the only way the House would be able to put together a bill in time for the Senate to act later in the session.

On that first day Bill Lippert pointed out that religious and moral judgments about homosexuality and gay marriage were not the committee's responsibility. The question before the committee following the court's ruling was how to grant the rights of marriage, not whether to do so.

Beth Robinson and Susan Murray both testified that day, insisting that anything short of marriage would deny important rights to gays and lesbians. As reported by Jack Hoffman in the *Rutland Herald,* Robinson noted that domestic partnerships would not be recognized in other states so the benefits of marriage secured through domestic partnerships would be limited. She and Murray also insisted that the word *marriage* was a benefit in itself. "Everybody knows what it means," Robinson said. "It's a powerful term."

In the coming days, the committee sat through testimony from a wide range of witnesses, many of whom were happy to provide moral judgments. During day two of testimony, members heard from opponents. Thomas McCormick, a Burlington lawyer, warned the committee that "when it comes to marriage, we are dealing with the very hub of our social order." He attacked the Supreme Court, saying the court had "violated the separation of powers." And he raised the slippery slope argument: "What do you say tomorrow when three or more people say we want to marry, we're in a committed relationship?"

McCormick proposed a solution that was gaining currency among some members of the Legislature: a constitutional amendment that would negate the effects of the Supreme Court ruling. It was a constitutional amendment, after all, that had ended the effort in Hawaii after the plaintiffs won court victories there.

But one of the reasons Vermont had been a promising place to press the case for gay marriage was that the process for amending the state constitution was more difficult than in virtually any other state. An amendment requires the approval of two separate Legislatures, which meet every two years, and then it requires ratification by the voters.

Another witness on January 12 came with a statement from a man who would become one of the most formidable foes of gay marriage—Bishop Kenneth Angell of the Roman Catholic diocese of Burlington.

> Our opposition to same-sex marriage is widely known. We believe that marriage is a sacred covenant between one man and one woman, entered into for life and open to the possibility of children and family. We believe that a stable, lifelong relationship of husband and wife best serves the procreation, care, and education of children. We believe further that redefining marriage, expanding it to include other private relationships, will ultimately attack the age-old truth that traditional marriages and stable families constitute the very foundation of our society.

Angell marshaled his arguments with cogency and force. He opposed any form of domestic partnership because, in his view, it would be a step toward same-sex marriage. And he defended those who objected to their tax dollars benefiting people living a lifestyle of which they disapproved.

> Is it acceptable that Vermont's highest court orders all citizens to pay for the benefits of a special interest group? Where is respect for the rights of taxpayers who, in conscience, cannot condone, much less support a lifestyle which is objectively wrong?

Twice in his statement, Angell used the term *objectively wrong*. But for some committee members what the bishop believed to be objectively wrong had no bearing on the task before them. Diane Carmolli, a devout and active Catholic, was among them. "If we legislate our beliefs," she said in an interview later, "we become a state like the Taliban." She paused. "That's pretty harsh," she said, "but we have to honor differences."

During the course of the debate on gay marriage, Carmolli received letters from priests and nuns supporting her efforts and opposing the bishop. Four years later she still felt obliged to protect the identity of the letter writers, but the writers included prominent members of the Catholic community.

"This is just a note of sincere commendation for your courage in this challenging Legislative session. I'm proud to be one of your former teachers. Your position has been one of charity and inclusiveness that is truly Christlike." That letter came from a nun active in the religious and political life of the state.

"Just wanted you to know we support you in your vote for the domestic partnership bill," wrote another nun. "I'm sure it was an agonizing situation for you, in light of the bishop's public stand and the feeling of the majority of Vermonters. . . . Perhaps our church leaders will learn a lesson from you!"

In Angell's view, however, approval of gay marriage

amounted to discrimination against those who viewed homosexuality to be wrong. "It is ironic that sometimes legislation
intended to end alleged discrimination against certain individuals ends up discriminating against others."

Angell urged the Legislature to go slow and to explore all
the alternatives. "If civil rights are being denied," he said, "the
matter needs to be addressed in some manner that does not
derogate the sanctity and time-honored place of marriage and
the family in our society," he said.

Unlike many opponents of gay marriage, Angell always included in his statements the admonition that homosexuals
must be accorded love and respect.

> We will maintain loving concern for people who oppose
> our position, including those who are homosexual. We
> preach that all persons are gifts from God, deserving of
> love and respect. However, we ask those who disagree to
> understand that one can love and respect others without
> accepting all their actions and without wanting the govern-
> ment to provide special incentives for their lifestyle.

No one was as eloquent in opposition as Angell nor as influential. Little had taken the unusual step of going to visit Angell at the diocese office in Burlington on the Monday before
testimony began. Angell made it clear to him that he believed
almost anything the Legislature could do would be a threat to
the institution of marriage. And Angell would continue to
make his position clear in public statements and the pastoral
messages he sent to the priests of the diocese.

As Little's committee continued with testimony other witnesses tried Little's patience. On that second day of testimony
Hal Goldman, who had filed the Supreme Court brief on behalf of Take It to the People, launched a broad attack against
the Supreme Court.

The *Baker* decision . . . attempts to set up the court not as
the safeguard of a democratic system, but as a benevolent
dictatorship where the justices have substituted their own
personal sense of right and wrong for that of the people
and felt free to violate the boundaries of power in so
doing.

Little wanted to give everyone a fair hearing, but in Little's
view Goldman's attack on the court served little purpose.
When Goldman was finished, Little chided him. His exagger-
ated views were doing him no good, Little told him.

3.

THE COMMITTEE continued to take testimony during the last
two weeks of January. Meanwhile, the drama grew stranger
and more intense outside the committee room. One day Representative Nancy Sheltra, the conservative member from
Derby, found Tom Little and asked him to come with her. She
had someone she wanted him to meet. Sheltra introduced
Little to a man in a dark fedora, explaining that he was a radio
talk-show host. Little had a brief chat with the man, who
seemed pleasant enough. Soon he realized he had met the man
who, for many legislators, came to embody the bigotry they
were working to contain, whose memory made them cringe
even three years later.

The talk-show host was Randall Terry, the founder of the
antiabortion group Operation Rescue. Terry lived in the Binghamton, New York, area, and he had come to Montpelier to
"mobilize the troops" against gay marriage or domestic partnership. His rhetoric was extreme, and his methods were

aggressive. He called homosexuality "inherently evil," and he vowed to help defeat legislators who voted to extend the rights of marriage to gays and lesbians. As he said in a *Rutland Herald* story, "I'm playing hardball."

For members of the Legislature he became a Mephistophelean character, lurking in the corridors of the State House in his hat, black overcoat, and reptile-skin shoes, a peculiar and alien getup for the State House in Montpelier. He shadowed legislators through the halls, whispering biblical injunctions at them. In the Judiciary Committee room he made a show of praying.

Diane Carmolli said that in committee hearings Terry had a practice of choosing one committee member and staring. "He was the personification of hate," she said.

Terry rented a three-room storefront office on State Street and vowed to stay until he had crushed efforts to pass a bill. But even opponents of gay marriage tried to distance themselves from him. The Catholic diocese released a statement saying, "The Bishop has confirmed that the Roman Catholic Diocese is in no way affiliated or supportive of Mr. Terry's campaign against same-sex marriage."

The president of Take It to the People, Michele Cummings, urged Terry to leave the issue to Vermonters. Cummings issued a statement, reported in the *Rutland Herald*:

> Your former affiliations with anti-abortion groups will only dilute and damage the thoughtful discussion about traditional marriage. Moreover, your political aspirations in New York and your commercial radio talk show do not bring anything positive to a discussion based on Vermonters' traditional values.

Terry had been an unsuccessful candidate for Congress from upstate New York in 1998, and he planned to broadcast his talk show from his storefront in Montpelier. But there was a strong belief at the State House that the marriage issue should be resolved by Vermonters. Senator Dick Sears told Frederick Bever, a reporter for the *Rutland Herald* and the Barre-Montpelier *Times Argus*, "I think one of the things that's been exemplary so far is that outside groups have not come in. Once we get outside groups involved, it becomes that much more difficult to find consensus." Sears said he was already concerned about the divisions within the state. With Terry's arrival, he said, "the polarization I've seen will become more pronounced."

Terry was not deterred by the hostility he was arousing. "He used to follow me around the State House," Bill Lippert remembered. "He would follow me into the committee room, and he would say—what's the term, sotto voce?—'Judgment Day is coming, Representative Lippert, Judgment Day is coming.'"

One day he confronted Judiciary Committee member Cathy Voyer, grabbing her hand and warning her she would be sorry if she voted for gay marriage. "We will make sure you never return," he told her.

Terry's menacing presence at the State House illustrated one of the most difficult problems facing those who opposed gay marriage. The behavior and language of some opponents were so offensive that they tarred the opposition and gave pause to undecided legislators. Nancy Sheltra was unapologetic in her view that her duty was to serve the word of God, and she led a small contingent of House members who were less concerned about counting votes and persuading fellow legislators than in bearing witness and making a statement.

It was hard for legislators to separate responsible opposition from the vicious torrent of abuse they were receiving in their mail, on the phone, and in the hallways of the State

House. An example was a letter Bill Lippert received from someone in Missouri:

> Gays are Filthy Disease carrying Rodents and all should be Shot! What a Ungodly—nauseous lifestyle. The Governor of Vermont must be a Fag to approve such Vulgar Legislation. You are a Filthy Rodent. Hopefully Vermont will Die of AIDS soon. Missouri had the Brains and Morality to squash such Filthy Legislation.

Such attacks were so vicious they might have been dismissed as irrelevant. But hate mail and phone calls are not easy to endure, and as judicious as the statements of Bishop Angell might have been, other less judicious opponents spread a poisonous atmosphere. Among the crowds in the hallways and committee rooms at the State House, Lippert could never know which faces were concealing hatred like that of the letter writer from Missouri.

By the middle of January, the *Rutland Herald* reported that the governor's office had already received 8,600 phone calls, faxes, and e-mails on the marriage issue. Generally, the office received about thirty calls a day.

At Diane Carmolli's house the phone calls left on the family's answering machine were so abusive her husband, Nick, erased them. She told him to leave them on the machine. She needed to hear what people were saying.

Cathy Voyer received calls telling her she was a terrible mother. She remembered one day she and her two children, nine and ten years old, were heading out the door on their way to school when a phone call came in and a voice began speaking to the answering machine. "What kind of parent are you?" the voice said. "You're worthless." She had to explain to her children that it was all part of her job as a legislator.

The committee continued to hear testimony through January from a variety of people, including lawyers, government officials, academics, and clergy. But the public was clamoring for a voice, and Little arranged with Dick Sears to hold a joint hearing of the House and Senate Judiciary Committees in the House chamber. The public was invited to comment, and committee members would devote the evening to listening. That hearing, and the one that followed a week later, drew thousands to the State House. The hearings were carried live on radio and television, and Vermonters throughout the state were riveted by hours of testimony from people searching for ways to talk about love, morality, fear, history, tradition, and justice. It was an extraordinary education, not just for the members of the two committees, but for the state as a whole.

4.

SECURITY officials were expecting as many as three thousand people at the State House the evening of January 25. Bishop Angell planned to hold a silent vigil in front of the State House, and he had arranged for a bus caravan to take opponents of gay marriage to Montpelier. Buses had been chartered from many parts of Vermont for both opponents and supporters, but weather forecasters were predicting a major blizzard, and as many as two dozen bus trips were canceled. So was the bishop's vigil.

Even so, people began to arrive as early as 1 P.M. They wanted to make sure they could find a place in the House chamber, which ordinarily seats 150 House members but has the capacity for as many as 500. By 6 P.M. the House was filled to capacity, and people were still arriving. They filled the corridors and the meeting rooms. That afternoon Bill Lippert went to Sergeant at Arms Kermit Spaulding to urge the installation of a speaker system that would bring the testimony to people crammed into rooms on the first and second floors. During the day Lippert had been on the phone to friends. You have to get here, he was telling them. This is going to be big. When he and fellow committee members headed down the hill toward State Street for something to eat that evening, people were still streaming up toward the State House.

Before the start of the hearing at 7 P.M., the eleven House members and the six senators gathered in the House committee room, and Tom Little discussed with them how he intended to run the hearing. Hearings of this sort often employ a list of speakers who would sign up either pro or con, but Little thought that this method would be too polarizing. Instead, he placed a box in the House chamber into which people put their names to be drawn at random.

There were two armed plainclothes police officers in the committee room, and that is when it hit Diane Carmolli that the tension and anger in the House chamber could reach dangerous levels. Before the members went out to the House chamber, the officers wanted a word with them. If we say to move, an officer said, then move. If there is trouble, follow us. We have an escape route through the exit behind the rostrum and into the cafeteria. For Carmolli, it was a sobering warning.

People kept arriving, shaking the snow off their coats and their hats, stamping their heavy boots, tucking gloves into pockets, and unwrapping scarves. At the doorways to the building, people stationed themselves to hand out stickers. There were white stickers that said DON'T MOCK MARRIAGE or SUPPORT TRADITIONAL MARRIAGE, and there were pink stickers that said I SUPPORT THE FREEDOM TO MARRY. People filled the meeting rooms, the reception rooms, the hallways. By the time the hearing began there were close to 1,500 people at the State House.

The committee members left the committee room and entered the short passageway that took them to an entrance at the left front of the House chamber. Tom Little felt as if he were walking into a stadium to play a football game. As they took their places, the members looked out on a sea of faces, young and old, men and women, people whom they might encounter at the supermarket, at their places of work, or in their neighborhood. Jackets and shirts were dotted with pink or white stickers in equal numbers. It was time to get under way, and after some preliminary tinkering with the sound system, Tom Little called the meeting to order.

"Good evening. Welcome to the people's House. Thanks for coming. My name is Tom Little."

The setting enforced a feeling of decorum and respect that would sometimes be lacking at other venues in the weeks to come. A sense of expectancy filled the chamber and the hallways and rooms beyond.

"Tonight we are engaging in the exercise of two fundamental principles established in our constitution," Little said. "The right to freedom of speech to address elected officials and the duty to assure that our laws apply to all citizens, that each of us is equal before the laws of the state."

To those who thought the committee might stray from its duty to ensure equality, they had just been advised otherwise.

"There is plenty of room for strong opinions and clear disagreements," he said, "but they can lead us to an eventual stronger consensus as a people if they are expressed with dignity and respect. At least in my view, we govern ourselves best, not by reading poll results but by listening carefully to the views and concerns of Vermont citizens."

Little warned the crowd that order would be maintained,

and he told them not to cheer or applaud or express displeasure. Such displays would have the opposite effect from that intended, he said. Each speaker would have two minutes to speak, and he suggested that they offer their ideas on how the committees should respond to the court's ruling.

The first two speakers set the tone and outlined the parameters of the two polar positions that would be expressed that evening. First was a woman in a bulky blue sweater and a blue turtleneck.

My name is Mary Wilkens. I'm from Burlington, Vermont. Thank you for letting us speak tonight. I only wish the decision were referred to as same-gender civil marriage. I am not asking for the church, any church, to condone or not condone civil marriage. Equality of marriage is something Vermonters can be proud of. It is in keeping with Vermont's tradition of defending human rights. Vermonters were the first to outlaw slavery. We acknowledge marriages of mixed races, and now many religions also acknowledge marriages of couples of differing religions.

I would also like to say that historically when people of other races or less typical sexual orientations were viewed as less than human, they were often denied their human rights as well. Hatred and prejudice born of ignorance have been and still are seen as traditional in some places. Let's be sure Vermont isn't one of them. Some traditions need to die out. Love isn't one of them.

I would also like to say that I would never mock marriage. I honor my parents, married nearly fifty years, my brothers half that time, and other family members. I do not see what married people, what families, have to fear when others are asking for the simple right that their love be acknowledged. Thank you.

The mixture of the historical and the personal was characteristic of the statements that would be heard from supporters. Mary Wilkens stood and walked away.

"Jim Lake? Is Mr. Lake here?" said Tom Little.

A portly man in a jacket, sweater, tie, and white sticker sat in front of the microphone.

Good evening. My name is Jim Lake. I'm a twenty-year resident of Berlin and the pastor of the Bible Baptist Church in Berlin. As a Bible-believing preacher of the Gospel of Jesus Christ, I want to say that I'm opposed to both proposals of same-sex marriages and any form of domestic partnership. Both of these proposed solutions present our society with yet another turn away from the morality that our country was founded upon. Historically, no society has remained strong that ever embraced sexual promiscuity as the norm, whether it be heterosexual adultery, common-law unions, or homosexuality. By allowing same-sex marriages the government of Vermont would be redefining marriage in a way which has never been recognized in history.

While I believe homosexual behavior to be wrong, I do not propose to persecute those who choose to practice it. However, I think and would ask that this body of lawmakers not bend to political pressure to legitimize this behavior by calling it marriage. Domestic partnership in many ways not only redefines marriage but in reality eliminates it.

Finally, I would like to encourage you to stand against what to me seems to be an abuse of judicial powers of the state Supreme Court. By the virtue of the separation of powers, an American ideology that preserves the balance of power, the judicial branch must not mandate any law to be written by any elected officials. If we

allow this to be, we tread down the path of judicial
tyranny. If you cannot find the ability to simply table this
issue, then for the sake of the freedoms we hold dear, let
the people vote in a referendum.

Lake's testimony contained many of the elements of the
opposing side, the appeal to Christian teaching, a view of history emphasizing moral values rather than egalitarian tradition, and resentment of the judiciary. His appeal for a
referendum suggested he believed popular opinion was on his
side, though Vermont had no mechanism, except the constitutional amendment process, for voting by referendum.

The committees began to get in a rhythm as speaker
followed speaker.

The Reverend Gary Kowalski, minister for the First Unitarian Universalist Society of Burlington, was next. He said he
spoke for eighty-two clergy members, and asked Tom Little if
they could all stand as he read their statement.

Little intended to maintain a firm hand. "I don't think
we're going to get into that," he said.

Kowalski continued. Perhaps anticipating Bible readings
condemning homosexuality, he read from the Song of Solomon:
"Many waters cannot quench love. Neither can the floods drown
it." He said marriage was strengthened by same-sex unions,
which "exemplify a moral good."

He was followed by speakers who thought otherwise.
Chris Bixby of Williston said traditional marriage was "the
glue that has held our society together." He said marriage was
not a civil right, and he finished with the popular rallying cry,
"Let's take it to the people."

Laurie Morrison, a woman from Norwich, followed Bixby
to the microphone.

She began tentatively, a slight quaver in her voice:

This is not an easy task for me to come before you publicly today. As a woman living in a committed, loving relationship with another woman with whom I am raising
her two sons, I live a secretive life out of fear.

The packed chamber was hushed, and the committee
members were attentive.

We are fortunate to live in an enlightened accepting
church and school community, where I am truly treated
equally as another parent, dealing with all the same child-
rearing issues everybody else is dealing with.

Despite this, my family still remains shackled by intolerance and inequality in many aspects of our lives. I
have never before spoken out for my own rights, due to
fear of hatred, slander, and, yes, fear of violence being directed toward my family.

Today I must take the risk this holds and break the silence which is the greatest violence to my civil liberties. I
want the right to provide the benefits and privileges to
my family and children that are now being denied only
because of unfounded prejudices. I want the right and
privilege to sit anywhere I wish on the bus with my
family.

Not too long ago, my youngest, who's now eleven,
would ask me when we, his parents, would be getting
married and when I would be hyphenating my name. He
has now been exposed to the fear and hatred of the world
around him and no longer asks this question. I want my
children to have the respect they deserve, to have parents
that are married and can fully provide for them. I call on
you as leaders of this state to accept the challenge that
the Vermont Supreme Court has courageously put before us, and I urge you to support the right for same-sex

couples to marry in order to ensure that my family is extended the same rights and privileges that opposite-sex couples enjoy.

There was no time or opportunity for the committee members to respond to the statements they were hearing. The audience was hanging on every word. In the hallways, people were leaning through doorways into committee rooms to hear the sound being piped into the speakers.

The witnesses continued to offer the committees guidance from history.

Tim Menk of Ryegate quoted the words of Lincoln: "Fellow citizens, we cannot escape history. The dogmas of the quiet past are inadequate to the stormy present. As our case is new, so we must think anew and act anew."

Some of the testimony contained surprises. Tom Luce of Barre, with white hair and white beard, sat before the committees. "I am a practicing Catholic," he said, "but I want my church to go back to the drawing board and reassess its teaching and its handling of this issue." As his two minutes drew to a close, he had a revelation to offer:

I want to close with another fact about myself. Whatever you wish to call the set of physical and emotional characteristics of homosexuality, I have them. I live with them now, and I have lived with them for as long as I can remember, and I'm sixty-one years old. I have, however, chosen not to live a gay lifestyle or to call myself gay. This is due in no small part to my Catholic upbringing. My choices work for me, not that it's been without difficulty. I was a priest in the Catholic diocese, and I've been married for thirty years this coming August. I want to say to you tonight I stand in unity with my gay and lesbian brothers and sisters as they demand their right to marry.

Revelation followed revelation. But some of the most significant revelations occurred among audience members. People with white stickers sat next to people with pink stickers, ordinary Vermonters in snow-dampened clothes. Were they gay, these people with their pink stickers? Actually, it was impossible to tell unless they said so. That was the revelation. People who might have been categorized as somehow *other* were now mixed in with everyone else. For this evening in this chamber, the other was a visible part of the community. They were not other at all.

Holly Puterbaugh and Lois Farnham remembered listening to the hearing on the radio. "I remember thinking, I can't believe the number of people who are outing themselves. There were a number of people we knew," Holly said. Holly and Lois had outed themselves at the press conference announcing their lawsuit. Now the people of Vermont were hearing similar revelations from dozens of people.

On both sides of the issue, anger strained against the decorum occasioned by the setting. Kevin Moss, a professor from Middlebury College, described how, growing up in New Orleans, he had been taught, according to the commonsense, traditional, and natural morality of the time, that racial integration and interracial marriage were bad.

"I've been there," he said. "It does feel good to think you're better than someone else. But what it really boils down to with the opposition to same-sex marriage is 'my relationship is better than yours and I'm better than you are.' That's what they really want to say behind all their appeals. And I'm sorry, I just can't accept that . . . Either we are equal in the eyes of the law or not."

There was also anger in the tone of Ruth Goodrich from Cabot, a sense that her values were under siege.

Vermont is world famous for cheese, maple syrup, scenic beauty, and traditional values. This is what people tell me when they come here to visit Vermont. My ancestors represented nine generations of this same traditional value. They believed that marriage was one man and one woman raising a family with good moral values, nurturing them, and teaching them honor, integrity, and trust. I believe that marriage is for procreation, for nurturing children, and for raising them to know the difference between right and wrong. Everyone in this room is an example of a traditional relationship. The institution of marriage has held the community and the fabric of the human community together since the dawn of time. No civilization in the history of the world has ever survived the decay of moral values. Once lost it can never be regained. Is this really what we want Vermont to be famous for? Already many are ridiculing us . . . I would ask the Legislature to define marriage as between one man and one woman and to uphold traditional values. This gives Vermont its strength and integrity.

Keith Ribnick offered another view.

The reason that I'm here today is that I want you to know that my partner and I understand the term *family*. We both had two wonderful parents, and I was fortunate enough, with my partner, to take care of both of my parents when they became gravely ill. Most recently my father moved to Vermont to live with both of us. And I have to tell you, we made some mistakes . . . But we understood what the term *family* means, and I have to say that when my father passed away, he knew we loved him. The entire time he lived here, he knew we loved him.

Now I come to you today, I wish I could give you
some answers regarding what you should do. But I can't.
I'll be very, very thrilled and happy to live in a state where
I could marry my partner who I love, who makes my life
complete. But if you choose to pass a domestic partnership bill, I will be happy with that. I will be thrilled with
that. Either way, I will be happy.

Many of the audience members were unmoved by the
confessional statements by those supporting gay marriage.
Mike Hennessey of South Burlington could scarcely contain
his anger. "Special interests are using us as a guinea pig," he
said. He added, "This whole thing with the Supreme Court is
so out of line it's a joke."

Donna Lescoe of Starksboro made a point that stuck with
committee members. She said, whatever they did, she hoped
they didn't use the term *domestic partner*. "It makes me feel like
domestic help."

Committee members still had not devised the term *civil
union,* but testimony at this hearing convinced them *domestic
partner* was a term to avoid.

After two hours of testimony, Little called for what he
hoped would be a four-minute break. If he was tending toward
adoption of a domestic partnership law, he had heard virtually
no support for that option so far that night. Freedom-to-marry
advocates were adamant about the right to marry, and they
spurned the second-class status of domestic partnership. Opponents believed domestic partnership to be just as wicked as
marriage. It was important, however, for the committee members to hear the polarized views of Vermonters in order to understand the social context within which they were acting. The
strong feelings on both sides would provide the rationale for
compromise.

After the brief recess testimony continued. Jonathan Radi-
gan of Burlington came to the hearing with his partner, Chris
Tebbetts, who was active with the Freedom to Marry Task
Force.

> I think that those who oppose equal access and civil rights
> for gay and lesbian Vermonters are often quick to point
> out that they don't hate us, just what we do. And I'm kind
> of confused by that because I think that people are de-
> fined by what they do. And I fear the opposition is a little
> bit confused at times. And even though such opinions
> have nothing to do with the issue at hand, I feel I must
> clarify a few things for the ill-informed.
>
> Here's what Chris and I do. We pay our taxes. We go
> to the farmers market. We visit the animal shelter, and
> we've adopted a dog recently. We donate money occa-
> sionally to the food shelf . . . But I need to tell you that
> there's an unhealthy obsession with what goes on in
> people's bedrooms. And that needs to stop. And we don't
> need to legislate in reaction to that unhealthy obsession.
> Let me tell you what Chris and I do in our bedroom. We
> sleep, like a lot of other people. Thank you so much for
> this opportunity. Please support marriage for gay people.

He was followed by Vanessa Merrill of Clarendon, who
said gay marriage was a "dramatic breakdown from what God
intended." She called God "the big boss" who "forbids destructive behavior."

The anger and the denunciations coming from opponents
were getting to some people. Jan Buker of Lincoln sat before
the microphone.

> Hatred, especially hatred in the name of Christ, is deeply
> sad and troubling to me. Standing outside in line I heard

diatribes that almost made me sick. I am a Christian woman who follows the Christ who says the greatest commandment is to love God and love your neighbor. Look around at your neighbors here. We're all wearing labels. We don't need labels. We're just human beings. Many of these people have endured a long, lonely road to come here, many at great risk. And they have spoken of that risk very eloquently tonight. They are as beautiful and important as you, desiring the same rights you have always taken for granted. To deny other human beings basic human rights, such as those in marriage, is to deny our own humanity.

The testimony continued until about 10:55 P.M. when Dick Sears read out a final list of names, including Randall Terry. But those remaining witnesses had left. The hearing was over. In all about one hundred people had testified. Sears thanked the crowd for their civility, and he adjourned the hearing. There was applause, but it soon became apparent that the explicit enunciation of opposing views had sharpened, not blunted, the hard edge of the conflict. People on both sides were appalled by what they had heard. Freedom-to-marry activists felt that, though decorum had been maintained, many of the comments had been enormously hurtful. At the same time, opponents were aghast that a point of view that threatened to rot the fabric of American society was gaining legitimacy in the political realm.

An incident occurred afterward that became part of the lore of the hearing. Jonathan Radigan, Chris Tebbetts, a sister, and a friend were traveling home to Burlington on Interstate 89, able to see no more than a car length in front of them in the heavy snow. On the highway they encountered a motorist with three passengers who had stalled in the blizzard. They and another motorist stopped to help, and reluctantly the four people in the stalled van agreed to accept the offer of a ride. They had all been to the hearing, and it was apparent they were on opposite sides of the question. The driver of the car rode with Radigan's group. They didn't talk about the hearing. They were neighbors helping neighbors.

The story seemed to suggest that Vermonters were able to put their differences aside when it counted. But it wasn't as easy as that. The anger and passion on display at the first hearing had not abated. Because the snowstorm had kept many people at home, Little and Sears scheduled another public hearing for the following week, and on February 1 the State House was packed once again.

For the second hearing bus caravans brought people from all corners of the state, and before the hearing began about one thousand people gathered for a rally on the steps of the State House where speaker after speaker voiced support for God's law.

Angell, speaking in orotund, preacherly tones, told the crowd that Vermonters should pray that the Legislature would know God's will and that laws meant nothing unless they were written under God's guidance. Angell urged support for a constitutional amendment saying marriage was limited to one man and one woman, and he handed out petitions in support of an amendment.

There were smaller counterdemonstrations in front of the State House. A group of religious leaders led supporters of gay marriage in a recitation of the Lord's Prayer, and chants of "equal rights for all" momentarily interrupted the speakers at the bishop's rally. A group of University of Vermont students brought their own portable speakers and announced they had a resolution of support for same-sex marriage. But they were drowned out by religious leaders who were opposed.

Inside the State House the corridors and hearing rooms filled up again, and about 750 people packed themselves into the House chamber. Once again the committees heard testimony from about 100 citizens, this time alternating between supporters and opponents of gay marriage. The second hearing unfolded much as the first had. The committees heard warnings that the voters would cast them out of office if they supported gay marriage, and they heard pleas to do the right thing despite the political consequences. They heard that Vermont would be subject to an influx of homosexuals if they approved gay marriage, and they heard that opponents were motivated by "fear of the unknown, fear of the different."

As painful as the testimony was for many and as polarizing as the debate became, the hearings succeeded in achieving, far beyond anything they could have planned, a major goal for the freedom-to-marry advocates. One of the important elements of the campaign by the Freedom to Marry Task Force had been public education. They believed it was important for gay Vermonters to go before the public to tell their stories. They had organized speakers' bureaus to place people in front of Rotary Clubs, church groups, and other organizations to put a human face on the issue of gay rights.

The task force may not have wanted to enter the "political cauldron" of the legislative process, but the public hearings had given them a megaphone unlike any other. Speaker after speaker had told personal stories about their lives, providing the ordinary, intimate details that painted in the human dimension.

More than twenty years before, Harvey Milk had urged gay and lesbian Americans to stand up proudly, to show America that homosexuality was not some dark undercurrent and homosexuals were not alien beings. They were everywhere in society, and their lives deserved respect.

Public education had also been a part of the methodology of Martin Luther King, Jr., who urged African Americans to stand up with dignity, to be proud of who they were, to show society at large that they deserved respect.

"There is something in the American ethos that responds to the strength of moral force," King wrote in *Why We Can't Wait*. "A nonviolent army has a magnificent universal quality."

A small nonviolent army had answered the call to stand up at the State House, declaring who they were before the cold stares of those who would condemn them. For the time being, the two sides were locked together in mutual incomprehension—uncomprehending because of differences in experience and belief, but locked together because, like it or not, they were neighbors. But the courage of the freedom-to-marry advocates began to have an effect. For some House members unsure of how to vote, fearful of the voters' wrath, unclear whether gay and lesbian Vermonters deserved the rights they were seeking, the moral force of the promarriage speakers at the two public hearings was persuasive.

CHAPTER SEVEN

ACT ANEW

I.

ROSS SNEYD was the State House reporter for the Associated Press, and in nearly a decade he had seen nothing like this controversy. During his years of reporting, a question of conscience sometimes arose that created a moment of drama in the Legislature. But from the beginning of the 2000 legislative session to the end, the drama was writ large every day, all day. Sneyd began to sense that the entire state of Vermont was listening in to every word spoken in the cramped quarters of the House Judiciary Committee.

Sneyd, who was thirty-eight years old at the time, had an added difficulty to contend with as he covered the gay marriage story. It was no secret that he was gay. He had served on the board of Mountain Pride Media, which published *Out in the Mountains,* the state's gay newspaper. Before long opponents of gay marriage began to question his objectivity and fairness. Randall Terry began to refer to him as "the homosexual reporter," and letters to the editor began appearing in papers around the state suggesting he was pursuing his own agenda.

Christopher Graff was correspondent for the Associated Press in Montpelier and Sneyd's boss. Whenever someone complained to him that Sneyd could not be fair, Graff asked for an example of an unfair story. No one ever came up with one. "We never wavered in our belief that he could do the job." Whether he wanted to do the job was another matter. Graff continued, "I went to a Randall Terry press conference one time and heard him spouting these horrible things about homosexuals, and there was Ross, three feet away from him. I'd go to Ross. I'd ask him, are you okay?" Sneyd stayed with the story.

Imputing bias to gays placed gay reporters under a special burden. But who was to say a heterosexual reporter would not be biased against gay rights? No one asked that question. In fact, Sneyd was not sure what he thought about gay marriage. Did gays really think it was a good idea to mimic an institution as plagued with trouble as marriage?

As the Judiciary Committee continued its deliberations, Sneyd was perched most days in the narrow confines of the committee room, where members were moving closer to a crucial decision. They called it the threshold decision: Would they write a bill authorizing marriage for gays and lesbians or would they create something else, a parallel institution, as yet unnamed?

Three days before they made that decision they had another visit from Susan Murray and Beth Robinson, who took this last opportunity to urge the committee not to give in to pressure by passing a domestic partnership law. As Robinson had said back in December, anything short of full equality would not be equality. The strain of the struggle was beginning to show. Murray, who was generally a cool and composed figure, spoke with unusual passion.

"It's really painful to hear people say, 'You're immoral, you're an abomination,'" she told the committee. Murray remembered the case of Susan Bellemare and the lengths to which Bellemare had to go in order to maintain custody of the child she had raised from birth. At a fundamental, human

level it was not fair. According to the *Rutland Herald* story by
Jack Hoffman, Murray echoed a statement made to the committee earlier by Episcopal Bishop Mary Adelia McLeod, who
had urged support for gay marriage. "Gays and lesbians are
the only group that are still politically correct to kick," Murray said.

Murray, fighting back tears, had to pause for a moment to
regain her composure. Tom Little, sitting opposite her in the
chairman's seat, told her gently, "Take a deep breath."

Murray recalled the opposition that was aroused by the
idea of interracial marriage. "The same arguments are being
heard fifty years later," Murray told the committee.

Little wanted to pursue the parallel with race and the
question of volition. There had been much discussion about
whether homosexuality was a choice or an inborn orientation.
Race was a given, he said, but people are able to exercise a degree of control over their sexual choices.

"What difference does it make?" Murray said. It was a
question that exasperated many gays and lesbians. Was it help-
ful for straight people to tolerate homosexuality because they
believed gays and lesbians couldn't help themselves? That sort
of tolerance derogated the choice of homosexuals to affirm
themselves as gays and lesbians.

When Beth Robinson spoke to the committee, she addressed the question of choice. She pointed out that religious
faith was a matter of choice, and people's religious choices
were considered under the law to be equally valid. Even if
homosexuality were a choice, one's choice of who to love would
be no excuse for unequal treatment. Interracial marriage is
legal, not because blacks are unable to change their skin color,
but because skin color doesn't matter, she said.

The grounding of the freedom-to-marry movement in
the history of the civil rights movement became evident as

Robinson summoned the memory of Martin Luther King, Jr., quoting extensively from King's famous "Letter from Birmingham Jail."

Robinson's voice took on the authority of America's greatest civil rights leader as she read his words:

> I have almost reached the regrettable conclusion that the Negro's great stumbling block on the stride toward freedom is not the White Citizen's Counciler or the Ku Klux Klanner, but the white moderate who is more devoted to "order" than to justice; who prefers a negative peace which is the absence of tension to a positive peace which is the presence of justice; who constantly says, "I agree with you in the goal you seek, but I can't agree with your methods of direct action"; who paternalistically feels that he can set the timetable for another man's freedom; who lives by the myth of time and who constantly advises the Negro to wait until a "more convenient season."

Bill Lippert, sitting next to Little at the head of the table, understood what Robinson was saying. His agony came from the awareness that he and fellow House members would require gay and lesbian Vermonters to continue to wait for their full freedom. Even so, he believed creating a domestic partnership law would be more than establishing a negative peace.

The committee's vote on the threshold decision was fast approaching. Supporters had not been silent, but the vitriol of opponents had been fierce. When Robinson and Murray were finished with their testimony, Tom Little, who had learned important lessons about civil rights years before from the Kake Walk controversy, told them, "The committee is screwing up its courage to move into phase two. That was a good pep talk. We're aware we're in a historical situation."

During the next few days Bill Lippert spoke to members of

the committee, telling them it was his belief that domestic partnership, whatever it was called, was the realistic choice for them to make. Go ahead and vote for it, he told them. But he also told them he was going to vote for marriage. He understood the validity of Murray and Robinson's arguments, and he was not going to go on record in favor of a compromise that derogated his rights. For his own credibility within the gay rights movement, he needed to vote for marriage.

John Edwards was approaching the decision he dreaded. He had thought that if action could be delayed until May or June, when the Legislature was due to adjourn, he would be off the hook. "I wanted to keep putting off the debate until the Legislature went home," he said later. But there was no escape. For weeks, the State House had teemed with advocates from both sides, and Edwards had become increasingly concerned about the safety of House members. He saw people in the crowds at the State House whom he was acquainted with from his years as a state police officer, people with criminal histories and a potential for violence. The Legislature had become "a zoo," he said. And yet he said the hearings in those four weeks had provided him with "a tremendous education."

Finally, in the midst of the tumult at the State House, Edwards had a moment of clarity. It happened in the Cedar Creek Room, a reception room on the second floor dominated by a ten-foot-by-twenty-foot painting of the Battle of Cedar Creek, where the Old Vermont Brigade had distinguished itself during the Civil War. There was much coming and going by legislators and the public through the Cedar Creek Room, but Edwards had nowhere else to go for privacy. So in the midst of the turmoil, he sat on a couch and took a moment for himself. He realized he had heard enough. The question was about respect. He saw then that he could not possibly do his gay and lesbian neighbors the disrespect of voting against a bill granting them their rights. It was quite a simple matter in the end. He made his decision, and from then on he was at peace with himself. He knew it would probably cost him his seat in the House. But as he said later, "Sometimes in life, you've got to stand up and do what's right."

The threshold decision came on February 7. Public interest was so extreme it was impossible to meet in the tiny Judiciary Committee room, and Tom Little arranged to hold the committee's meeting that day in a large meeting room downstairs. The room was packed with one hundred or more onlookers as the committee members took their places at the tables that had been arranged for them.

By this time, many of the committee members had concluded that marriage was the right thing to do but that it would be impossible to win passage for a marriage bill in the House. Representative Michael Vinton, like Edwards, was a retired state trooper and was part of a small group of conservative Democrats who called themselves the Blue Dogs. He had sat in the committee hearings waiting for the opponents to give him a reason to oppose the bill, and he continued to be disappointed. "I could have gone right ahead for marriage," he said later, "but I didn't think we could have got it through the House."

Committee members went around the table one by one, explaining their positions at great length. Reporter Ross Sneyd had the impression that the comments of many members took shape as a kind of apology to Bill Lippert, their fellow committee member.

Representative Judy Livingston, a Republican from Manchester, said the previous month had been "the most intense educational experience" of her life. And she said she thought one day civil marriage would be available to those who were not interested in a religious ceremony. But for now civil marriage for gays and lesbians should take the form of domestic partnership.

John Edwards, Michael Vinton, Cathy Voyer, Alice Nitka, Michael Kainen, and Diane Carmolli all made statements recognizing that domestic partnership was a compromise, but a necessary one.

Bill Lippert held out for marriage. "The diversity that gay and lesbian people bring to the state of Vermont strengthens the state of Vermont in my view," he said. "Indeed, as Justice Amestoy said, our common humanity calls for our being fully welcomed into the community of Vermont."

Still, he understood the committee would not be voting for marriage.

"I trust that whatever next step we take collectively that we take it in the direction of continuing to dismantle the institutionalized discrimination and prejudice against gay people and gay families. I hope and I ask that we do that by amending the marriage statute."

Two other committee members took a strong stand for marriage. Representative Steve Hintgen of Burlington was a member of a left-leaning third party, the Progressives, and he warned that choosing domestic partnership would be giving in to hate.

For all those who have come before this committee preaching hate in all its poor disguises, whether with a Bible, a law degree, or Ph.D. in hand, those who have filled our ears with hate, they will not be sent a message of rebuke by this committee by us choosing domestic partnership. The hateful will have been strengthened by our decision. Pursuing the domestic partnership path validates the hate. It does more than validate it. It institutionalizes the bigotry and affirmatively creates an apartheid system of family recognition in Vermont.

Tom Little was the last of the committee members to speak that day, summing up in unapologetic terms the need for taking a step shaped by the pragmatic view of a realistic politician.

> Leadership requires a keen sense of what ought to be done in the context of what can be done, what is achievable. Leadership untempered by careful assessment of the world we live in is not sound leadership. What is achievable in this General Assembly and this body politic this year is a broad civil rights bill and, speaking for myself, that does not cross the threshold of marriage.

Cathy Voyer, a Republican member of the committee, was shattered by the vote she felt compelled to take that day. "In your heart you believed it should be full marriage," she said later, "but you knew it wouldn't be accepted."

When the hearing adjourned, she burst into tears, threw her arms around Bill Lippert, and apologized. "I'm sorry," she said. "I just couldn't get to gay marriage. I just can't do it. I'm sorry."

By not advocating aggressively for marriage, Lippert had allowed his fellow committee members to reach the conclusion for themselves that marriage was the only way to provide full vindication of the rights of gays and lesbians. He had become the conscience of the committee.

Ross Sneyd wrote a story that day, and later he regretted the direction his story had taken. His story emphasized the fact that the committee had refused to endorse gay marriage. In fact, he wished he had focused on the fact that the committee members had all endorsed action to provide the benefits and rights of marriage to gay and lesbian Vermonters. Little's strategy had worked. He had allowed committee members time to listen and consider before taking a position, and after they had done so, Republicans and Democrats and one Progressive had unanimously concluded that the gays and lesbians of Vermont deserved the rights of marriage. They had decided to compromise, and they would call it something else. But no committee member had sided with the opposition. It was a historic day.

2.

IT WAS DURING this period that Representative Bob Kinsey showed up one afternoon with his ducklings.

He did it every year, and the year 2000 would be no exception. He liked to buy a dozen white Peking ducklings so they could patrol the pond beside his house in Craftsbury during the summer. He called them his "Swiss navy." He put his order in with Agway in Montpelier, and when the ducklings were ready he went over at noon to fetch them, bringing them back to the House chamber and setting them in a box next to his seat. It was a reminder for fellow House members that spring was on the way and that outside the granite walls of the State House Vermont remained a rural place where the cycles of life recurred each year. Members of both parties visited Kinsey at his desk toward the back of the chamber to check out the tiny birds. It was Kinsey's way of lightening the mood. One year when the Senate Appropriations Committee was particularly miffed at him, he went to mollify the committee chairman, and he pulled what he called a Casey Stengel stunt. Kinsey borrowed a colleague's hat, and when he said hello to the unhappy senator, he lifted his hat, revealing a duckling on the top of his head. (Casey Stengel, the legendary baseball manager, performed the same trick for an umpire years before, though not with a Peking duckling.)

Kinsey and his ducklings helped foster a human connection among House members at a level deeper than the political bonds or the political conflicts that were part of their daily work. In recent years Kinsey, a Republican, had resisted pressure from the ideologically conservative wing of his party, and he had begun to take some heat for his independent ways. Not too long before, someone had stolen his car from his dooryard in Craftsbury, trashed it, and left it in a gravel pit in the nearby town of Coventry. Such a thing had never happened to him before. Kinsey had cast several votes that went contrary to the wishes of local people affiliated with the group known as POST, and he suspected that one or more of his unhappy constituents had decided to teach him a lesson. One of those votes was for Act 60, the education funding reform law, and another was for the bill to regulate clear-cutting on large parcels. Both bills provoked resentment among those who believed Montpelier was extending its power too far.

He couldn't be sure who was responsible for the car theft. But then on a summer morning, his tepee burned. He had constructed the wooden tepee as a warming hut for skaters in the winter. It was a sizable structure that no one on the road to South Albany could miss. There was no electricity near the tepee, and there had been no lightning. When it went up in flames, he had his suspicions. He had become embroiled in heated discussions with constituents about those two controversial bills and also about the issue of gay rights. He could not prove that the tepee had been destroyed by arson, but the political climate in his part of the state suggested to him that the fire had been deliberately set.

The summer the tepee burned, fifteen or so fellow House members came up to Craftsbury to help him rebuild it. They were Republican and Democrat, and they included Diane Carmolli. Carmolli remembered that while they were there Kinsey took them up the road above his farmhouse to the grave of his son Everett. He had dug it by hand in frozen ground on a cold November night in 1995. His son, suffering from clinical depression, had taken his own life.

With characteristic understatement, Kinsey recalled that day. "That was about the worst day of my life," he said.

His son was "exceedingly sharp," he said. He had thought of becoming a lawyer but had come home to run the farm instead. He had been hospitalized several times for depression, and at the time of his death he had stopped taking his medication. Kinsey wanted his colleagues to see the grave on the hillside. For all the posturing and gamesmanship that occurred within the State House, the lives of these small-town politicians, like the lives of everyone else, were touched by tragedy and animated by human sympathy.

Unless asked, Kinsey did not talk about his son's death. But when asked, he was not shy about telling the story. His was a combination of reticence and frankness valued in the state's rural precincts.

It was important for Carmolli and Little to win over legislators like Kinsey if they were going to pass a domestic partnership bill. In Kinsey's case, it turned out to be an easy sell. Kinsey was in touch with Tom Little about the issue, and by the time the issue took shape he had reached a conclusion of his own. "I told him if he would leave religion out of the bill, I would support it."

It was the human dimension of the gay marriage bill that touched him. The pieties of his neighbor to the north, Representative Nancy Sheltra, were irksome to him, as was the conservative ideology of his angrier constituents. He and his wife, Eunice, had attended the same Presbyterian church for more than fifty years. They had learned something about life and love and death. No one was going to instruct him about right and wrong or the disposition of his soul.

———

IT WAS NOT apparent in the wake of the Supreme Court's ruling that the Republican Party would oppose a bill for domestic partnership. In early January Representative Walter Freed, House Republican leader, met with Speaker Obuchowski and assured him he could rely on about thirty Republican votes.

Meanwhile, Peg Flory, a freshman Republican from Pittsford, was troubled by the *Baker* decision. "To award benefits based on perceived sexual activity didn't seem appropriate," she said.

She was Catholic, but hers was not a moral objection. Rather, she was concerned about the state's role in marriage. In her view, the state had no business granting benefits to people because they had sex together. That was a distinction the state was not suited to making. It should suffice that the pair were committed partners, sexual or not: two brothers, an uncle and a nephew, a mother and a daughter, or a homosexual couple.

Thus it was that Flory drafted a bill of her own even before the House convened in January. She was pushing what became known as reciprocal partnerships, and she became the leader of those Republicans who were uncomfortable with the moral absolutism of Nancy Sheltra and her allies and who understood that the Legislature had to fashion some kind of response to the *Baker* decision.

Flory, like so many others, quickly became an enemy of Randall Terry. "I made a conscious effort to distance myself as much as possible from him," she said. "He tried to tell me what a sinner I was. He was not a pleasant person. He was harmful to the whole campaign."

Before long, Walter Freed met again with Obuchowski and Little, suggesting that rather than thirty Republican votes, he might be able to guarantee only twenty. It was apparent to Obuchowski that Freed was under pressure from the Republican caucus and was making his own political calculations. It wasn't long before Freed came to the speaker and told him he was on his own. The Republican leadership had no help to offer.

Meanwhile, Beth Robinson and Susan Murray had to decide how to respond to the crushing defeat they had suffered when the House Judiciary Committee voted to pursue domestic partnership rather than marriage. They had hired one of Montpelier's most prestigious lobbying firms to advise them on the legislative process. "One of the most significant decisions I helped them make was when to compromise," recalled lobbyist Steve Kimbell, partner with Kimbell, Sherman, Ellis. But compromise would not be easy, and Robinson, Murray, and their allies disappeared from the State House following the committee's threshold vote in order to consider their next move.

During those days, Bill Lippert was feeling terribly alone. He had been in frequent contact with Robinson and Murray, and now they were gone from the State House. He knew they were devastated by the committee's vote, and he understood the question of principle with which they were wrestling. But without their presence at the State House, he was missing his closest allies.

At the time, his closest allies were not feeling so close to him. Dorothy Mammen of Middlebury was statewide coordinator for the Freedom to Marry Task Force. "We were really mad at Bill Lippert," she said later. Lippert may have voted for marriage in the committee vote, but they knew he was willing to settle for domestic partnership. "We felt he let us down big time," Mammen said.

For nearly two weeks Robinson and Murray were on the phone with task force members around the state. The organization had developed a sophisticated and extensive grassroots network that included regional councils in all parts of the state and regional coordinators who could contact supporters by telephone or e-mail. "We spent hundreds of dollars in conference calls," Mammen said.

The lawyers met with the plaintiffs in the *Baker* case to determine if they were willing to settle for legislative action that provided something less than marriage. Holly Puterbaugh was among those disappointed with the committee's decision to compromise. "I felt they were copping out. I felt they were saying you deserve it, but we don't have the courage to use the words. So, yeah, we're going to make it legal, but we're going to make you second-class citizens."

For the plaintiffs, it was an "agonizing decision," Holly said. But eventually they decided to support domestic partnership. "There was no guarantee what the court would do," Holly said. So the plaintiffs decided they ought to settle for "half a loaf."

Robinson consulted with other task force members as well, trying to determine whether the task force should support a domestic partnership bill or withdraw support and try to sink it. "Beth didn't say where she stood," Mammen said. "She played the devil's advocate's part. It was important that the task force board not make a decision and tell the gay community what they were going to do." A top-down decision would fracture the gay community, Mammen said. "Gradually, this thing kind of percolated till we knew what we had to do."

TO MEMBERS of the Judiciary Committee, their decision to support a domestic partnership bill may have seemed like a compromise, but it did nothing to mollify opponents who believed any law recognizing the legitimacy of homosexual relationships was a violation of God's law.

Nancy Sheltra remained the leader of a small group of conservative House members who would do anything to derail action on a domestic partnership bill. She and about a dozen legislators signed a resolution urging the impeachment of the entire Supreme Court. They refused to acknowledge marriage as an issue of civil rights. "This is a choice of lifestyle," she said.

One of her allies was Representative Neil Randall, a Libertarian from Bradford. She and Randall were also pushing a constitutional amendment that would forbid both gay marriage and domestic partnership. An amendment barring gay marriage had already been introduced in the Senate, but because it did not ban domestic partnership, Sheltra didn't think it went far enough.

During this period Randall Terry brought in a half dozen ministers from out of state to patrol the halls of the State House. They wore black, as Terry did, and they sought to pressure the legislators, surrounding them in groups and interrogating them. House members began to call them the "God squad."

Lippert remembered one day when the God squad had encircled Diane Carmolli, thinking they could intimidate her. But Carmolli, an articulate and thoughtful Catholic, was not about to let anyone dictate morality to her. Lippert smiled as he thought back to the way that Carmolli returned the fire of the God squad. She had given a good deal of thought to the division between church and state and how, since Vatican II, the church had given Catholics a great deal of "discernment" about reaching their own conclusions on political issues. "There is no doctrine or encyclical that tells a legislator what political path or agenda to follow," she said. "My salvific vision is not what I'm there to legislate." She was certainly not there to legislate the salvific vision of Randall Terry or the God squad.

Terry was having salvific problems of his own. Shortly after the threshold vote by the Judiciary Committee, the *Rutland Herald* reported in a story by Diane Derby that Terry's church in Binghamton had censured him three months earlier because he had left his wife. Terry called the censure "garbage," though, according to Derby, he also acknowledged, reluctantly, that he was no longer living with his wife.

Derby spoke with Dan Little, the pastor of the Landmark Church, who said, "To go out and speak and challenge people to live and think biblically, you have to begin at home. If you can't do it at home, why go to Vermont? Stay home and get it right and then go out and say what you want."

According to Derby's story, Dan Little cited signs of what he saw as spiritual deterioration, including "anger and self-will which manifested itself in what I would characterize as a lack of purity in speech and lifestyle."

Meanwhile, Terry and his God squad continued to make a poor impression in the State House. Speaker Obuchowski increased security because of the feeling of intimidation that Terry and his followers had created. Representative Mary-Ann Parizo, a Democrat from Essex, complained that she had to walk a gauntlet of God squad members every time she left her committee room. House members learned Terry was keeping a chart in his State Street office, marking in red supporters of gay rights. In response, some House members began to wear red stickers on their lapels.

Terry was unrepentant. "We're mobilizing people in this state and around the country, and that intimidates them," he told Fred Bever of the *Rutland Herald* and *Times Argus*. "So they're trying to make me the issue."

Increasingly, Terry was the issue. One legislator told Bever he had heard Terry refer to Bill Lippert as "that flaming faggot."

"They are taking advantage of the historical openness of this State House," Lippert told Bever. "Our expression of civility is being violated by intimidation and threats laced with religious bigotry."

Lippert was dismayed that Sheltra and her allies were backing Terry and his methods, but Sheltra defended Terry and his friends. "They are just asking members where they stand. They might not want to be asked, but they need to be."

For the God squad and friends, the piety of their preachments about marriage did not square with the reality of their lives. House members knew that Nancy Sheltra had been divorced. Nor was Michael Vinton impressed by the God squad when he saw them late one night at the Thrush Tavern, a bar near the State House. "They were all half in the bag, smoking cigars, putting the hit on the waitress," he said. It was closing time, but the gathered clergy were making no move to leave. The waitresses were becoming exasperated, so Vinton approached the group. "Why don't you get on your coats and get out of here," he said to them.

Randall Terry responded, "You're on that committee, aren't you."

"Yeah, you've got a problem with that?" Vinton said.

The God squad left. Vinton had noticed that in the State House they generally did not approach him or other male legislators. "He would go after the women."

WITH AN increasingly polarized atmosphere enveloping the State House, the House Judiciary Committee had to settle into the work of actually writing a law. It was a daunting task, and there were several ways the committee might have proceeded.

But one of the important decisions the committee had to make was what to call the new institution it was creating. Domestic partnership was out. Committee members had been persuaded that the term *domestic* derogated the relationships at issue. It was on a Friday when the topic came up for discussion by the committee. Tom Little was absent, and Bill Lippert was chairing the meeting.

"We needed a new term that represented the significance of what we were doing," Lippert said.

France had created what it called a *pacte civil,* and the word *civil* conveyed the important idea that a secular rather than a religious institution was being created. Lippert remembered that Representative Judy Livingston suggested *civil accord,* but the phrase reminded members of a Japanese car. They went around the table searching for a new phrase. Most committee members were unsure who was first to utter the phrase *civil union.* William Eskridge wrote in his book *Equality Practice* that it was Cathy Voyer who first said the words. Asked if that was true, Voyer said, "Yes, I think I was."

Union was a powerful word. It was more than a partnership. It conveyed the joining, the merging, that occurs as a result of the emotional and sexual commitment of a marriage. Marriage itself was a union, and it was the intent of the committee to make civil unions as close to marriage as possible without calling it marriage. The term *civil union* did not exist before that Friday, but it quickly entered the lexicon. People solemnized a marriage. They would certify a civil union. Once the committee members happened on that phrase, they knew it was right, and from then on that is what they called it.

But creating civil unions in law was a daunting task. Would the committee have time to sift through all thirty-three volumes of the Vermont statutes to change every reference to marriage so it also applied to civil unions? There were hundreds of references, and such an overhaul of state law would be virtually impossible given the pressure to respond in a timely fashion to the *Baker* decision.

Lippert credited Tom Little with finding the solution. He called it "amendment by reference," which meant rather than amending each statute that referred to marriage, the bill would state that all provisions of a statute related to marriage also applied to civil unions.

Opponents criticized this approach, saying it showed that civil unions were nothing other than marriage by another name. If it walks like a duck and sounds like a duck, they said, it's a duck.

In fact, the committee wanted civil unions to be like marriage. That was the whole point.

In drafting the bill, Little first set out the legislative findings that were the basis for the committee's actions. Point by point, in neatly logical fashion, the findings distilled the case for civil unions down to eleven paragraphs.

The first paragraph contained a concession to opponents. "Civil marriage under Vermont's marriage statutes consists of a union between a man and a woman." From there, the findings laid out the case clearly and succinctly. They described Vermont's history of equal treatment and the importance of civil marriage. They noted that gay and lesbian parents were allowed to adopt and that the state had an interest in promoting family stability, including families of gays and lesbians. The findings pointed out that civil unions were not the same as marriage and did not interfere with religious freedom.

Extending the benefits and protections of marriage to same-sex couples through a system of civil unions preserves the fundamental constitutional right of each of the multitude of religious faiths in Vermont to choose freely and without state interference to whom to grant the religious status, sacrament, or blessing of marriage under the rules, practices, or traditions of such faith.

The logic of those paragraphs would not persuade Nancy Sheltra, Randall Terry, or their allies. But the reasoned approach that Little brought to the task created a zone of comfort for Republicans John Edwards, Cathy Voyer, and Judy Livingston and Blue Dog Democrats like Michael Vinton.

For those weeks in February, the committee had the job of drawing up a bill establishing the procedures for civil unions and describing what a civil union would be. The committee determined that town clerks would issue civil union licenses and that parties to a civil union would have "the same benefits, protections, and responsibilities under the law . . . as are granted to spouses in a marriage." These included laws relating to property ownership, causes of action such as wrongful death, probate, adoption, insurance, spouse abuse, discrimination, victim's compensation, workers' compensation, medical care, family leave, public assistance, taxes, immunity from compelled testimony, and veterans' loans. The list went on. Parties to a civil union could establish prenuptial agreements, and if they wanted to dissolve a civil union, they would have to follow the same family court procedures that heterosexual couples followed to obtain a divorce.

After a couple received a civil union license, they could employ a judge, justice of the peace, or member of the clergy to perform the appropriate ceremony and certify the civil union. The parties would then return the civil union certificate to the town clerk, who would record the civil union as part of the town's vital records. Vermont residents would obtain a license from the town clerk where one of the two parties lived. Couples from out of state could go to the town clerk of their choosing. The law also allowed assistant town clerks to issue licenses in place of town clerks. Legislators knew some town clerks would object to the mandate requiring them to issue civil union licenses, and in those cases they would be permitted to hand over the duty to an assistant.

To Beth Robinson, Susan Murray, and the Freedom to Marry Task Force, establishing a separate procedure for civil unions, even if parallel to marriage, implied a second-class status made necessary only because of the prejudice of the majority. It was a galling compromise, a form of segregation. So for those days in February, the Freedom to Marry Task Force remained on the sidelines far from the corridors of the State House while task force members decided what to do next.

Bill Lippert knew that if civil unions were going to pass, he would need help. "We need to have the support of individuals and allies who have spoken so eloquently and forcefully about marriage," he said in an Associated Press story by Ross Sneyd. "What we have in front of us in our draft is a very, very significant piece of legislation that would establish comprehensive rights for gay and lesbian couples, that merits active, positive support."

That is what the Freedom to Marry Task Force eventually concluded as well. With the support of the six plaintiffs and the membership of the task force, Robinson and Murray came out in favor of civil unions. "Ultimately, obviously, the goal is and always has been genuine equity, which is inclusion in the marriage statutes," Robinson said in Sneyd's story. "But we've seen the political reality. Certainly, if the right domestic partnership bill comes out of that committee and it's a positive step toward marriage, then of course we'd support it."

Members of the task force had decided they couldn't walk away from the fight. "We decided we had to be at the table," Dorothy Mammen said. "If we weren't at the table, it had the potential to be a bad bill." There were members who likened a civil union bill to "institutionalized apartheid," Mammen said, but for now the task force would work for the incremental gain of a civil unions bill. Those who disagreed with the decision to support civil unions faded into the background, Mammen said. They let the fight continue on behalf of civil unions, but they didn't have the heart to take part. Still, the organizational skill and determined advocacy of the Freedom to Marry Task Force would continue to be an essential ingredient in winning passage of a civil unions bill. Political reality may have dictated that the committee back civil unions rather than marriage, but it was by no means certain that even civil unions would win legislative approval.

AS THE CIVIL unions bill neared final action by the House Judiciary Committee, the public uproar continued to build. An unprecedented wave of letters to the editor came to me at the *Rutland Herald,* and I tried to print as many as I could. There were hundreds of them, and I devoted extra pages strictly to letters about what our logo referred to as "same-gender marriage."

The letters touched on many of the same points that had been repeated again and again during the previous weeks, but as the din of the struggle welled up, individual Vermonters felt the need to take sides so their side wouldn't be drowned out.

Within the *Rutland Herald,* I was insulated from the murmurs of dissension that were heard in the advertising and circulation departments. The advertising sales staff had the unpleasant task of facing business owners hostile to civil unions, and the circulation staff had to take calls cancelling subscriptions. There was even concern within the news department that I was paying too much attention to the issue. But it never occurred to our publisher, John Mitchell, to soften our editorial position. He had taken over as publisher following the death of his father, Robert Mitchell, in 1993. Going back decades, Robert

Mitchell's editorials had established the paper as an early opponent of McCarthyism and an early supporter of civil rights.
Support for civil unions was in line with this tradition.

Meanwhile, the public had another avenue for voicing its
views on the issue of gay marriage. Town meeting would be
held that year on March 6, and voters in some towns would
have the chance to cast a ballot expressing support or opposition to same-sex marriage and domestic partnership. The resolutions would not be binding, but Senator John Bloomer of
Rutland County, Senate minority leader, was promoting the
town meeting votes. It was a way to make life difficult for the
Democrats. (His father, as chairman of the Judiciary Committee eight years before, had been an opponent of the antidiscrimination bill. The elder John Bloomer had died in a car
crash, and young John had been elected in his place.)

As Town Meeting Day approached, more than 50 of Vermont's 246 cities and towns were scheduled to vote on questions
related to gay marriage or civil unions, and Tom Little was in a
quandary. House members ordinarily visited the town meetings
in their districts to talk with voters about the issues of the day. So
should the Judiciary Committee vote on a civil union bill before
town meeting or after it? If they waited until after town meeting, they might be accused of trying to avoid the voters' wrath.
If they voted before town meeting, they could be accused of acting before the voters had a chance to express their will.

Little decided the committee would vote on the bill before
town meeting so that in appearances before voters committee
members could say in straightforward fashion where they
stood. Thus, March 1 became a history-making day, though
not as dramatic as the day of the threshold vote. The committee members knew what they were going to do.

They met in the small room upstairs where they had devoted untold hours to the bill over the past two months. The

room was packed as usual with the press and other onlookers, including Randall Terry who took up a position standing directly behind Cathy Voyer. In the tight confines of the room, he loomed above her only inches away, and she finally lost her patience. "Go away," she told him. "Go away from me."

Michael Vinton was seated near the door, and he summoned a deputy sheriff who was standing outside. Terry was forced to move.

"We all knew we were doing something incredibly important," Bill Lippert remembered. They had come so far, they had heard so much impassioned testimony and so much abuse. There was excitement, exhilaration, and apprehension, Lippert said. When they had tallied their votes, it was 10–1 in favor of the bill.

The lone dissenter was William McKinnon, a Democrat from Sharon, who continued to hold out for a bill allowing for marriage. McKinnon's vote drew criticism from fellow committee members, who accused him of grandstanding. Lippert said McKinnon was guilty of "a failure to engage in the political process."

"I voted for marriage, I spoke for marriage, and I think I probably recognized earlier on than many others the wisdom of what was politically achievable," Lippert said in the *Rutland Herald*. "And quite frankly, I've worked to help others understand that we would achieve far, far more for gay and lesbian Vermonters—as well as gay and lesbian people across the country—by working to create a well-crafted, comprehensive bill that grants rights and benefits than by holding fast to a so-called principled position and have nothing."

It was the realistic appraisal of a politician who understood better than most the cost of the compromise.

Now action would come quickly. Speaker Obuchowski saw no reason for delay. The voters of some towns would have their say on Town Meeting Day, and the full House would take up the issue nine days later. Obuchowski, Little, Lippert, and Carmolli would be the team guiding the bill toward passage in the House, but with members of the House still coming to grips with the vote before them, there was no guarantee the bill would win.

3.

TOWN MEETING was still a revered tradition in Vermont, allowing voters to gather each year to carry out the mundane business of local government. Should the town buy a new dump truck? Should the town refurbish its library? Voters also had the power to petition their select boards to place items on the town meeting ballot, including nonbinding resolutions on issues as diverse as nuclear weapons or war in El Salvador. The non-binding resolutions allowed voters to stand up and argue among themselves and then cast their ballots. Though the results were not a representative sampling, they carried the authoritative stamp of grassroots democracy.

The results of the voting at town meeting in 2000 provided ammunition for those who accused the Legislature of refusing to listen to the people. Of the fifty towns voting, none supported the creation of same-sex marriage. In addition, thirty-eight towns voted against and eleven towns voted in favor of domestic partnerships. The tiny town of Tinmouth in southern Rutland County tied on the question of domestic partnership. The vote was 23–23.

The *Rutland Herald* made an unofficial tally of the aggregate vote, finding that about 15,000 voters had said no to domestic partnership and 10,000 voters had said yes. But this total included voters from only about one-fifth of Vermont's municipalities and did not include many of the large cities and towns where support for civil unions was the strongest.

In some towns and cities the balloting showed that legislators who favored civil unions would face enormous difficulties in November. In Rutland City, residents voted 3,507–814 against marriage and 3,022–1,283 against domestic partnership. For the four Rutland City Democrats who planned to support civil unions, including Diane Carmolli, the town meeting vote foreshadowed trouble.

In more liberal precincts, the voters showed that civil unions were not without support. Montpelier voters rejected marriage but approved domestic partnership, 1,657–1,158. In the small mountain town of Lincoln, voters rejected marriage 244–141 but approved domestic partnership 216–172.

Town meeting allowed voters who might not have spoken up at other venues to carry on the highly charged debate that had gripped the state for two months. Anger boiled over in some places. The small town of Athens was an example. There the town clerk, Darlene Wyman, told voters she would quit her job rather than sign a civil union certificate. "They will have to find a new town clerk. I will not do it," she said, according to the *Rutland Herald* account.

Once town meeting was over, Obuchowski, Little, Lippert, and Carmolli buckled down to the job of rounding up the votes they would need to pass a civil unions law. Obuchowski decided he would bring the bill before the House on March 15. In the few days remaining before the vote, he, Little, Lippert, and Carmolli met every day in Obuchowski's office, and reviewed the tally that Carmolli was keeping of where members stood on the issue. They viewed her count as reliable. ("You're not going to lie to Diane Carmolli," Tom Little said.) But a number of House members had not made up their minds.

Meanwhile, the opposition was growing more determined. Outside the House, opponents included Ruth Dwyer, a Republican former House member and previous candidate for governor. She would be running for governor again this year, and she chose March 13 as the day to launch what she called a "listening tour" of Vermont. By doing so, she was placing herself at the head of a parade of increasingly angry Vermonters, who felt disenfranchised by events in Montpelier. It had been the trademark of her political history—trying to exploit the discontent of the voters to her advantage. She warned that passage of the civil unions bill would "tear this state apart." Her critics would claim it was her divisive style of politics that was tearing the state apart.

"I don't want to campaign in an angry society," she said. "And I'm afraid that's what will happen if they pass this law." Yet by jumping into the campaign on the week of the House vote, she stood to reap the benefits of the anger that was sure to follow. By now the Republicans had seen their opportunity, and they were getting ready to take it.

Obuchowski and Little, meanwhile, had decided they would not bring the bill to the floor unless they had determined in advance that they had a margin of at least ten votes. They knew some House members might crumble under the pressure, and they needed to know they had a safe margin. They would have to fend off a variety of amendments designed to delay or kill the bill, and Little was gearing up to lead a long parliamentary battle on the floor of the House.

Members of the Judiciary Committee continued to talk to fellow House members, trying to round up the needed votes. Lippert remembered that John Edwards and Michael Vinton, two former cops, had credibility with some of the men who may have been uncomfortable talking with Lippert about gay rights.

One member who seemed unlikely to vote for civil unions was Albert Perry, a Democrat from the town of Richford near the Canadian border. Perry, a former submarine commander who had retired to his hometown, told voters at town meeting that he thought the Legislature should not move so fast on the issue, and he talked himself into believing that a vote on the bill would be delayed.

He and John Edwards shared an apartment in Montpelier during the legislative session, and they had become good friends. Perry understood where Edwards stood, but he shared Peg Flory's view that some sort of reciprocal benefits arrangement was better than an institution that singled out gay and lesbian couples for benefits. At the same time, he had enormous respect for Edwards, who supported the civil unions bill.

Many House members faced formidable pressure from their home districts to vote against civil unions, and the list of members endangered by a yes vote was long.

Marion Milne, a Republican from the small town of Washington, was a popular legislator serving her third term. She had attended the first large public hearing on the night of the blizzard, and she had returned home where she did "a lot of tossing and turning" through the night. The words of one of the speakers stuck with her: "Please don't let the majority decide for the minority." She knew she might lose her seat, but she was leaning toward a yes vote.

Richard Mallary, a Republican from Brookfield, had been preparing a domestic partnership bill even before the *Baker* decision came down, and there was no question in his mind that he would vote yes. He was a venerable figure among Republicans. He had served as speaker of the House back in the 1960s and then had served a term in Congress. "I didn't know what the repercussions would be," he said later, though he knew a substantial majority of his constituents opposed civil unions.

When the leadership met in Obuchowski's office on March 14, Lippert was discouraged. It appeared they could rely on only sixty-eight or sixty-nine votes, and they needed seventy-six. What should they do? They didn't have the ten-vote margin they had been hoping for. Should they pull the plug on the whole effort?

They looked at each other that day. It had been nearly three months since the day in December when the Supreme Court had issued the ruling that had transformed the political landscape. These four were a disparate group, but they had some things in common. They had all heard the clamor of religious denunciation, but all four were religious people. Obuchowski, a Harvard-educated Polish American from a working-class background, was Catholic. Carmolli was a Catholic who had witnessed the bitter division within her church between the hierarchy and many of the faithful. Little was chancellor of his Episcopal diocese. Lippert was the son of a minister.

Obuchowski was firmly behind the bill and also was pleased with the job Little had done. Little had earned wide praise for the steadiness and calm with which he had brought the bill forward. He had refused to be drawn into the emotional tumult of direct confrontation with Nancy Sheltra or Randall Terry.

Meanwhile, Lippert's outward restraint masked an impassioned man who in private could express outrage and astonishment at those who blithely insulted him and other gays and lesbians. He had dedicated his life to his community, and now more than anything he wanted to deliver a political victory. How could they possibly pull the plug on their effort now? To back away, even with the outcome in doubt, would be an unconscionable betrayal of thousands of people who had been willing to take a stand against a mounting storm of hatred. What would they say to Beth Robinson and Susan Murray?

Lippert had argued that marriage would be impossible to achieve and that compromise was necessary. Failing to achieve that compromise was an outcome too awful to contemplate. The anger sweeping the state was palpable, but so was the hope of those who, like Lippert, countered bigotry with a demand for respect. A previously scorned minority had finally found its voice, and it was a voice that had gained an undeniable moral force.

They could not back away from a vote. They had taken steps to win over wavering members, including two separate declarations within the bill defining marriage as a bond between a man and a woman and a section creating a limited number of benefits for reciprocal partners, including blood relatives.

Diane Carmolli was more optimistic than Lippert about the outcome. "We had the votes," she said. "I knew we had the votes."

Tom Little said later that he thought they had sixty-five solid votes and would have to secure the remaining margin during the debate on the floor of the House the next day.

One thing Bill Lippert knew was that at some point during the day on March 15 he would have to give a speech. He had spoken up forcefully from time to time during the debate, but he did not place himself out front in advocating for the law. By not making himself an advocate, he had won the respect of many members who understood his views but appreciated that he let them come to their own conclusions on the law. Still, on the final day, many in the House would be looking for him to say something. It would be his moment. It was a daunting prospect.

But on the evening of March 14 he realized in a panic that he hadn't written a speech. He was with Little and Carmolli. He remembered their reassurances. Don't worry, they said. Just say the things you've been saying to us. You have it all in your heart.

He was staying in Montpelier that night. He had brought with him the Bible his parents had given him, a Revised Standard Version with his name emblazoned in gold on the front cover. No one was going to hijack the Bible to use against him. He might want to quote Scripture himself. That night in his hotel room he called a gay friend in California, but the friend wasn't there. Lippert left a message. "I'm sorry," he said. "I just wanted to talk to someone who would understand how important it is what I have to do."

The debate would last all the next day and into the evening. Once again the public packed the State House, filling the gallery, the lobbies, and the chairs in the back and the front of the chamber. I did not often go to Montpelier, but that day I made the hour-and-a-half drive and took up a place in the crowded press gallery on the right side of the chamber.

Obuchowski wielded the gavel from the rostrum; the monotone of his voice suggested this was just another day's business, but everyone knew it was more than that. Little was at his desk in the center of the chamber. He hoped Carmolli was right when she said they had the votes.

Little brought up the bill for debate that morning. "What we have here in front of us are Vermonters who are different from some other Vermonters [but] nevertheless equal members of our state under the law," he said. "We're not asking anyone to grant special [protections] to anyone. We're only asking for equal protection under the law."

The first action came from John Robb, who along with John Edwards represented the two-member district of Swanton. He offered a resolution urging the Senate to pass a constitutional amendment declaring marriage to be between a man and a woman. Amendments must originate in the Senate, and in order for the House to have a chance to vote on the amendment that session, the Senate needed to act.

His resolution was referred to the House Judiciary Committee.

After lunch the House took up the civil unions bill in earnest. The first serious challenge to the bill came from Representative Tom Koch, a Republican from Barre, who proposed an amendment that would strike the bill and replace it with a call for a constitutional convention to respond to the *Baker* decision. Several legislators questioned whether the procedure was constitutional; others saw it as an abdication of the Legislature's responsibility.

But supporters of the amendment urged its passage. One of them was Oreste Valsangiacomo, a Democrat from Barre and the longtime chairman of the House Ways and Means Committee. "Are you afraid of the people?" Valsangiacomo asked fellow House members.

Among those listening to Valsangiacomo was Nina Beck, who had taken a place in the front of the chamber, holding her baby, Seth, in a red cloth sling. She remembered Valsangiacomo launching into a bitter tirade against civil unions. Then in the midst of his speech, he happened to glance over at Nina and Seth, smiling at the image of mother and child. He had no inkling of who she was.

The amendment on a constitutional convention would be the first test of where the votes might fall on the issue, and as the clerk began to call the roll, people throughout the chamber, including me, kept a running tally, marking down yeas and nays as the members announced their votes. The convention went down to a solid defeat, 103–45. It was no sure guide of the final outcome, but supporters breathed a sigh of relief.

Next came the amendment from Peg Flory, George Schiavone of Shelburne, and Robert Starr of Troy. It would replace civil unions with what they called "domestic units," which could include gay and lesbian couples or blood relatives who

wanted to join in a kind of partnership. Flory, a freshman legislator, had been through a trying ordeal as the member seeking to head off civil unions. "It was terrible to stand there and
be called a bigot and a homophobe," she said later. As neither
a supporter of civil unions nor a moral absolutist in opposition, she felt she was in "no-man's-land."

As someone in the middle, she had a hard time lining up
support either from the right or the left. Sheltra and the extreme right opposed reciprocal benefits that would sanction
homosexual relationships, and supporters of civil unions opposed the bill as well. But her bill became the principal alternative to the civil unions bill.

Earlier in the afternoon, Little had wandered over to the
right-hand side of the chamber to Bill Lippert's desk. "I think
you need to speak soon," he said. Lippert had only a collection
of notes for the speech he was going to give. He needed more
time. But as a vote on the Flory amendment approached, Little
came over to Lippert's desk again. "Bill, it's time. You need to
speak."

Lippert knew it was time. He would speak from the heart.
He would speak for his community. From the speaker's rostrum, Obuchowski recognized the member from Hinesburg,
who took a deep breath as he stood up.

> Thank you, Mr. Speaker. Representative Flory's strike-all
> amendment, she indicates, is designed in part to remove
> "sexual activity" from the bill. At the same time, Repre-
> sentative Flory's strike-all amendment, unlike the bill of
> the House Judiciary Committee, fails to acknowledge
> that there has been discrimination and inequity toward
> gay and lesbian couples, currently or historically.

The chamber was silent but for Lippert's voice. In the press
gallery, I was sitting next to Ross Sneyd, whose fingers were

tapping furiously at the keyboard of his laptop computer. The power of this moment, long anticipated, was apparent to everyone. The House was rapt.

> I think it's important to put a face on this. I think it's important to ask who it is that we're talking about, who it is that we've been discussing.
>
> I've had the privilege in my own life of coming to the process—through a struggle at times—the process of coming to identify myself as a gay man. I've had the privilege of developing a deep, devoted, loving, caring relationship with another man. I think it's very important as we listen, as we debate, and as we make decisions, that you understand what the reality is about gay and lesbian people, gay and lesbian couples.

Lippert seldom talked about his personal life or made a point of his sexual orientation. In hours of interviews with me, he protected the identity of his partner and said little about his relationship. To come forward with this personal information was all the more powerful because of his customary restraint.

> Our mailboxes have been filled with letter after letter talking about abomination, talking about sinfulness, talking about Judgment Day coming soon. I'm here to tell you that gay and lesbian people and gay and lesbian couples deserve not only rights, they deserve to be celebrated. Our lives in the midst of historic prejudice and historic discrimination are to my view, in some ways, miracles.

The House members had seen the hate filling their mailboxes. It was dawning on many who had not thought much about it before that if that was the kind of hate that gay people felt every day, then something was surely wrong.

Think what kind of relationship you would try to establish and how successful it would be to find a loving,
committed partner in an environment where you have
been barraged on a daily basis, from birth, saying you are
sinful or wrong, that something is fundamentally flawed
in your nature. It is, in truth, the goodness of gay and
lesbian people and of gay and lesbian couples that is a triumph—*is a triumph*—against discrimination and prejudice. We are not a threat. We are not a threat to traditional
marriage. We're not a threat to your communities. We
are, in fact, an asset. We deserve to be welcomed because
we are your neighbors. We are your friends. Indeed, we
are your family.

Numbers of people here have come up and talked to
me privately about their gay brother, or lesbian sister, or
their child or their uncle. Part of those conversations are
private, at times, because in fact prejudice and discrimination continue to exist in this society. Not everyone
feels, even with the laws we have on our books now,
not everyone feels able to say with openness and with
pride, "Yes, my family member is a gay man or a lesbian
woman."

We have made incredible progress in Vermont. And
up until the last two-and-a-half months I would have said
Vermont has more progress than any other state in this
country. I have proudly said that. Our nondiscrimination
laws, our hate crime laws, our adoption laws, they all
make us proud.

But Lippert was angry. He had vowed to keep his composure, but the truth of what he felt at this moment was complex. What he and fellow House members had endured during
the past few months was outrageous to him.

There remains afoot in Vermont prejudice against gay men and lesbians. In the last two-and-a-half months I have seen and I have heard, I have been called names in this chamber, in this building, the likes of which I have never experienced in my life—my personal life or my political life. And I've watched come true what I have always known to be true, that those who stand beside gay and lesbian people as their allies, as people who are going to stand up and say, "Yes, this is wrong," and "Yes, there should be rights," they get targeted, too. Because for some people the hate runs that deep, the prejudice runs that far.

He knew gays and lesbians could not win their rights without allies in the straight community, and he wanted to express his gratitude to them.

I've watched while members of my committee have made brave political decisions to support equality for gay and lesbian people, for gay and lesbian couples and rights for us, and I have watched them be attacked. I have stood there and listened while they have been threatened personally and politically, and I've had members of my committee say, "I couldn't sleep at night. I've had knots in my stomach." I wouldn't have wished this on any of them, but I am deeply appreciative of the work of my committee members who listened, who struggled, came to hard-reached decisions that it's the right thing to do.

Passing the bill that the House Judiciary Committee has brought forward will not end discrimination. It will not end prejudice. It will not end hate, but it will grant rights.

He had heard Republican opponents repeating the line that had become their mantra: that the issue was not about civil rights, it was about benefits.

We argue about whether they are civil rights or other rights, but I'll tell you this, they are rights that I don't have right now and most everyone else in this chamber does.

There's something strange about sitting in the midst of a deliberative body that is trying to decide whether I and my fellow gay and lesbian Vermonters should get our rights now; should we wait a little longer; should we ask all the people whether or not we deserve to have those rights?

Who are we? We are committed, caring, loving individuals in a time when desire for greater commitment, greater love, greater fidelity is needed in our society, and I find it so ironic that rather than being embraced and welcomed we are seen as a threat.

We are people, some of us, that in recent times endured the scourge of a terrible epidemic, and even in the midst of that epidemic have reached out and formed relationships, cared for each other, holding each other, sometimes as death has arrived. Don't tell me about what a committed relationship is and isn't. I've watched my gay brothers care for each other deeply and my lesbian sisters nurse and care. There is no love and no commitment any greater than what I've seen, what I know.

He paused to take a breath. At that moment he might have dissolved into tears. Tears were brimming in the eyes of onlookers, including me. Ross Sneyd continued to type.

Our relationships deserve every protection that our bill would grant. Our relationships deserve those rights, those protections. We don't need to study it any longer. We don't need to put it off and let someone else decide. We have a historic opportunity, and I ask us to put aside this amendment, which I trust is well-intentioned, but I think flawed. I ask you to put aside the rest of these amendments as well. Let us move forward, putting into law a bill that will set aside traditional marriage in order to meet the needs of those who somehow feel threatened, but will find a way through this thicket and will grant rights, will give a message to our community that it is time to take another piece of the hatred and the discrimination and the prejudice and remove it, and at the same time give an affirmation to our community about what it means to have full inclusivity, to embrace our neighbors, to affirm committed, loving relationships and to affirm our common humanity.

Thank you, Mr. Speaker.

Lippert sat down.

"Mr. Speaker!" A voice came from the back of the chamber, and before Obuchowski could even recognize him, Robert Kinsey was on his feet. He had not come to Montpelier thirty years before with the idea that he would be voting one day about rights for homosexuals. But he had not remained lodged in the past, and he understood the importance of the moment. "I just heard the greatest speech I've heard in thirty years," he told the packed chamber. "And that's why I'm glad to be a friend of the member from Hinesburg, and that's why I'm glad to be on his side."

It wasn't in vain that Sam Schneider had taken that pail of water in the face.

When the Flory amendment came to a vote, it failed to attract significant support on the right or the left, and it was defeated, 118–29.

The debate would continue into the evening, House members offering impassioned testimony on both sides of the issue. Mary Mazzariello, a Democrat from Rutland, held back tears as she talked about her two lesbian daughters. "They did not choose to be different," she said. "Their pain and their inability to fit the mold has been our pain as well. Please help to remove the stigma."

The crowds who had come to watch the debate and witness the historic vote continued to wait inside and outside the State House. After dark, supporters rallying on the State House steps lit candles. During the evening Lippert left the chamber for a moment and walked across the lobby to the second-story windows that looked down between those massive columns to the crowd on the steps. He saw a sea of flickering candles. On a small scale it was like the sea of candles in San Francisco twenty-two years before, but these candles were lit in hope, not in grief and despair. Lippert had been in San Francisco a few years before, and he made a point of going to City Hall. He wandered the marble corridors of the building, unsure exactly where it was that Harvey Milk had been gunned down. For Lippert, Milk's death was a kind of martyrdom, a life that, after it was taken, came to represent the courage and commitment needed to lift the mantle of oppression from millions of people. The shadow of violence had not been far from the debate during the past two and a half months, and Lippert understood the risks he was taking by speaking out.

Finally, all the arguments had been heard, and it was time for Obuchowski to call for a vote. Each legislator would hear his or her name called and would have to call out aye or nay. The complicated calculus of personal belief, political expedience, and constitutional law would come down to a decision many wanted to avoid. Finally, there was no avoiding it.

There were some surprises as the names were called. Al Perry, the Democrat who was John Edwards's roommate, had finally acknowledged to himself that the issue was one of civil rights, though he thought the Legislature should move more

slowly. As the clerk began to call the roll, Perry was still undecided on how he would vote. When he voted yes, Carmolli and
others were astonished. The four Democrats from Rutland
all voted yes. Marion Milne, the Republican from Washington,
voted yes. Richard Mallary of Brookfield voted yes. Robert
Kinsey voted yes. Democrats from conservative districts,
people such as William Wisell of Bristol and Joyce Barbieri of
Wallingford, voted yes. In all fifteen Republicans voted yes, and
sixteen Democrats voted no. When the result was announced,
it was closer than the outcome on any of the amendments.
The vote was 79–68. The bill had won.

Members swarmed around Bill Lippert that night, hugging
him and thanking him for what he had said. When he left
the House floor, a reporter approached him, and Lippert saw
the man was verging on tears. He pulled the reporter into the
Cedar Creek Room. "I'm a reporter," the man said. "We're not
supposed to have feelings, but Bill, you don't know how important it is what you said tonight." The reporter, whom Lippert
would not identify even three years later, was heterosexual.
Lippert gave the man a hug.

That evening was "the most exhilarating time of my life,"
he said. He and his colleagues went out for drinks, but during
the evening his jubilation grew more muted when he remembered the fight was not over. The vote on March 15 had been
the second reading, which meant the bill would have to survive a final vote the next day. Opponents would make a final
push to change people's minds. Lippert and his allies would
have to be ready to meet the challenge. But now they knew
they could win.

The next day proved to be a grueling ordeal for Bill Lippert and his allies. They had won the day before with seventy-
nine votes, but if opponents could change the minds of five

House members, or persuade a few to take a walk, there was an outside chance they could kill the bill on its final reading. At the least, they would continue to offer potentially damaging amendments.

Lippert's composure was tested a final time when Fred Maslack, a Republican from Poultney, offered an amendment requiring anyone requesting a civil union license to undergo an HIV test. If one of the two partners tested positive, civil union would be prohibited.

As Maslack spoke on his amendment, Lippert fell into a quiet fury. This was the last straw. Then Nancy Sheltra rose. She looked directly at Lippert as she declared that homosexuals needed to be protected "from their own epidemic." It was the familiar attack, blaming gays for the disease that was killing them. Diane Carmolli came over to sit with Lippert as Sheltra spoke, hoping to keep him calm. Lippert was aghast at the ignorance and viciousness of what he was hearing. In his speech on the floor the day before, he had spoken of his partner; he had not mentioned that his partner had lived with AIDS for years and that he had devoted years to keeping his partner alive. He was not going to take it anymore.

After Sheltra spoke, Lippert rose, enraged. "This is the most offensive amendment I have ever heard offered on the floor of the House," he said. "This is the kind of blatant discrimination we should have no part of."

When he was finished speaking, he rushed from the chamber, looking for a friendly face. When he found Susan Murray, he grabbed her and took her into a hallway behind the speaker's rostrum. There he put his arms around her and wept.

It turned out his fellow House members wanted no part of the Maslack amendment. It was defeated, 136–2. Maslack and Sheltra were the only two who supported it.

During the afternoon there were further efforts to delay the bill and more speeches from House members. But when it came time for the third and final reading, the bill passed 76–69.

Tom Little's comments afterward revealed how fluid the situation on the House floor had been. "I think there were some profoundly moving speeches on the floor that helped the members that had not previously had a chance to think deeply about it," he told reporter Jack Hoffman. "To hear ten or fifteen hours of debate I think made a difference for those people."

It had been an exhausting ordeal for many members of the House. They credited the leadership of Little and the example of Lippert as keys to the bill's success. In the minds of many, the moral force of statements by Lippert, Mary Mazzariello, and others made a difference, especially compared to the angry, moralistic tone of the more extreme opponents.

Now the bill was headed for the more liberal Senate, where many observers thought passage of the bill would be far easier than in the House. I was one of them. I didn't know at the time how close it would come to defeat. The furies that had swept through the House only intensified the pressure felt by the senators as the bill went over to that quiet club of thirty.

CHAPTER EIGHT

A LOVER'S QUARREL

I.

DICK SEARS had a burly physique and a gruff manner that contrasted with the more cerebral and even-tempered approach of his counterpart in the House, Tom Little. Sears had made a career running a residence for troubled kids, and he was used to the rough-and-tumble of human affairs. But now he was worried. He had seen the level of anger that the civil unions bill had generated throughout the state. He represented Bennington County in the southwestern corner of Vermont, a mixture of liberal and conservative, Bennington College intellectuals and blue-collar factory workers. Most of the House delegation from Bennington County had voted against civil unions, and Sears was sensitive to the strong feelings against the bill among his constituents.

Peter Shumlin, leader of the Democrats in the Senate, continued to be fearful of the effect the furor over civil unions would have on Democratic prospects in November. He had felt the brunt of public opposition. Christian radio stations had broadcast the phone number of his office, and he was receiving a continuous barrage of calls from across the nation. "You couldn't hang up the phone without it ringing again," he said. Shumlin knew of Sears's trepidation about the bill. "The place was crumbling," Shumlin said. "I remember Dick Sears saying, 'We just can't do this bill.'"

Shumlin had experienced his own evolution on the issue. As of December 19, the day before the *Baker* decision, Shumlin said the issue of gay marriage wasn't even on his radar screen. He had an ambitious agenda for the Senate; he was particularly concerned with health care issues. Gay marriage was far from a priority.

After the *Baker* decision, Shumlin attended meetings with Beth Robinson and Susan Murray, and he said he felt the need to lower expectations. Even before the House had taken up the bill, Shumlin told Robinson and Murray that marriage would never pass. "Beth must have thought I was the most sold-out, compromising politician," he said. But he said she was new to the political process, and he described her as "starry-eyed." It was a description that did not fit the tenacious and hard-nosed advocacy that Robinson practiced throughout the court case and the legislative battle. But Shumlin had a keen eye for political difficulties and potential ramifications, and he had cast himself in the role of the realist.

So the civil unions bill faced a different problem in the Senate than in the House. In the House the leadership had been eager to press for a bill, and the rank and file needed to be cajoled. In the Senate, which had a 17–13 Democratic majority, the leadership was fearful while many rank-and-file Democrats would have been happy to press for marriage. These included two of the six members of the Senate Judiciary Committee, Richard McCormack, a folk singer, and James Leddy, a mental health administrator and former priest.

Eventually, during the long weeks of debate in the House, Shumlin began to see the issue of civil unions as a "moral imperative." But he and Sears were also concerned about the imperative of maintaining Democratic power. So they decided to pay a visit to Governor Dean. They didn't want anyone to know about the meeting; Shumlin insisted that the governor's staff assistants leave the room. "I didn't want to read stories about how Shumlin and Sears were chickening out."

In fact, they were chickening out. They wanted to know if it was possible to delay action on the bill. Shumlin and Sears had different memories of the options under discussion: Shumlin said they discussed the appointment of a study commission, and Sears said they discussed having the Judiciary Committee study the issue over the summer, letting the new Legislature take up the issue in January.

But further delay was not likely to help matters for the Democrats. To study the bill over the summer would only prolong the agony and would require the newly elected House to go through the whole process of passing a bill again. After everything the House had gone through, there would have been a massive outcry if the Senate backed down. But in Shumlin's view, facing the voters in November after adopting a civil unions law would imperil the Democrats' hold on power.

Shumlin and Sears rode the elevator up to the fifth floor of the Pavilion Building where Dean had his offices. They knew Dean to be a supremely pragmatic politician able to weigh the options realistically. But Dean was attuned to more than pragmatic considerations. Shumlin said that when he brought up the idea of delay, Dean's neck and face turned red. "The veins were popping out of his neck," Shumlin said. As Shumlin remembered it, Dean told them, "Peter and Dick, every once in a while you have an opportunity to change history and do the right thing. And that's what we're going to do." Shumlin said Dean was not ordinarily an emotional man, but in this instance he was furious. Shumlin and Sears left the meeting knowing there was no choice but to act.

Publicly, Shumlin remained optimistic about the bill's

prospects. "We will pass a bill this year," he said in the *Rutland Herald*. At the same time, he said, "I expect things to get much more intense as it comes over to the Senate. I've told the members to get ready."

By the time the Senate Judiciary Committee took up the bill it was late March. Sears let it be known that he was not going to rubber-stamp the House bill, and he scheduled a new round of testimony, pro and con, on how best to proceed. He viewed himself as a moderate who liked to find ways to bring people together.

But he was a moderate with a temper, and his temper faced an extra test during those days. The strain of the controversy had caused him to ignore a worsening cold until he feared he had pneumonia. With Sears's patience stretched thin and his health worsening, Shumlin feared Sears might scuttle the entire bill. So a few weeks into the process Shumlin told Senator Ann Cummings, a member of the Judiciary Committee, that she should persuade Sears to take a day off to go home to rest.

Yet the hold that Sears and Shumlin had on the enthusiasm of their more liberal colleagues was tenuous. In Sears's absence Dick McCormack, vice chairman of the Judiciary Committee, brought a bill before the committee designed to protect the rights of the transgendered. Much to Shumlin's dismay, the committee approved the bill.

McCormack was an unapologetic liberal who had voiced support early and forcefully for gay marriage. And yet he was able to mock his own ideological purity. "The ideological liberal kind of waltzes through life, delighted with his virtue," McCormack said. He knew the bill on the rights of the transgendered had the makings of a political disaster, and he was not surprised when Shumlin demanded that he give up the bill. The bill would not come up for debate if it did not make it to

the Senate calendar. And it would not make it to the Senate calendar if it was stuck in Shumlin's pocket. It was a rarely employed parliamentary tactic, but in an effort to prevent a public
outcry, Shumlin pocketed the bill.

Sears's illness was an acute case of bronchitis, not pneumonia, and he stayed on the job except for that brief sojourn at
home. During late March and early April, the Judiciary Committee continued to take testimony, including an appearance
by Nina Beck.

It was March 22, the eighth anniversary of the day when
Beck and Stacy Jolles had celebrated their union in the Oakland hills. Stacy Jolles, holding Seth, looked on as Beck testified
before the Senate committee. Holly Puterbaugh also made a
rare appearance at the State House to witness the committee
hearing.

"Stacy and I have been through everything a couple can
imagine," Beck told the senators. "We share a deep love for
each other, have shared in the joy of the birth of our two children, and the devastating grief at the loss of our firstborn. We
survived that loss because of the strength of the bond between
us and in no small part because of the vows we exchanged
eight years ago."

As described in Ross Sneyd's story for the Associated Press,
many in the audience grew tearful as Beck told of the loss of
their son Noah.

"Civil marriage can strengthen the fabric of our society as
it protects and nurtures the bonds between a couple and a family," Beck told the senators.

Bishop Angell also came before Sears's committee and
spoke in uncompromising terms. "Do not let the court or anybody else push you around," Angell said. "You have no duty,
moral or constitutional, to weaken the institution of marriage.
If the court thinks otherwise, then let the people overrule the

court. This is the United States of America. We are not ruled by kings, whether on a throne or in a courtroom."

Sears lost his patience that day in a colloquy with a conservative minister from Bennington. According to Ross Sneyd's story, he told the Reverend Glen Bayley that he didn't like being told by opponents that support for civil unions would send him to hell.

"But they're not telling you to go there. And they're encouraging you to go in a different direction," Bayley said. "I do believe you'll be judged one day and so will I."

"I have confidence that this vote is not going to make the difference," Sears retorted acidly.

Though they rejected the advice of the bishop, Sears and Ann Cummings, another Democratic committee member, continued to hold out hope they could craft some kind of compromise that would mollify the bill's opponents. In particular, Sears wanted to include a residency requirement, allowing civil unions for Vermont residents only. That way he might win over Senator John Bloomer, one of two Republican members of the Judiciary Committee. But Beth Robinson and Susan Murray strongly opposed a residency requirement, arguing that it would write discrimination into the law.

Dick McCormack saw another problem with the residency requirement. He feared that if the Senate included a residency requirement, liberals in the House would abandon the bill, and the bill would fail. He even suspected Sears and Shumlin, still concerned about the election in the fall, of secretly hoping the bill would fail in the House. That way they might escape the wrath of the voters.

In any event, the Freedom to Marry Task Force was not about to let Dick Sears off the hook. Beth Robinson and Susan Murray were not aware of the secret visit Sears and Shumlin had made to Dean. But they sensed Sears's weakness on the issue, and they wanted to show him it was safe for him to back a civil unions bill. So when Sears announced that he and the other senator from Bennington County, Gerald Morrissey, would hold a public hearing at the firehouse in Bennington, the task force went into action. The battle for Dick Sears's support would be joined in his hometown.

2.

BENNINGTON has a history that reaches back to Vermont's beginnings. It had been the center of activity for Ethan Allen and the Green Mountain Boys, and the Americans and the British had fought an important battle of the Revolutionary War on the outskirts of Bennington. Today the largest collection of art by Grandma Moses, a painter who celebrated the simplicities of rural life, is contained at the Bennington Museum just up the road to the west of the firehouse. A bit further up the road in the Old Bennington cemetery a gravestone rests over the ashes of Robert Frost. Chiseled into the stone are Frost's words: "I had a lover's quarrel with the world."

Vermont would bring its newest quarrel to the firehouse on River Street on a Saturday in April. The Freedom to Marry Task Force had 2,500 people on its e-mail list, and according to Dorothy Mammen, the word went out that people had to get themselves to Bennington.

Opponents were also making plans. A lobbyist for Take It to the People warned Peter Shumlin that the group was organizing bus caravans and there would be 5,000 people at the Bennington meeting. He was wrong.

The fire department had removed the five fire trucks from their positions inside the firehouse, and by the time the meeting

began, 350 people had filled the firehouse floor. Another 100
were standing against the walls or in the large bays at the front
of the station. Pink stickers were plentiful throughout the
crowd, and with the names of speakers drawn at random, it was
apparent that supporters of civil unions outnumbered opponents by about two to one.

The war over civil unions was no longer a matter of new
arguments or evidence. The ground had been tilled many
times. The point was to show up in force and to persuade legislators that your side was strong, that in the power struggle of
democratic action the legislators were not alone. It was particularly important for the Freedom to Marry Task Force to deliver that message to Dick Sears.

At the Bennington meeting, it was easy to see the kind of
pressure that Sears was facing in his home district. Joe Wolfe, a
friend of Sears, told the meeting: "This issue has taken on for
some of us aspects of a holy war, and holy wars don't go away.
Come election time, it won't be forgotten."

After two hours of discussion inside the Bennington firehouse, Sears told the crowd, "Unfortunately, I really do have
good friends on both sides of the issue. Unfortunately, I have
to make a decision that isn't going to make all of my friends
happy. If after eight years, I no longer have the opportunity to
serve you, so be it."

He was going to vote for some sort of civil unions bill, and
they could throw him out of office if they liked. The firehouse
crowd erupted in cheers. Looking back, Sears said he was astonished at the support evident for civil unions in his hometown. The Task Force strategy had worked.

But each step of the way, feelings only seemed to intensify.
In the lobby of the State House, the week after the meeting in
Bennington, Ross Sneyd got into a shouting match with Ger-
ald Morrissey. As Sneyd described it, Morrissey was angry that

Sneyd had not quoted him in his story about the Bennington meeting. Sneyd told Morrissey the reason he had not been quoted was that he hadn't said anything worth quoting. As the shouting continued, it occurred to Sneyd that he and Morrissey might come to blows. Kermit Spaulding, sergeant at arms of the Legislature, approached them, but the argument stopped before Spaulding had to intervene. It was another sign of the political and emotional pressures building in the State House and throughout the state.

Certainly, opponents of civil unions were not about to ease the pressure. On April 6, five days after the meeting in Bennington, Nancy Sheltra led a rally of opponents on the steps of the State House. They had gathered for what Sheltra called a "Jericho march," during which protesters circled the State House seven times, emulating those who brought down the walls of the biblical city.

Alan Keyes, a radio talk-show host and a Republican candidate for president in 2000, made an appearance at Sheltra's rally that day. Senator John Bloomer, the Republican leader, had invited Keyes to Montpelier with the idea he could testify before the Judiciary Committee, despite the ground rules established by Sears limiting testimony to Vermonters. Sears refused to change the rules for Keyes, but Keyes took the opportunity to address the crowd Nancy Sheltra had organized outside the State House.

On the presidential campaign trail, Keyes was distinguished by his provocative rhetoric. "So shall we have to forgo all discrimination against all adulterers now?" he asked that day in Montpelier. "Shall we forgo all discrimination against people who exploit children? Shall we forgo all discrimination against rapists and people of this kind? Where do you stop in your willingness to say that human sexual behavior is a condition and not a choice?"

As Tracy Schmaler's account in the *Rutland Herald* described it, Keyes's speech drew howls of approbation from the crowd: "I can say clearly on my own behalf as an adult person—you take it back into the bedroom where it belongs," he said. "If you bring it out into the public arena, we must fight you."

Sheltra was just as angry. "I think it's time to turn Vermont around," she told the crowd. "Claim Vermont for godly purposes . . . One hundred years ago, the Christian community, the moral people, they were the ones that controlled the media, controlled the government, and they controlled the schools. Hey, we were a great nation then, folks, weren't we? What's happening now?"

The crowd was charged up as it dispersed and entered the halls of the State House. There they found Dick Sears in the corridor outside a committee room. A few of them began to talk with Sears, and he joined in a discussion with them. But soon the crowd in the hallway grew to about eighty, and the discussion deteriorated into a familiar harangue about Sears's sinfulness and the immorality of the bill his committee was considering. The anger of the crowd made Sears worry for a moment about the potential for violence. They were not letting up on him. He was ill with bronchitis, and he was exhausted from the ordeal of the past few weeks, and finally his patience snapped. "Look," he said, "they don't pay me enough to take this shit." And he walked away.

In the days that remained before the Judiciary Committee took action on a bill, the residency requirement remained a central unresolved question. The two Republicans on the committee, John Bloomer and Vincent Illuzzi, supported the residency requirement, and the two liberal Democrats, Dick McCormack and James Leddy, opposed it. Sears and Ann Cummings continued to believe that compromise was possible, but that hope crumbled after a notorious meeting on a snowy night in St. Albans. Looking back three years later, McCormack, Cummings, Sears, and others said St. Albans turned the tide.

3.

ANN CUMMINGS headed out in a snowstorm for St. Albans on April 11 with her dog, Dominic, in the car beside her. Dominic was a mutt with a resemblance to a German shepherd, and Cummings thought his presence in the car served as a measure of protection. She was heading to a public meeting in St. Albans, organized by Senator Sara Kittell, a Democrat from Franklin County, where legislators involved in the civil unions controversy could answer questions from the public.

Cummings, a former mayor of Montpelier, had a sense of humor about the controversy that had engulfed the Senate. Her daughter told her she was probably the only member of the Legislature who framed her hate mail. But it would be hard to maintain a sense of humor about what happened that night in St. Albans.

St. Albans is a town of under 8,000 in the northwestern corner of the state where one of the main events of the year is the maple festival in the spring. The patron saint of St. Albans might be John LeClair, a St. Albans native and a star in the National Hockey League. The only action on Vermont soil during the Civil War took place in St. Albans, when a band of rebels swooped down from Canada and robbed three banks.

Like other old railroad towns, St. Albans had experienced a decline after the railroads went out of business, but during the 1990s, the town enjoyed an industrial revival. Even so, Franklin County was a long way from Windham County, the liberal bastion in the southeast that was Peter Shumlin's home. Dairying, sugaring, and hockey remained central to life in Franklin County, and the Catholic Church was still influential among its sizable population of French-Canadians.

More than the demographics, it was probably the momentum of the debate about civil unions that provoked the anger that erupted that evening in St. Albans. Opponents had repeated their objections in every possible forum. Voters had rejected civil unions at town meeting. But nothing seemed to halt the drive to pass a bill. Among opponents, a feeling of helplessness had engendered a growing rage.

The meeting was held in the auditorium of Bellows Free Academy, a private institution that served as the public high school for the St. Albans region. The school, built in the 1930s, retained an antique charm, with period light fixtures still in place. The yellow-walled auditorium, which seated about four hundred, had a steep balcony and a proscenium stage. Ann Cummings pulled into the parking lot beside the school; leaving Dominic in the car, she made her way through the maze of hallways. A huge crowd was streaming into the school, and soon the entire auditorium, including the balcony, was full. Unlike the atmosphere of the State House, the school did not enforce a sense of decorum. The angry residents of Franklin County were on their home territory, and they were going to make their feelings known.

Bill Lippert also drove to St. Albans that night, as did John Edwards, whose hometown of Swanton was just to the north. They were looking forward to the kind of give-and-take that might ease tensions about the issue.

But the audience was in no mood for give-and-take. They were ready only to give. Eight legislators stood in front of the stage, facing the crowd, and when John Edwards was introduced, the audience erupted in a torrent of boos. Edwards was a popular legislator and a likable, friendly man who was known to many in the audience. The hostility directed at him was a sign of what was to come. From then on the crowd refused to hear what the legislators had to say. When Ann Cummings began to speak, hoping to explain the process in the Senate, she was jeered and howled into silence. "It's the first time I had a Vermont crowd that wouldn't even let me speak. People sitting in front of me were saying the rosary," she said.

When Bill Lippert began to speak, the crowd shouted him down. The whole meeting was veering out of control.

Emerson Lynn, the publisher of the *St. Albans Messenger,* was moderator of the event, and he called a halt to the question-and-answer portion of the meeting. Instead, the audience took over, making statements at a microphone. The decorum did not improve.

"How would you like to see deviants walk hand in hand?" asked the first speaker. He had seen such a thing in San Francisco. "I don't care if I go to jail for one thousand years. I won't tolerate it."

When a teenager told the audience that she had two lesbian parents, audience members shouted obscenities. According to the account in the *Messenger,* someone hollered, "Child abuse!" Someone else shouted, "What do they do to you at night?"

Someone told the legislators they had no right to vote according to their consciences. "The people sent you not to vote your conscience but the consensus of the majority," one man said. "We will remove you from your positions of authority."

Objections raised politely at the State House hearings were hurled toward the stage at St. Albans with alarming vehemence and anger.

Francis Howrigan, a former senator, warned about what would happen if a gay man were allowed to become the guardian of a boy. "You know what that boy will be in twelve or thirteen years," he said.

Civil unions had their defenders. A woman from Fairfield began to list the rights that civil unions would provide for gay and lesbian couples, but jeers from the balcony silenced her.

Sara Kittell, who had organized the forum, was shocked by the behavior of her constituents. Ever since she first ran for office in 1996, she had been a supporter of gay marriage, and she planned to vote for the civil unions bill. Now she realized she had been naive about the depth of the hostility the bill had provoked.

Dick McCormack tried to make the point that the rights of the minority deserved protection. But the audience wasn't listening. McCormack and the other legislators were stunned and worried. There were no police officers in evidence.

"There was no easy exit out of that place," Cummings said. "Bill Lippert was there, and I was concerned for him."

Looking back, Lippert said, "That was as close to a lynch mob as I have ever experienced. It was scary stuff. I remember thinking, if somebody doesn't get beat up tonight, it's a miracle."

No one got beat up, but when Ann Cummings emerged from the school that night, Dick McCormack recalled, her jaw was set, and she had a steely resolve. "There's no point in compromise," she told McCormack. "Those people aren't interested in compromise. And I'll be damned if I'm going to compromise."

As she headed home with her dog beside her, she was furious. She and Dick Sears had wanted to be reasonable, to craft language of some sort that would show opponents they were willing to listen. Already the House had compromised by choosing civil unions instead of marriage, but she and Sears had hoped the residency requirement or some kind of additional language would appease angry voters. At St. Albans she had listened, and she had heard enough. Compromise? No way. That is what she told Sears when she got back to Montpelier. And with Cummings joining McCormack and Leddy in opposing a residency requirement, Sears saw the idea was dead.

From McCormack's point of view, abandoning the residency requirement saved the bill. He quoted a favorite historian: "Everything that happened almost didn't." He thought most people were unaware of how close civil unions came to not happening. "The bigots of St. Albans should know we have them to thank for civil unions," he said.

It was two days after the St. Albans meeting, April 13, that the Judiciary Committee finally approved the civil unions bill. The committee decided it was important for civil unions to mirror marriage as closely as possible, and they rejected the residency requirement, approving a bill that ended up varying only slightly from the House bill. The most significant change was the effective date, which the Senate moved up from September 1 to July 1. The committee's vote reflected the partisan split developing around the bill. It passed 4–2, with the two Republicans opposed.

4.

BARBARA MacDonald of Williamstown had served in the Vermont House for only three-and-a-half months when she died in a car crash on snow-covered roads in April 1983. Her son, Mark, was a teacher at Randolph Union High School, and soon after Barbara's death, Governor Richard Snelling appointed Mark to take her place in the House.

Mark MacDonald had spent his youth in Princeton, New Jersey; Washington, D.C.; Turkey; and France. After high school in Washington, he flunked out of Syracuse University and was in and out of other colleges before he was drafted into the army in 1968. He served aboard a helicopter in Vietnam, returning in 1970 when he went to work on a shrimp boat in Florida. He eventually returned to Vermont, where his family had a second home, and received his teaching certificate.

He was elected to the Vermont Senate from Orange County in 1996. He was a Democrat in a largely conservative district, but he was a likable, hardworking public official who took his work seriously. When he heard about the Supreme Court's *Baker* decision, he thought the court had done the right thing, but when he realized the court had dumped the issue into the lap of the Legislature, he knew he was in trouble.

By the time the bill came over from the House to the Senate, MacDonald's Senate mail box was filling up with hateful messages from all over the country, telling him he was evil, that he would go to hell if he voted for the civil unions bill. He spent every evening at home on the phone fielding calls from constituents. Some would threaten him, others would try to reason with him. He remembered one caller: "Mark, heads are going to roll. I'm calling you as a friend."

After the Judiciary Committee had voted out the civil unions bill, Peter Shumlin approached MacDonald and told him he didn't have to vote for the bill when it came to the floor. The Democrats had enough votes without him. If he thought he needed to vote no in order to save his seat, he could do so. Even Governor Dean sent a message to MacDonald through a third party, saying Dean would understand if MacDonald voted against the bill.

MacDonald spoke with Sara Kittell, the senator from Franklin County. Shumlin had given Kittell the same message: Vote no if you need to. It was advice she was hearing from friends and family members, too. Now MacDonald said to her,

"If you don't vote for it, I won't vote for it." He said she didn't give him an answer. "She was embarrassed that I had said such a thing," MacDonald said. Kittell said later it hadn't occurred to her to vote against the bill.

On the weekend before the bill came to a vote in the Senate, MacDonald visited with constituents out mowing their lawns, playing ball, or dropping off trash at the dump. No, he wasn't going to vote for the civil unions bill, he told them. Most of those he encountered were glad of that. But there were some who had urged him to support the bill, so on a Monday evening he made a few calls to them. They don't need my vote, he explained. He wanted his friends to know the Senate leadership had told him he could vote against the bill in order to hold on to his seat and help maintain a Democratic majority.

After a half dozen calls, one of his friends called him back. His friend said to him, "Mark, what are you going to tell your school kids? How are you going to tell them you voted for something you don't believe in just to get reelected?"

The bill came to the Senate floor on April 18, just a week after the tumultuous hearing in St. Albans. There was little doubt about the outcome; Shumlin was right about the Democratic majority in favor of the bill. But Mark MacDonald had something he wanted to say.

> I spoke to my state representative last night and told her that it would be wise for me not to vote for this bill . . . I could tell people . . . that if I got reelected easily, I would be in a position to help educate the others that need time to deal with this. I told my wife that, heck, my constituents in polls are against this bill, and after all, I should vote for what my constituents want.

He told the senators about the calls he had made and about the friend who had reminded him about his students. "Someone called back and said, 'You know, Mark, you teach eighth-grade social studies. What are you going to tell the kids when you get back to school?' And I cursed him . . ."

> I thought of my mom—I'm not in the habit of talking to my mother late at night—I said this isn't fair. I got drafted once . . . They sent me because it was the right thing to do, it was moral, and when I came home, they didn't care much, and told me for years and years that I was a fool for having gone. I thought you only had to do that once in your life, but I've been drafted again. My mother said, I always told you that life wasn't fair. I said, now I've got to speak to my kids when I get back to school. She said, you'll know the right thing to tell them when you get back to school.

MacDonald voted for the bill, as did every other Democrat, including Sara Kittell, and two Republicans, Peter Brownell and Helen Riehle of Chittenden County. The same day the Senate rejected a constitutional amendment that would have established marriage as a heterosexual union. The front page of the *Rutland Herald* the next day showed a four-column photograph of Dick McCormack hugging Mark MacDonald. They both knew the political storm to come during the election might claim one or both of them. But they had no regrets.

The next day, the Senate gave final approval to the civil unions bill with Stan Baker and Peter Harrigan watching from the gallery. It had been a long road for them. The state of Vermont had been engulfed for months in the bitterest controversy anybody could remember, all because of the case they had launched four years before when they went to obtain a marriage license from their town clerk.

Beth Robinson watched the Senate action that day from the rear of the chamber. She was never one to let herself go too far. She knew there were always more battles to be fought; the House still had to vote on the bill as modified by the Senate. But the political cauldron she had entered so reluctantly four months before had yielded a victory, and she had words of praise for the senators.

> The vote really turned on the soul-searching that each individual senator did. I was moved by the speeches, particularly by the legislators who really seemed to get it, that this is an issue of civil rights.

The struggle reached its culmination on April 25 when the House voted 79–68 to accept the bill sent to them by the Senate. Once again the galleries were packed, and all six of the plaintiffs in the *Baker* case were there, along with five-month-old Seth. Holly Puterbaugh and Lois Farnham were seated in the red upholstered seats lining the front of the chamber to the speaker's left. "I remember watching Lois keeping track of the vote," Holly said, "and when I saw we had enough votes, it was—chills. There were a few tears on my part."

The photo in the *Rutland Herald* the next day showed all six plaintiffs on the floor of the House chamber, beaming with happiness (little Seth looking more dismayed than happy). In a smaller photo Peter Harrigan was seen hugging a smiling Bill Lippert, the man who had carried the banner through the months of sound and fury.

No one doubted that the election in the fall would offer opponents of the bill the chance to exact their revenge. But those who had brought the civil unions bill along its tortuous path toward passage believed it was their finest hour. These included House Speaker Michael Obuchowski, who understood by now that his speakership was imperiled, and the numerous legislators who were already acquainted with the level of anger that awaited them on the campaign trail.

Governor Howard Dean did not wait long before signing the bill. On April 26, the day after final passage by the House, he gathered his staff together in the privacy of his office. There were no reporters or photographers to record the event. Legislative leaders, usually invited to celebrate historic bill signings, were not there. No advocates or supporters were allowed to witness the signing. He signed the bill in the closet.

Or so his critics said. After signing the bill, Dean called a press conference where he described the bill as a triumph and where he explained that he did not want to indulge in the triumphalism that usually accompanies bill signings. Vermont had been through too much, and the feelings of Vermonters were too raw. He was proud to sign the bill, but he did not want to aggravate the wounds that were still stinging so many people.

> There is much to celebrate about this bill. Those celebrations, as the subject matter of this bill, will be private. They will be celebrated by couples and their families, by people making commitments to each other.

But even if Dean chose to sign the bill behind closed doors, he was plain and out front about his support for the bill.

> I chose to sign this bill because I fundamentally believe it's the right thing to do, and I also fundamentally believe that in the long run it's the right thing for the state of Vermont and the United States of America . . .
>
> This bill enriches not just the very small percentage of gay and lesbian Vermonters who take advantage of this partnership and get the rights that the court has determined that they are due. I believe this bill enriches all of us as we look with new eyes at a group of people who have been outcasts for many, many generations.

At his press conference the legislative leaders who had brought the bill through to passage stood lined up to Dean's left: Bill Lippert, Tom Little, Dick McCormack, and Dick Sears.

When the press conference broke up, reporters gathered around Bill Lippert, wondering what he thought of Dean's decision to sign the bill in private. Had he signed the bill in the closet? Lippert was reluctant to criticize the governor at this historic moment, but what could he say? He left the governor's ceremonial office, worrying that the press would overlook the historic nature of the bill by dwelling on the private signing. Then as he entered the Cedar Creek Room across the hallway from the governor's office, he abruptly turned back. Dean was just emerging from his office, and the two of them were surrounded by the press. Lippert extended his hand and said for all to hear: "Governor Dean, congratulations on being the governor to sign the most comprehensive bill for gay rights in the nation."

Lippert was furious that even this moment of triumph had to contend with the cloud of antigay bias. But Dean beamed at Lippert's magnanimous gesture. The next morning outside the State House cafeteria Lippert ran into Dean. As Lippert recalled it, Dean told him, "Man, you saved my ass last night."

Lippert was less interested in protecting the governor politically than in keeping the focus where it belonged: on the historic advance represented by the governor's signature.

After Dean signed the bill, I wrote that he had also signed away any prospect of running for president of the United States. He had explored the possibility of a campaign in 2000, but it seemed to me that the governor who had signed a civil unions bill would be hard-pressed to win support in the more conservative regions of the nation. Three years later in the early stages of the primary election, Dean emerged as an important contender, portraying his decision to sign the civil unions bill as an indication of his courage.

At the time he signed the bill, however, a furious political backlash was already taking shape. Dean was facing a stiff challenge in his race for governor, and a grassroots movement, using the slogan "Take Back Vermont," was attacking members of the Legislature who they said had refused to listen to the people. If the backlash succeeded in ousting a sufficient number of legislators, the civil unions bill could be overturned. For many Vermonters, however, there was more at stake in the 2000 election than a piece of legislation. The election that followed passage of the law became in the minds of many Vermonters a battle for the soul of their state.

CHAPTER NINE

WHAT IS THE HARM?

I.

ANNETTE CAPPY, town clerk of Brattleboro, received a call in June 2000 from a local woman who wanted to have a civil union ceremony as soon as the new law took effect—at midnight on July 1. It would be Cappy's job to issue civil union licenses, administer the required oath, and receive the application fees. Unfortunately, as she told the caller, July 1 was a Saturday, and her office wasn't open on Saturdays. The caller sounded disappointed, and Cappy said she would give the matter more thought. Maybe there was something she could do.

Carolyn Conrad, thirty years old, was associate dean of students at nearby Marlboro College. Kathleen Peterson, an electrician known to her friends as KP, had been Conrad's partner for four years. They had held a private marriagelike ceremony two years before, but after the civil unions bill became law, they decided to make their partnership legal. Peterson, who was forty-one years old, remembered that a friend had said to them, "You're going to do it at midnight, aren't you?"

Soon Annette Cappy called back and said she had decided she would open the doors of the town clerk's office at midnight, July 1. She felt bad about having to delay their ceremony. So she and the two women began to make arrangements for the first civil union ceremony in Vermont's history.

Word got out quickly, and soon it became apparent the ceremony would become a major media event. The national press found its way to Brattleboro, as did reporters from Japan and Norway. The two women fielded numerous phone calls, including a call from a reporter in South America who asked how they could be sure they would be safe. Peterson remembered thinking, "Wow, I don't have any advice for people whose life is in danger." They were expecting a crowd of protesters to show up at the ceremony, but the town police made preparations to ensure there would be no disruptions.

Meanwhile, Cappy devised a plan that would allow Conrad and Peterson to avoid the crowd of reporters waiting at the municipal building before the ceremony. They arranged to meet at 11:30 P.M. on Main Street. At the municipal building, the front door remained locked, and the police opened the back door, where a scrum of reporters interviewed a pair of Massachusetts men who planned to apply for a civil union license after Conrad and Peterson had received theirs.

Cappy and her husband, Jim, joined Conrad, Peterson, and about a dozen friends and family on Main Street at the appointed time, and they headed up to the town offices. The municipal building is an imposing two-story brick structure with high, sloping slate roofs looming over the intersection of Linden and Main Streets. The group walked up twenty-nine concrete steps to the front door of the building where a police officer inside opened the door and let them in. The reporters out back had no clue the group had arrived.

Cappy and the wedding party waited in the town clerk's office, watching the clock, and just before midnight the police let the press inside. When midnight came, Cappy gave the two women the piece of paper they had been waiting for. They had filled out the application beforehand; it was similar to the application for a marriage license. Then Cappy delivered the oath:

> Do you both certify that the information on this form is
> correct to the best of your knowledge and belief and that
> you are both free to enter into a civil union in the state of
> Vermont?

Conrad and Peterson said that they did. Then they went across Linden Street to a small public park to hold their civil union ceremony in the open air. The park forms a triangle, and at the point of the triangle there is a fountain surmounted by two Corinthian columns.

As KP Peterson remembered it, the town had been buzzing with news of the event, and that evening word had circulated that a group of protesters would be coming to town. As midnight neared, a sympathetic crowd of about fifty townspeople walked down to the park to make sure the protesters did not cause trouble.

It turned out that a group of about fifteen protesters had made the two-hour drive from Rutland, and police kept them across the street from the ceremony. They remained civil during the ceremony, Peterson said. They were there to register their point of view, nothing more.

T. Hunter Wilson, a friend of the couple from Marlboro College who was a justice of the peace, performed the civil union ceremony. A friend sang, and Conrad and Peterson read statements pledging themselves to each other. Soon the ceremony was over. All that was left was for the justice of the peace to certify the civil union and to return the certificate to the town clerk. Conrad was so grateful to Annette Cappy for her help that she gave Cappy the bouquet of flowers she had held during the ceremony. Then Conrad and Peterson went home where they shared a bottle of champagne with their friends.

Cappy decided she would open her office on Saturday after all, and that day she issued four more civil union licenses. She remembered a man in his seventies who was so happy to receive his license that he reached over the counter and took Cappy's hand. "You'll just never know what this means," he said. The man started to cry, and then Cappy started to cry. She went around the counter, and the two embraced, both of them in tears. "That's when I realized how important this was," she said.

Civil unions quickly became woven into the everyday duties of Vermont's town and city clerks and on tax forms and other legal documents where Vermonters were asked to indicate their marital status. Figures from the state Department of Health showed that in the last half of 2000 there were 1,704 civil unions, followed by another 1,875 in 2001.

Out of that eighteen-month total of 3,579 civil unions, 2,954 involved out-of-state couples, and 625 involved Vermonters. In that period couples came from every state but Montana and North Dakota. There were thirty-two from Canada. The figures also showed that of that eighteen-month total of 3,579, women accounted for 2,366 couples and men for 1,213.

By 2003 the total of civil unions numbered 5,560; 833 of those involved Vermont couples.

Outside of Vermont, civil unions became a legal issue when couples tried to dissolve them. As with divorce, Vermont law allowed for dissolution of a civil union only for Vermont residents. But when couples asked judges in Connecticut, Georgia, and Texas to dissolve their civil unions, the judges refused to recognize civil unions even for the purpose of ending them. Civil unions gained a measure of legal standing in a New York case in which a judge ruled that a civil union partner had the right to sue a New York hospital in a wrongful death case involving his partner.

2.

EVAN WOLFSON occupied a small office overlooking West 22nd Street in Manhattan where he worked as executive director of the Freedom to Marry Collaborative. In the aftermath of Vermont's experience in passing the civil unions law, he was adamant in his view. "What Vermont did was a tremendous step forward," he said. "But I don't think what Vermont did was the right thing."

Wolfson was the lawyer who had served as co-counsel in the Hawaii case for the Lambda Legal Defense and Education Fund. He called the *Baker* decision "positive." But it was not the right result. Beth Robinson and Susan Murray eventually convinced themselves of the need to settle for civil unions, but for Wolfson, whose goal was the freedom to marry, civil union was not good enough.

"The court did not do its duty," he said. "Separate but equal is wrong, and the court should not have shirked its responsibility."

There were two portraits on Wolfson's office walls when I visited him—Abraham Lincoln and Martin Luther King, Jr. "Like every other successful civil rights movement, we must see our struggle as long-term and must set affirmative goals, marshal sustained strategies and concerted efforts, and enlist new allies and resources," Wolfson wrote in an article that appeared in the *Advocate* on September 11, 2001.

The movement should not settle for civil unions, he said. "If we are going to have to face opposition and work to engage the middle no matter what we strive for, why not ask for all we deserve?" he wrote.

"It is worth remembering that we didn't get civil unions by asking for civil unions. We got this separate but unequal status by pressing for the freedom to marry . . . We do ourselves no favor when we enter this civil rights discussion bargaining against ourselves."

He said Vermont's experience had shifted the debate. Before civil unions, most Americans opposed any recognition of gay partners. But afterward, the majority adopted an "all-but-marriage" position, willing to recognize partnerships as long as those partnerships were not labelled marriage.

Wolfson's view paralleled those of Beth Robinson and Justice Denise Johnson. The only justification for withholding the right to marry was bias, and that was no justification at all.

"In Vermont we won gay marriage," he told me. By that he meant, Vermonters had won a specially designed new category of marriage for gays and lesbians called civil unions. "But I don't want gay marriage," he said. "I want marriage."

In the wake of the Vermont experience, William N. Eskridge, Jr., the John A. Garver professor of jurisprudence at Yale Law School, wrote a book examining civil unions from the liberal perspective. In his book, *Equality Practice: Civil Unions and the Future of Gay Rights,* Eskridge rejected the notion that civil unions paralleled the "separate but equal" regime of the Jim Crow South.

"The case of Vermont," he wrote, "illustrates a central tension between liberal theory and liberal practice, which lawyers would express as a tension between *right* and *remedy* or (more abstractly) between the *substance* of equality and the *procedure* required to get there. In a heterogeneous polity, immediate equality is usually not attainable, but sometimes *equality practice* is." Over time, in Eskridge's view, Vermonters would learn, by practice, that equal rights for gays and lesbians were not damaging to Vermont society or values, and eventually the practice of equality would lead to the full realization of constitutional rights. There was no justification for denying gays and lesbians the right to marry, but it may be counterproductive to roil the community so badly that resentment and prejudice are magnified. "So equality," Eskridge wrote, "comes on little cat's feet."

Following passage of civil unions in Vermont, advocates around the country considered what to do next. Legal challenges began to move forward in some places, and legislative action took place in others. Meanwhile, in Vermont, the civil unions law faced its first challenge in the election of November 2000. If civil unions represented a civil rights revolution, that revolution still had a ways to go before victory could be declared.

3.

EVEN BEFORE Howard Dean had signed the civil unions bill in April, Richard Lambert, a farmer from the town of Washington, had begun to print and distribute signs with the words TAKE BACK VERMONT in stark black, uppercase letters on a white background. Soon TAKE BACK VERMONT signs began to appear everywhere in Vermont—along busy highways and quiet back roads, tacked to trees, nailed to the sides of houses, propped up on lawns. By fall, Lambert had distributed about five thousand signs, and their presence represented a thumb in the eye of anyone who had supported civil unions.

Another slogan appeared on numerous bumpers during those months: REMEMBER IN NOVEMBER. And soon there were others: TAKE VERMONT FORWARD and KEEP VERMONT CIVIL. The coming election would be a referendum on civil unions, and the war of lawn signs and bumper stickers was a constant reminder of how intensely people felt about the issue. On a back road in the town of Huntington, a landowner had erected a large hand-painted sign viciously attacking Governor Dean, calling him, among other things, "our anus governor."

But the attacks by opponents of civil unions were provoking anger on the other side, as well. No one expressed that anger more eloquently than Sharon Underwood of White River Junction, who wrote an opinion piece carried in April by the *Valley News,* the daily paper in Lebanon, New Hampshire. Defenders of civil unions had long sought to contain their anger at the harsh language of opponents. They thought it was in their interest to avoid stridency, to remain reasonable, to maintain their dignity. But in her op-ed piece Underwood let loose, expressing what many people felt but were unwilling to say, and her piece quickly spread on the Internet to readers around the world:

> Many letters have been sent to the Forum concerning the homosexual menace in our state. I am the mother of a gay son, and I've taken enough from you good people.
>
> I'm tired of your foolish rhetoric about the "homosexual agenda" and your allegations that accepting homosexuality is the same thing as advocating sex with children. You are cruel and you are ignorant. You have been robbing me of the joys of motherhood ever since my children were tiny. My firstborn son started suffering at the hands of the moral little thugs from your moral, upright families from the time he was in the first grade. He was physically and verbally abused from first grade straight through high school because he was perceived to

be gay. He never professed to be gay or had any association with anything gay, but he had the misfortune not to
walk or have gestures like the other boys. He was called
"fag" incessantly, starting when he was six.

In high school, while your children were doing what
kids that age should be doing, mine labored over a suicide note, drafting and redrafting it to be sure his family
knew how much he loved them. My sobbing seventeen-
year-old tore the heart out of me as he choked out that he
just couldn't bear to continue living any longer, that he
didn't want to be gay and that he couldn't face a life with
no dignity.

You have the audacity to talk about protecting families and children from the homosexual menace, while
you yourselves tear apart families and drive children to
despair. I don't know why my son is gay, but I do know
that God didn't put him, and millions like him, on this
Earth to give you someone to abuse. God gave you
brains so that you could think, and it's about time you
started doing that.

At the core of your misguided beliefs is the belief
that this could never happen to you, that there is some
kind of subculture out there that people have chosen to
join. The fact is that if it can happen to my family, it can
happen to yours, and you won't get to choose. Whether
it is genetic or whether something occurs during a critical
time of fetal development, I don't know. I can only tell
you with an absolute certainty that it is inborn . . .

You religious folk just can't bear the thought that as
my son emerges from the hell that was his childhood he
might like to find a lifelong companion and have a measure of happiness. It offends your sensibilities that he
should request the right to visit that companion in the

hospital, to make medical decisions for him or to benefit from tax laws governing inheritance. How dare he . . . these outrageous requests would threaten the very existence of your family, would undermine the sanctity of marriage.

You use religion to abdicate your responsibility to be thinking human beings. There are vast numbers of religious people who find your attitudes repugnant. God is not for the privileged majority, and God knows my son has committed no sin.

The deep-thinking author of a letter to the Forum on April 12 who lectures about homosexual sin and tells us about "those of us who have been blessed with the benefits of a religious upbringing" asks, "Whatever happened to the idea of striving . . . to be better human beings than we are?"

Indeed, sir, whatever happened to that?

This piece came to me at the *Rutland Herald* shortly after Dean signed the civil unions law, but I chose not to run it on our op-ed page because I hoped to lower the temperature of the anger in the state. I always regretted not publishing it, however, because it expressed better than anything I had seen the outrage many people felt about the hypocrisy and self-righteousness of those who had adopted a moral tone to condemn and attack their neighbors.

That summer, as in years past, the Freedom to Marry Task Force set up their booth at county fairs throughout the state and at the state fair in Rutland. Dorothy Mammen said the task force instructed members staffing the booth in the protocol of responding to people who were attacking them. They were to listen to the attack, to affirm that they understood what the person was saying, and to respond calmly. "You're never going to change their minds," Mammen said. "But how you conduct yourself matters." Borrowing a page from the civil rights movement of King's era, it was their intention to take the high road and to maintain their dignity.

"It was unbelievable how mean people could be," Mammen said. "And it was unbelievable how warm people could be."

At the Bondville Fair Mammen was sitting at the booth with her son, Ian, who was eleven years old at the time. Ian was reading the latest Harry Potter book when a woman approached the booth. "I can't believe they let shit like you in here," the woman said.

Mammen was speechless. "I thought, *Who's the shit here? I'm just sitting here with my son,*" she said later.

At the Vermont State Fair in Rutland, another woman approached the booth, spewing obscenities. As she was walking away, the man who was with her, presumably her father, turned to Mammen and said quietly, "I think people should marry who they want."

At the Tunbridge Fair that summer, there had been a good deal of drinking on Saturday night, and Mammen was alone at the booth around 9 P.M. The Take Back Vermont booth was across the way, distributing signs, and six big men hoisting signs up on their shoulders began to march back and forth in front of the Freedom to Marry booth. After a few minutes, one of the men leaned over the booth toward Mammen and said, "You're not welcome here. Can you hear? You're not welcome." Mammen, frightened by the threatening behavior, said nothing. Eventually security officials came and moved the men along. Later the same night someone sprayed pepper spray into the tent, and the entire tent had to be cleared out.

House members who had voted for civil unions also faced harsh treatment. Diane Carmolli had stopped attending Immaculate Heart of Mary Church, where she had been a parishioner for decades, because of the unfriendliness of fellow church

members. For months, she attended Mass at churches in surrounding towns.

Ruth Dwyer, the Republican candidate for governor, drew
enthusiastic crowds of Take Back Vermont sympathizers and
was able to capitalize on their anger. During one term on the
Thetford school board, she had been a divisive force, and during the campaign for governor scores of Thetford residents issued statements trying to warn the people of Vermont about
how destructive Dwyer could be. She was accustomed to making unsubstantiated accusations, such as her statement in the
campaign two years before that state welfare officials were purposely distorting figures on child abuse in order to make Dean
look good. She had no evidence that was true.

Dwyer's hyperbolic language coincided with the fears
and anger of the Take Back Vermont crowd, and within that
circle she drew an enthusiastic response. To supporters of civil
unions, the last thing Vermonters needed was a politician fan-
ning the flames of anger. And yet the Republicans had pinned
their hopes on their ability to tap into that anger. It might give
them control of the Legislature for the first time in years.

Governor Dean faced an additional challenge because of
the presence in the race of Anthony Pollina, a candidate from
the Progressive Party who was likely to strip away votes from
Dean on the left. If Dean did not win more than 50 percent of
the votes, the governor's race would be decided by the Legislature, and if anti–civil union elements took over the Legislature, no one knew what might happen.

Dwyer had to survive a primary challenge by Rutland
lawyer William Meub, who tried to position himself as a moderate. Meub opposed civil unions, but he repudiated the bigotry that had attached itself to the opposition. It turned out,
however, that the grassroots support Dwyer enjoyed among
the Take Back Vermont movement prevented Meub from win-

ning wide support, and Dwyer easily defeated him in the primary election on September 12.

The primary also claimed a first round of civil union supporters in the Legislature. In a number of districts Republicans challenged fellow Republicans. On primary day, Diane Carmolli, who had no Democratic opponent, prepared a pot of soup and took it up to Swanton as a gesture of support for John Edwards, who was facing a Republican challenge. It was a drive of more than two hours, and when she got to Swanton, she found Edwards standing forlornly outside the polling place. He told Carmolli it had been a lonely day for him in Swanton. He lost the race.

In Craftsbury, the vice president of POST, Kevin Goodridge, defeated Robert Kinsey in the Republican primary. Representative Marion Milne of Washington was also among those who lost. Representative Richard Mallary of Brookfield, the former member of Congress, decided he wouldn't even compete in the Republican primary. A popular former state senator who opposed civil unions had decided to seek Mallary's House seat, and Mallary knew he had no chance. So he decided to run as an independent in November.

During the primary, Republican supporters of civil unions had been targeted by a conservative Christian group who accused them in a direct-mail campaign of being antifamily. The chairman of the Republican Party in Vermont, Patrick Garahan, refused to criticize the group's tactics, which embittered some Republicans. Among those who came under attack was Barbara Snelling, the former lieutenant governor. She had launched a campaign for governor in 1996 but had withdrawn after suffering a stroke. Now she was a candidate for the Senate, and she declared that if she had been a senator in 2000 she would have voted in favor of civil unions. An incumbent Republican senator from Chittenden County, Peter

Brownell, lost in the primary, but Snelling, running in the same district, managed to survive. Still, her treatment at the hands of fellow Republicans prompted Governor Dean, a Democrat, to come to her defense.

"I was really offended by the way the right wing went after Barbara," Dean told the press. "I think at some point the Republican leadership should apologize to her."

The schism among Republicans became more evident two days after the primary, when Bernard Rome, who had opposed Dwyer in the Republican primary of 1998, revealed to reporter Peter Freyne that Dwyer had made anti-Semitic remarks to him in a phone conversation two years before. According to Freyne, a columnist for the Burlington weekly *Seven Days,* Rome and Dwyer had been talking about the favorable press coverage they thought Dean was receiving. When Dwyer said she thought the press was protecting Dean, Rome asked her why the press would do that. According to Rome, Dwyer said, "Because he's Jewish and the press is Jewish."

It was apparent Dwyer didn't know that Rome was Jewish. When he pointed out to her that Dean was not Jewish, Dwyer said, "Well, no, but his wife is, and they're raising their kids Jewish." Dwyer was also mistaken about the Montpelier press corps, which had only one Jew among its number.

Rome said he brought up the conversation two years after the fact because he thought Dwyer was "polarizing and intolerant." But his comments ignited a furious response from the Republican establishment, who accused him of sour grapes. Dwyer dismissed Rome's comments as "hearsay."

During the campaign Dwyer continued to draw adoring crowds, but she did not do so well when facing critics. In one interview, she said, "I know a lot of women on welfare, and, believe me, they're out with their boyfriends and the kids are stuck at home in front of the TV with a bunch of Cheerios." In response to criticism about her comments, she said, "Get a life."

Howard Dean was facing critics of his own. In one famous encounter Dean emerged from a meeting in Williamstown only to be surrounded by a crowd unhappy about his support for civil unions. The encounter was captured on radio, and it revealed Dean as someone willing to engage in give-and-take with voters. Someone in the crowd at Williamstown charged that Vermont schools were promoting homosexuality. Dean said he didn't think the charge was true but if they could show him a school that was doing so he would do something about it. One man asked Dean if he was bisexual. Unfazed, Dean answered no. Such encounters were common during the campaign, and over time Dean won the respect of voters who saw he was unafraid to talk with them directly, hear their thoughts, and stand up for his own position.

As the campaign progressed, Dean became more energized and Dwyer became more dispirited. The biggest event of the year in Rutland was the Halloween parade, and Dean was there, ebullient, hopeful. Dwyer was not. She had begun to cut her campaign days short, returning early to her horse farm in Thetford.

On November 1 an elder statesman among Vermont Republicans emerged in an effort to counter the drift of his party toward anger and intolerance. Robert Stafford, then eighty-seven years old, was a former governor and United States senator whose name was familiar to millions of Americans because of the Stafford education loans taken out by college students all across the country. In 2000 he was in frail health, but he had something he wanted to say, and he held a press conference at the Rutland police station.

"I believe that love is one of the great forces in our society and in the state of Vermont," he said. "And everyone in this country is better off living in a society based on love."

He described the bond he shared with his wife, Helen, which had lasted through all those years of public service. And in a voice quavering with emotion, he made a heartfelt plea:

"And even if a same-sex couple unites with true love, what is the harm in that? What is the harm?"

What is the harm? That question was the center of a statewide debate that carried all the way through the election. If the legislative debate about civil unions had been a crash course in equal rights and the nature of love, the 2000 election campaign had extended that debate to every meeting hall and diner in the state.

The election results reflected the divisions created by the issue of civil unions. Dean won 50.4 percent of the vote, and Dwyer won 37.9 percent. Dean's vote total, combined with the 9.5 percent that went to Progressive Anthony Pollina, represented a strong majority in favor of candidates who supported civil unions.

But in those conservative pockets where resistance to civil unions was strong, pro–civil union House members paid the price. Sixteen incumbents in the House who had supported civil unions lost. Among them was Diane Carmolli, who was philosophical about her defeat. Maybe it would allow the state to heal, she thought.

Robert Kinsey ran in the general election as an independent and a Democrat after losing in the Republican primary, and he lost. Richard Mallary, running as an independent, lost. Mary Mazzariello, who had spoken up on the floor of the House for her two lesbian daughters, lost.

Tom Little had hoped to retire from the Legislature in 2000, but he did not want to appear to be backing away from a challenge. He defeated a Republican opponent in the primary, and he won in the general election.

Republicans took control of the House, and in the next session, Walter Freed became speaker. Peg Flory, who had introduced the reciprocal benefits legislation as an alternative to civil unions, became chairwoman of the Judiciary Committee.

Broader constituencies showed greater acceptance of civil unions and of the politicians who had supported the new law. Dick McCormack, the liberal Democratic senator from Windsor County, survived, as did the other two Democrats from his district.

Mark MacDonald lost, but Democrats maintained control of the Senate by the slimmest of margins, 16–14. Sara Kittell from St. Albans held on to her Senate seat, as did Dick Sears in Bennington. Civil union supporters unhappy about the defeat of so many pro–civil union candidates in the House took comfort in the Senate results and in the reelection of Dean and Lieutenant Governor Douglas Racine, a Democrat.

Chief Justice Jeffrey Amestoy thought that subjecting the question of gay marriage to the political process would have a salutary effect on Vermont democracy, and he was right. By the end of the 2000 election campaign, Vermonters were politically exhausted, but no one came away believing the issue of civil unions had not received a fair hearing. Take Back Vermont signs remained in place for months, reminding Vermonters of the vitriol that had consumed their state. But gradually the signs began to come down. Three years later, the occasional Take Back Vermont sign on the side of a barn was a jolting reminder of that season of conflict. The high tide of the anti–civil unions backlash had swept in, changed the political landscape, and then it had receded. The civil unions law would face new challenges. In the legislative session that followed, the House passed a reciprocal benefits bill intended to replace civil unions, but Dick Sears and the Senate Judiciary Committee didn't even give it a look. In the election of 2002, the candidates for governor, including Republican James Douglas, barely mentioned civil unions. Neither did the voters. Douglas was the winner in a three-way race, and he had no intention of changing the civil unions law.

The anti–civil union electorate could take satisfaction in the fact that the system had allowed them their say. But in 2002 there was a backlash against the backlash, and voters tossed out a number of legislators elected in 2000 as opponents of civil unions. Republican control of the House was sharply reduced. In the Senate Mark MacDonald took back his seat, and the Democrats expanded their control. During the 2002 campaign, some voters told MacDonald they wanted to punish him in 2000 but now it was time to return him to office.

The backlash had run its course. It had not failed entirely, but civil unions were the law of the land, at least in Vermont. Meanwhile, advocates elsewhere in the nation were looking beyond Vermont, and they were looking beyond civil unions.

4.

ON MARCH 4, 2003, Mary Bonauto stepped before the Supreme Judicial Court in Boston to argue the case of *Goodridge v. Department of Health,* in which she was seeking the right to marry for seven gay and lesbian couples. There were court cases in two other states, but the case in Massachusetts had now advanced to the state's highest court and represented the first chance after passage of civil unions in Vermont for gay and lesbian couples to secure the right to marry. Vermont had stood on the shoulders of Hawaii, Bonauto said, and now she hoped Massachusetts would stand on the shoulders of Vermont.

There were differences between the *Goodridge* and *Baker* cases, but they involved the same core issue, Bonauto said. That issue was the fundamental right to choose a marriage partner without interference from the state. Unlike the *Baker* case, the *Goodridge* case emphasized the right of privacy when making important personal choices, a right that had been supported in numerous federal and state cases.

The Massachusetts Constitution provided more expansive liberty protections than the Vermont Constitution did, according to Bonauto. Equal rights are most explicitly protected in Article I of the Declaration of Rights, which states:

> All people are born free and equal and have certain natural, essential and unalienable rights; among which may be reckoned the right of enjoying and defending their lives and liberties . . . Equality under law shall not be denied or abridged because of sex, race, color, creed or national origin.

The constitution is meant to protect "the sanctity of individual free choice and self-determination," Bonauto wrote in her brief for the Supreme Judicial Court. And free choice in marriage was essential to the free pursuit of happiness.

Quoting the United States Supreme Court in *Planned Parenthood v. Casey,* an abortion case, she wrote:

> The Constitution protects against unwarranted state interference with "personal decisions relating to marriage, procreation, contraception, family relationships, child rearing, and education." These matters, involving the most intimate and personal choices a person may make in a lifetime, choices central to personal dignity and

autonomy, are central to the liberty protected by the
Fourteenth Amendment.

Bonauto made many of the same arguments heard in the
Baker case, calling marriage a fundamental right and arguing
that the exclusion of gays and lesbians represented sex discrimination. In addition, she cited a Massachusetts case in which
the court had found that decisions about procreation were an
area that ought to be free from governmental intrusion.

She also sought to head off any inclination by the court to
follow Chief Justice Amestoy's example by handing the case
over to the legislature or declaring that a choice short of marriage would be satisfactory. She included in her brief a discussion of the court's history with regard to remedy: The court
either declared a law unconstitutional or it extended the
law to those previously excluded. She wanted to be sure the
court did not "separate the word *marriage* from the benefits it
provides."

The Supreme Judicial Court was quick to interrupt Bonauto during her presentation on March 4. Justice Judith
Cowin asked her, "Why should we do something that virtually
no other state has done?"

"This court should do so because it is the right thing to
do," Bonauto answered. "The exclusion of the plaintiffs from
marriage . . . violates the fundamental right that these plaintiffs enjoy with all others in this commonwealth."

Justice Martha Sosman asked her whether allowing same-
sex marriage would lead to the legalization of polygamy.

Bonauto answered Justice Sosman by saying that neither
the legislature nor the court had ever suggested marriage
should involve more than two people.

Assistant Attorney General Judith Yogman faced skeptical
questioning from the justices as she defended the position of

the state. Justice John Greaney suggested there was a paradox in allowing gay and lesbian couples to form families through adoption but not to marry. Yogman denied the contradiction: "Marriage has many other responsibilities and benefits associated with it other than child rearing," she said.

When pressed by the justices, Yogman conceded that there was a constitutional right to privacy, though the justices did not press her to agree that right ought to protect the choice of marriage partner. Yogman's time ran out before she had given her summation, and quickly the arguments before the court were over.

As spring turned to summer Bonauto awaited a ruling in the *Goodridge* case, which she said could break a "logjam" on the marriage issue. If Massachusetts were to recognize the right to marriage for gays and lesbians, couples from other states could be married in Massachusetts then challenge federal and state laws refusing recognition of their marriages.

But before the Supreme Judicial Court issued its ruling in *Goodridge*, the United States Supreme Court issued a landmark decision in the case of *Lawrence v. Texas*, striking down a Texas law forbidding homosexual sodomy. The *Lawrence* decision overturned the court's 1986 ruling in *Bowers v. Hardwick* when the court had upheld an antisodomy law in Georgia. The court's reasoning in the *Lawrence* case paralleled the reasoning of the plaintiffs in the *Goodridge* case, particularly in its emphasis on the right to privacy in decisions about intimate conduct.

"The petitioners are entitled to respect for their private lives," Justice Anthony Kennedy wrote in the *Lawrence* case. "The state cannot demean their existence or control their destiny by making their private sexual conduct a crime."

It was not clear whether the rights established in the *Lawrence* decision would necessarily extend as far as the right to marry, but in one extraordinary paragraph, Kennedy set down the justification for a jurisprudence responsive to changing social mores:

> Had those who drew and ratified the Due Process Clauses of the Fifth Amendment or the Fourteenth Amendment known the components of liberty in its manifold possibilities, they might have been more specific. They did not presume to have this insight. They knew times can blind us to certain truths and later generations can see that laws once thought necessary and proper in fact serve only to oppress. As the Constitution endures, persons in every generation can invoke its principles in their own search for greater freedom.

The *Lawrence* decision came down on June 26, 2003. The Supreme Judicial Court in Massachusetts had been expected to decide the *Goodridge* case sometime in July, but following *Lawrence,* the court delayed its ruling.

Meanwhile, the *Lawrence* ruling, combined with the prospect for a ruling in Massachusetts, had brought gay marriage to the fore as a political issue. In July 2003 President George W. Bush outlined his position. "I believe marriage is between a man and a woman, and I believe we ought to codify that one way or the other, and we have lawyers looking at the best way to do that," he said at a press conference.

At the same time, there were challenges under way to the marriage statutes in other states. In May 2003 a Superior Court judge in Marion County, Indiana, dismissed a case brought on behalf of three couples, two of whom had already received civil unions in Vermont. The judge in the case cited the state's interest in encouraging procreation. The lawyer for the plaintiffs, Ken Falk, said he would appeal.

In New Jersey David Buckel of the Lambda Legal Defense and Education Fund filed a case on behalf of seven couples seeking the right to marry, and in the spring of 2003 the New Jersey attorney general had filed a motion to dismiss. Buckel had responded to that motion and was awaiting oral arguments sometime that summer.

Buckel said in an interview that New Jersey was a good place for a marriage case because of the state's history in recognizing gay rights. It was one of the first states to provide protection against discrimination based on sexual orientation, to allow for second-parent adoption, and to increase penalties for hate crimes directed at gays and lesbians. As in Vermont and Massachusetts, activists had conducted an extensive public education campaign to pave the way for public acceptance of gay marriage.

In Connecticut advocates were pressing in the legislature for the right to marry or at least for civil unions. Mary Bonauto was among those who testified before the Connecticut legislature, and there had been public hearings with emotional testimony from people on both sides of the question. Legislators in other states introduced bills for marriage or civil unions, even if, as in Montana, the legislation had little prospect of passage.

California had established a registry for domestic partners in 1999, but it offered only a handful of benefits related to healthcare and adoption. Then in September 2003 Governor Gray Davis signed a bill granting a long list of benefits and responsibilities to domestic partners. California's new law came closer to civil unions than the laws of any other state, though domestic partners did not have to hold a ceremony to certify their union; they needed merely to register with the state. The newly expanded benefits had to do with debt, parenthood, community property, family finances, and a broad array of benefits that usually accompany marriage.

Advocates in California had not moved ahead with a lawsuit challenging the marriage law, in part because of the danger of provoking a backlash. Jenny Pizer, senior staff attorney for the Lambda Legal Defense and Education Fund in California, was well aware of the results of Proposition 22, a ballot initiative approved by voters in 2000 that barred recognition of marriages between gays and lesbians. A lawsuit challenging the marriage law might lead to a ballot initiative that would undo the progress already made. So Pizer had pushed for expanded domestic partner benefits. "It's half a loaf," she said, "but to a population that's starving, you grab it."

In his book *Equality Practice* William Eskridge documented the progress that had been made in many Western nations in establishing the rights of marriage. The Scandinavian countries had been first in recognizing gay partnerships and providing benefits. France established *pactes civiles* for homosexual and heterosexual couples who were interested in a status short of marriage. Germany established a registry for domestic partnerships. The Netherlands was the first nation to allow gays and lesbians to marry.

Then in June 2003 the Court of Appeal for Ontario, Canada, upheld a lower court ruling granting the right to marry to gays and lesbians. The court wrote: "The restriction against same-sex marriage is an offense to the dignity of lesbians and gays, because it limits the range of relationship options to them."

That same day Michael Leshner and Mike Stark, who had been plaintiffs in the case, were married in Toronto. The Ontario court had not stayed the effect of its decision, and soon the government of Prime Minister Jean Chretien announced it would not challenge the ruling of the provincial court.

Evan Wolfson in New York told the *Boston Globe*:

The Ontario ruling is hugely significant because it could spur similar civil rights advances in the United States. The

Canadians aren't settling for lesser steps, such as civil unions, but demanding the real deal. Americans will look north to Canada and see that the sky isn't falling when gays and lesbian couples wed.

Conservative politicians continued to show that they believed it was wrong at a fundamental level to sanction any form of homosexual behavior. Senator Rick Santorum, a Republican from Pennsylvania, sparked a furor in the spring of 2003 by discussing the Texas sodomy case, saying that if the state lost the right to ban homosexual behavior then it would lose the right to ban adultery, bestiality, or incest. In Santorum's view, the right to privacy did not extend to intimate relations between people of the same sex.

There were proposals in Congress for constitutional amendments forbidding same-sex marriage or defining marriage as a union of a man and a woman. Those amendments had the potential of continuing the war at the national level on the issue of gay marriage.

5.

THE CIVIL unions in Brattleboro were not the only ones to take place on July 1, 2000. At 9 A.M. that morning Holly Puterbaugh and Lois Farnham headed for the city clerk's office on Dorset Street to pick up their civil union license. They had moved from Milton to South Burlington in 1999, and Margaret Picard, the South Burlington city clerk, was at her office that morning to help out. Holly and Lois were full of both anticipation and apprehension. There had been threats as July 1 approached, and one Burlington church had been defaced by graffiti. But July 1 was a peaceful, sunny day. Picard issued their civil union license and administered the oath. Then Holly and Lois faced the press who had gathered for the event. They spoke about what the day meant to them, then they asked the press to let them enjoy the rest of the day in peace, to let them have their civil union ceremony that morning away from the watchful eyes of the media.

Then they returned home to their townhouse on the lake and got dressed for the ceremony. Lois was elegant in a purple pantsuit. Holly wore a long flowered skirt, raspberry pink. Their daughter, Kim, wore a long green skirt. Lois said later the colors all went together like a single floral bouquet.

They had sent out about two hundred invitations, and they drove early to the church in downtown Burlington to make sure all the arrangements had been taken care of. The First Congregational Church in Burlington is a massive brick building with six white wooden Ionic columns supporting a large white pediment in front. As the time for the ceremony drew near, Lois, Holly, and Kim stood next to those columns, greeting guests as they arrived for the ceremony. They included Bill Lippert, Stan Baker, Peter Harrigan, Stacy Jolles, and Nina Beck. It was a glorious summer day, and everyone was ready for a celebration.

For the ceremony Lois's brother, Maurice Earl "Sonny" Farnham, did the readings. He read from the Book of Ruth: "Do not press me to leave you or to turn back from following you! Where you go, I will go; where you lodge, I will lodge; your people shall be my people, and your God my God." And he read from 1 Corinthians: "Love is patient; love is kind; love is not envious or boastful or arrogant or rude. It does not insist on its own way; it is not irritable or resentful; it does not rejoice in wrongdoing, but rejoices in the truth. It bears all things, believes all things, hopes all things, endures all things."

Their daughter Kim was the only attendant for the ceremony, and they gave her a medallion of three connected
circles, signifying their family of three.

Afterward there was a reception upstairs at the church.
Lois was particularly pleased that attendance at their ceremony
exceeded attendance at an anti–civil union rally held that day in
Montpelier.

"It was really affirming to stand there in church and declare
our vows in front of everybody," Lois remembered.

Other civil union ceremonies followed throughout the
state. Stan Baker and Peter Harrigan held their service at St.
Paul's Episcopal Cathedral in Burlington on August 13, 2000.
Stacy Jolles and Nina Beck waited until March 22, 2001, the
ninth anniversary of the marriage ceremony held in the Oakland hills. They had no guests. Ann Pugh, a member of the
Vermont House and a justice of the peace, came to their
house, said the appropriate words, and signed the papers. As
far as Stacy and Nina were concerned, their real wedding had
occurred in 1992 in the Oakland hills, and their civil union was
a formality.

THE STEEP driveway to Bill Lippert's house had already been
sanded after a snowstorm on a winter morning in 2003. Inside
his house the woodstove kept the living room warm, and the
sunlight shot through the stained-glass snowflake hanging in
his window. Lippert was remembering the struggle of three
years before. He was grateful for the steady hand of Tom Little
and for the other members of the House Judiciary Committee.
He had spoken on the House floor of the pain endured by
those willing to support civil unions, and he thought back to
the two former state troopers, John Edwards and Michael Vinton. "You wanted John Edwards on your side," he said. "You
wanted Michael Vinton on your side." Cathy Voyer and Judy

Livingston, two Republican committee members, were essential to the struggle, he said. "The success of civil unions in Vermont is a tribute to the ability of heterosexual allies to rise to
the occasion and demonstrate a level of political courage that
will rarely be asked of anyone," he said that morning. "I was
one vote."

This was my third interview at Lippert's home. He was describing an experience that went deep for him. He spoke of the
vitriolic, denigrating arguments that he heard over and over,
the hate mail, and the threats. "People came up to me, my
friends, and they said, 'How can you do it, Bill? How can you
be in the midst of this and not lose your cool?'"

He paused.

> It took an enormous toll on me. I'm still recovering from
> it. I had no idea how hard it had been on me till afterward.
> I heard the most virulent, most hateful attacks on me and
> my people. And I was going to fight it off. I was going to
> fight. I knew I had the ability to fight for it and articulate it
> and think strategically. There was no grand plan. This was
> completely new ground. Day after day after day, both
> fending off the hatefulness and trying simultaneously to
> help people figure out how to move forward.

Now the struggle over civil unions was three years past,
and Lippert, still a member of the Judiciary Committee, was
working on other issues. But the memories were fresh. And so
was the pride he felt about what he and his colleagues had
accomplished.

> I think what we did was huge. It changed people's lives.
> The advocates of gay marriage, who were so deeply dis-
> appointed, deserve enormous credit for finding their way
> to something, even though short of gay marriage, that
> moved us forward in a quantum way.

There were chickadees at the feeder outside and sunlight on the fresh snow. A disgruntled minority would always oppose civil unions or any measure to protect the rights of gay and lesbian Vermonters. But even the new Republican governor and the Republican House were willing now to let it go. Dr. King had said: "A movement that changes both people and institutions is a revolution."

Vermont had had its revolution.

THE APPLE trees were in bloom behind Bob Kinsey's farmhouse in Craftsbury, and in the garden across the South Albany Road the sweet corn was just coming up. The peas were up, and the potatoes, seven different varieties, were muscling their way through the soil. A few slender shoots of asparagus had shown themselves. Kinsey's son Jeffrey, who ran the farm operation now, planted sixty-three acres of corn that Saturday in the fields near the house and in a small field up the Andersonville Road near the cemetery. The previous year army worms had gone through the meadow surrounding the cemetery, destroying the second and third hay crop. Jeff had reseeded the field, and the hay was doing well. The cemetery was full of Andersons and Youngs and Uries. Toward the back of the cemetery was the grave Bob had dug for his son Everett. Next to it Bob had placed the base for another gravestone, though he hadn't yet put the stone in place. That would be his resting place. He and his son would face west toward an expansive view of meadows and woods extending for miles. In late May the pale green of maple and birch just leafing out was mixed with the darker green of conifers and the brilliant green of meadows brushed by the yellow of dandelions. On that Saturday the clouds draped low over the land, and there was a gentle rain. Jeff said a neighbor had joked that when they were all at rest here they could have a party, as in the play *Our Town*. In the timeless landscape of northeastern Vermont out on the Andersonville Road, it did not seem like so far-fetched an idea.

Bob Kinsey did not do much of the farm work anymore. But he had his projects, fixing up the rebuilt wooden tepee, tending to his flock of Peking ducks. He hadn't yet released the ducks, and a neighbor's dog had gotten into them, killing nine of the twelve. And someone had taken the new generator he had placed down by the tepee for electric power. "Son of a bitch stole it," he said when he discovered it was missing. Getting into his car again, he said, "That kind of takes the fun out of the day. We'll fix up something so they can't take it. Can't let them win."

He missed serving in the Legislature. After losing in 2000, he had run again in 2002, this time as a Democrat, and he lost. There were BRING BACK BOB stickers on his red 1949 McCormick Farmall tractor and also stickers that said: KICK A BAD HABIT. THROW OUT THE 6 PACK. The 6 Pack was the group of six conservative House members from the Northeast Kingdom, including Nancy Sheltra, who had taken office in 2000. The voters threw out one of them in 2002.

Jeff was milking 116 cows that May, though he expected he would have 140 milkers in production by fall. "He's a far better dairyman than I ever was," Bob said of his son.

Life went on. The furor over civil unions was one moment in a long history. Bob Kinsey was proud of his grandson, Everett's son, who had just graduated that spring with straight A's from Brown University. Kinsey's eyes gazed out over the breathtaking vista where he had been farming all his life. He had done the right thing, voting for civil unions. He might run for office again. He couldn't say for sure. "Don't get old," he said, squeezing his aching body behind the wheel of his car.

———

WALK DOWN Main Street from the Congregational Church in Middlebury. Stand where Bill Lippert stood that day in the fall of 1972 when he came to Calvi's, the soda fountain with the phone booth in back. Turn and look up Merchants Row toward the Painter House, which still overlooks the small village. Were he still alive, Gamaliel Painter, the town founder, could look down from the monitor atop the roof of his house onto a much-changed place. In the course of two hundred years, the ramshackle mills and shops and the muddy streets have become a handsome little village. But that is not all that has changed. Painter would be astonished and perhaps appalled that the language he signed in 1777 guaranteeing equal treatment under the law had been used to grant legal standing to homosexual couples. History suggests he was a man of conventional morality. Strict constructionists who say we should interpret the Constitution in accordance with the intentions of the founders could well imagine the scorn with which Painter would view his world after passage of the civil unions law.

But as long as we are imagining what Painter might have thought, it is possible to imagine something else. Imagine that he had not died in 1819. Imagine instead that he had lived on, witnessing the expanding evil of slavery and the advent of the Underground Railroad, which brought runaway slaves through Middlebury, up to Rokeby in Ferrisburgh, and onward to Canada. If he had lived on, he would have seen the principles of equality in the Vermont Constitution tested in a bloody Civil War, during which thousands of Vermonters gave their lives. And a hundred years later he would have seen those principles tested again when the descendants of slaves finally demanded their full rights of citizenship. Painter might have learned these lessons over those many years, and then when gay and lesbian Vermonters began to claim their own rights, he would have given the matter some thought. Maybe, to use Howard Dean's word, he would feel *uncomfortable* about the idea of gay marriage. But if he were still living in 2000, it is possible to imagine him as willing to look at the truth of the lives of his neighbors, people who had never before revealed anything about their sexuality. This was something new. There were the two lawyers at the law office just down the street. What was he to think of them and their demand for equal rights? How long would he imprison himself within the prejudices of the past? He had signed his name to a constitution that included these words: "That government is, or ought to be, instituted for the common benefit, protection, and security of the people, nation, or community." If he had witnessed that long history and then looked into the hearts of his neighbors, he might well have drawn a lesson that surprised him. He knew about grief. His son had drowned at age twenty-five, and more than two hundred years later the gravestone could still be seen at the old cemetery. There was enough grief in the world. Love bears all things. He had read that in 1 Corinthians. It should no longer have to bear the scorn of people unwilling to recognize the humanity of their neighbors. And maybe he would look down on his village after all those years and admit to himself that he had learned something from his neighbors about the way that democracy must grow with the understanding of the people, allowing wider scope for the expanding claims of human compassion.

AFTERWORD

ON A WARM AFTERNOON in October 2004, Jeffrey Amestoy sat in his office at the John F. Kennedy School of Government at Harvard University. He had retired as chief justice in Vermont two months before, and he was at Harvard to teach a seminar on the law and politics of same-sex marriage. Five years had passed since the Vermont Supreme Court had handed down its ruling in the *Baker* case, and at Harvard Amestoy was in a good position to reflect on the historic changes that had followed upon that landmark decision.

One of the most significant changes was the ruling in November 2003 by the Supreme Judicial Court of Massachusetts in *Goodridge v. the Department of Public Health*. In that case the court established that under the Massachusetts Constitution gay and lesbian couples had the right to marry. It was the victory toward which freedom-to-marry advocates had been striving for years. According to Amestoy, the *Baker* decision laid the groundwork for the ruling in *Goodridge*, though *Goodridge* went further than *Baker*, finding that civil unions would not be an adequate substitute for marriage. Asked to discuss the legal reasoning in *Goodridge*, Amestoy was circumspect. But he did say that the turbulent aftermath of *Goodridge* underscored his point that even a case decided by the court with finality is often not final at all.

"Certainly, looking at the fallout from *Goodridge*, one of the considerations is: Has it inhibited or advanced the argument for gay marriage?" Amestoy explained. After *Goodridge*, that was a question gay-rights advocates and their opponents were both trying to answer.

Amestoy elaborated that the central lesson of the Vermont experience had to do less with constitutional reasoning than it did with the way democracy works. Vermont had shown it was "possible to construct a space to conduct a civil dialogue on homosexuality."

A clamorous national dialogue—sometimes civil, sometimes not—has been one result of *Goodridge*. The dialogue intensified in February 2004 when San Francisco Mayor Gavin Newsom began to issue marriage licenses to same-sex couples without waiting for sanction from the courts or the legislature. Newsom's action unleashed an exuberant festival of matrimony: During the month that followed an estimated four thousand gay and lesbian couples received marriage licenses in San Francisco. That winter officials elsewhere followed Newsom's example. Gay and lesbian couples were married in Portland, Oregon; New Paltz and Nyack, New York; and Sandoval County, New Mexico, before courts stepped in to stop the weddings.

Amestoy observed these events from the perspective of a jurist who had always been mindful of how judicial rulings are part of the larger democratic process. In *Baker*, he hoped to foster the democratic engagement of the people of Vermont with the issue of gay marriage. The protracted battle that led to the creation of civil unions was democratic engagement in its fullest sense, and it helped move the public toward greater acceptance and understanding of gay and lesbian relationships.

The ruling in *Goodridge* went a step further by mandating marriage, but even so, *Goodridge* did not resolve the issue. Instead it served as the catalyst for a divisive struggle that extended far beyond Massachusetts and continued through the election of November 2004.

FOLLOWING THE *Goodridge* decision, Massachusetts became embroiled in a furious debate that echoed the struggle in Vermont four years before. Politicians fearful of the wrath of the voters immediately began to look for a way to circumvent the court's mandate for gay marriage. The result was an amendment to the state constitution, passed four months after the court's ruling, prohibiting marriage and establishing civil unions for gay and lesbian couples. Debate on the amendment drew thousands of partisans from both sides to Boston. Crowds filled the corridors of the State House and lined the streets of Beacon Hill, chanting, singing, shouting, praying. As in Vermont four years before, passions were high, and the state quickly became polarized between supporters and opponents of gay marriage.

The amendment in Massachusetts would have to be approved by a succeeding legislature and then would have to go before the voters in a referendum. Because of this, final action on the amendment will not happen before the election of 2006. In the meantime, gays and lesbians began to be married on May 17, 2004, and by 2006 there will be thousands of legally married gay and lesbian couples.

Thus, education on the issue of gay marriage is not over for the people of Massachusetts. According to Amestoy, Massachusetts residents are likely to see that gay marriage has not caused the sky to fall, and in the end it is far from certain they will pass an amendment to overturn *Goodridge*.

Meanwhile, the *Goodridge* decision and the marriages in San Francisco reinvigorated the opponents of gay marriage, while some gay rights activists worried that events were spinning out of control. Representative Barney Frank, the Democrat from Massachusetts, expressed the fear that the marriages in San

Francisco would provoke hostile actions in Congress and in state legislatures around the country. "These aren't legal marriages," he said with exasperation.

Freedom-to-marry advocates viewed the marriages in San Francisco as an opportunity for the nation to learn about the reality of gay relationships. Evan Wolfson, executive director of Freedom to Marry, called the outburst of marriages in San Francisco a "civil rights moment," in which people took it upon themselves to challenge unjust laws.

President George W. Bush responded to the *Goodridge* decision and the onset of gay marriage around the country by inveighing against "activist judges" and others who would put in jeopardy the institution of marriage. As the presidential campaign got under way in 2004, Bush announced he would support an amendment to the United States Constitution prohibiting same-sex marriage and civil unions.

The United States Senate took up the amendment that summer, but the Republicans had nowhere near the number of votes needed to adopt the amendment or even to continue debate. Nevertheless, the Republican Party endorsed the amendment in its platform adopted at the Republican National Convention in September. In the end, Bush's decision to call attention to gay marriage was a crucial component of his reelection strategy. Exit interviews reported after the election that "moral issues" were the most important concern for many voters, motivating many Bush supporters to go to the polls. Because gay marriage was the most visible moral issue in the race, opposition to gay marriage may have been one of the keys to Bush's reelection.

The social ferment surrounding gay marriage was widespread. Missouri and Louisiana adopted state constitutional amendments barring gay marriage (though in October 2004 a Louisiana district judge threw out the amendment as it was drawn up and passed in that state). Then in November 2004, eleven additional states approved amendments: Arkansas, Georgia, Kentucky, Michigan, Mississippi, Michigan, Montana, North Dakota, Ohio, Oklahoma, Oregon, and Utah. In fact, the amendment in Ohio may have contributed to Bush's margin of victory there.

IN NOVEMBER 2004 Bill Lippert was elected to another term as a member of the Vermont House of Representatives. Not only that, the Democrats regained control of the Vermont House for the first time since the struggle over civil unions four years before. Lippert was especially pleased that the Legislature elected in 2004 included four openly gay House members and one openly gay senator.

As he looked back at all that had followed the passage of Vermont's civil unions law, he was encouraged by the progress he saw. "It has been the most exciting time in history for the advance of civil rights and freedom for lesbian and gay people in the United States," he said.

Lippert pointed to the *Lawrence* decision by the United States Supreme Court, which overturned laws criminalizing intimate gay relations, as a major milesone; another was the ordination of the Reverend V. Eugene Robinson as Episcopal bishop of New Hampshire. And the advent of gay marriage in Massachusetts was a historic step forward. At the same time Lippert found Bush's successful exploitation of the issue of gay marriage to be "very discouraging."

"He wouldn't have won without doing it," Lippert said. Massachusetts had provided the ammunition for Bush adviser Karl Rove to "motivate the base."

Lippert cautioned against the instinct by gays and lesbians to blame themselves for provoking a backlash. Self-blame is a sort of internalized homophobia, he said. The real problem is

"externalized homophobia" that works to limit the rights of
gays and lesbians.

Despite Bush's success, Lippert had words of hope. He and
his allies had suffered setbacks following the adoption of civil
unions. "But in four years we turned it around," he said. Lippert recalled an encounter with Howard Dean in the summer
of 2004 when Dean was in the midst of his presidential campaign. "He shook my hand, and he said, 'Who would have
thought that in a few short years civil union would be called the
moderate-to-conservative alternative?'"

Lippert said he was more aware than ever that achieving justice was "never a linear process." He had drawn inspiration from
the women's suffrage movement of the nineteenth and early
twentieth centuries. It took many decades for women to gain
the right to vote, and many leaders of the suffrage movement
never lived to see it happen. "In many ways it strikes me that
we've made more progress in a shorter period of time," he said.
"Decades went by, and they didn't give up the struggle." He referred to the anti-marriage amendments passed in numerous
states as "inequality by geography." But the battle over those
amendments had done a great deal to heighten awareness, even
in states where the battle for marriage rights was lost. "More
people are stepping up to fight the fight," Lippert said.

THREE DAYS BEFORE I sat down with Amestoy at his Harvard office, Supreme Court Justice Antonin Scalia visited the
Kennedy School, delivering a speech in which he excoriated the
view that the Constitution ought to be viewed as a "living" document. Scalia considers himself an "originalist," which means
he believes it is the task of judges to look to the original intent
of the Framers and to refrain from reading new meanings into
the language of the Constitution. He gave emphatic expression
to that view in his dissent in the *Lawrence* case.

"It is clear from this that the Court has taken sides in the culture war, departing from its role of assuring, as neutral observer, that the democratic rules of engagement are observed," Scalia wrote. "Many Americans do not want persons who openly engage in homosexual conduct as partners in their business, as scoutmasters for their children, as teachers in their children's schools, or as boarders in their home. They view this as protecting themselves and their families from a lifestyle that they believe to be immoral and destructive. The Court views it as 'discrimination' which it is the function of our judgments to deter."

When George W. Bush denounces "activist" judges, he is lining up with Scalia. Critics of the *Baker* and *Goodridge* decisions charge that the courts in Vermont and Massachusetts have found rights in their state constitutions that were not intended by the Founders and do not exist. Amestoy rejects that approach to the law, saying the Constitution must not be viewed as a "static" document. In *Baker* he wrote that it was the court's job to "distill the essence, the motivating ideal of the framers" and "to remain faithful to that historical ideal, while addressing contemporary issues that the framers undoubtedly could never imagine."

Justice Kennedy's majority opinion in the *Lawrence* case offered a justification for judicial activism similar to that expressed by Amestoy in *Baker*. "As the Constitution endures," he wrote, "persons in every generation can invoke its principles in their own search for greater freedom."

It should not be surprising that the issue of gay marriage should rest squarely atop the political and legal fault line caused by clashing views of how to read the Constitution. The Vermont and Massachusetts courts have responded to demands for equality that touch on deeply rooted fears shared by many people. And as Amestoy suggested, it is an issue far beyond the imaginings of the Framers.

Amestoy pointed to the landmark school desegregation case *Brown v. the Board of Education* as an important example of how courts can play a constructive role when the other branches of government fail to address injustice. At the same time, he said that ultimately the issue of gay marriage will not be resolved by the courts. He crafted his language in the *Baker* case in order to advance the understanding of society. "Our common humanity" was a phrase designed to "resonate with those who are going to be responsible for taking the next step," he said. He espouses a legal approach he calls "pragmatic constitutionalism." By pragmatism he did not mean a capitulation to popular sentiment. Rather, it was recognition that the courts are part of a democracy in which the people have the power to overturn the effects of a court's ruling. If the reelection of George W. Bush was due in part to the *Goodridge* ruling and its effects, the election result may underscore the prescience of Amestoy's pragmatic view.

It is clear that the social ferment surrounding gay marriage will be with us for years. Freedom-to-marry advocates see their cause moving ahead on many fronts. Court cases in California, Washington, Oregon, New York, New Jersey, and elsewhere will keep the issue in front of the public. Action in state legislatures, both pro and con, will confront officeholders across the country with a debate as emotionally fraught as the debates in Vermont and Massachusetts. Gay couples will continue their struggle to achieve the love and respect that others take for granted.

Understanding on the part of the public at large will inevitably grow during this turbulent process, as it has grown over the past thirty years. But progress in understanding will also be shadowed by fear. After all, fear is the shadow of love, and all great advances in civil rights have occurred when love has stood up to fear. That is the struggle that is under way today.

ACKNOWLEDGMENTS

THE ISSUE OF gay marriage is a volatile combination of the political and the personal. I could not have written this book without the courage, openness, and trust of many people who were willing to talk to me about matters of great personal sensitivity. I am grateful to them. The names of those who helped me are found throughout the book, but I am also grateful for the help of those not named who provided valuable background information, both political and personal.

The quotations in this book are taken from my interviews and from conversations remembered by those whom I interviewed. Many quotations also come from news sources, principally the *Rutland Herald,* where I have worked for twenty-one years.

I want to thank my many colleagues and former colleagues at the *Herald* who have worked with me over the years, handling my copy and sharing a life in the news. Many of them contributed to the exemplary coverage of this story as it happened. They include John Van Hoesen, Jo-Anne MacKenzie, Kendall Wild, John Mitchell, Jack Hoffman, Diane Derby, Tracy Schmaler, Susan Smallheer, Stephen Baumann, John Dolan, Tim Clemens, Bruce Edwards, Albert J. Marro, Vyto Starinskas, Dirk Van Susteren, Jim Falzarano, Yvonne Daley, Heather Stephenson, Fred Bever, Jessica Smith, Jack Crowther, Cynthia Mayer, and Faye Wener.

I am also grateful for the pioneering work of the journalists and scholars who have led the way in the area of gay rights, including the work of Randy Shilts, Dudley Clendinen and Adam Nagourney, Andrew Sullivan, and William N. Eskridge, Jr.

In writing this book I enjoyed the help and support of many people. I want to thank those who offered encouragement and suggestions at the outset, including Edward "Sandy" Martin, Edgar May, and John Barstow. And I want to thank my friend William Sessions for his help looking over several chapters.

I want to thank my agent, Fredrica S. Friedman, for believing in this book and for providing valuable editorial guidance and encouragement. And I want to thank my editor at Harcourt, Andrea Schulz, for her meticulous attention to and faith in the manuscript, which, I believe, shows a special polish because of her.

I want to express gratitude for the steadfast friendship of Janie Wulff and her son, Colin. Janie was there even when she wasn't there.

Most important for me in everything I do is the presence in my life of my three children, Jared, Thatcher, and Nina Moats. They are most excellent.

BIBLIOGRAPHY

Andres, Glenn M. *A Walking History of Middlebury*. Middlebury, Vt.: The Sheldon Museum, 1997.

Armstrong, Karen. *The Battle for God*. New York: Alfred A. Knopf, 2000.

Berry, Wendell. *The Unsettling of America: Culture and Agriculture*. San Francisco: Sierra Club Books, 1977.

Clendinen, Dudley, and Adam Nagourney. *Out for Good: The Struggle to Build a Gay Rights Movement in America*. New York: Simon & Schuster, 1999.

Duberman, Martin B. *Stonewall*. New York: Dutton, 1993.

Duffy, John J., ed. *Ethan Allen and His Kin: Correspondence, 1772–1819*. Hanover, N.H.: University Press of New England, 1998.

Eskridge, Jr., William N. *The Case for Same-Sex Marriage: From Sexual Liberty to Civilized Commitment*. New York: Free Press, 1996.

Eskridge, Jr., William N. *Gaylaw: Challenging the Apartheid of the Closet*. Cambridge, Mass.: Harvard University Press, 1999.

Eskridge, Jr., William N. *Equality Practice: Civil Unions and the Future of Gay Rights*. New York: Routledge, 2002.

Hollingdale, Linda. *Creating Civil Unions: Opening Hearts and Minds*. Hinesburg, Vt.: Common Humanity Press, 2002.

King, Jr., Martin Luther. *Why We Can't Wait*. New York: Harper & Row, Publishers, 1963, 1964.

Kunin, Madeleine. *Living a Political Life*. New York: Alfred A. Knopf, 1994.

Langrock, Peter. *Beyond the Courthouse.* Forest Dale, Vt.: Paul S. Eriksson, Publisher, 1999.

Lee, W. Storrs. *Gamaliel Painter: Biography of a Town Father.* Forest Dale, Vt.: Paul S. Ericksson, Publisher, 1952, 2001.

Ludlum, David McWilliams. *Social Ferment in Vermont, 1791–1850.* New York: Columbia University Press, 1939.

Murdoch, Joyce, and Deb Price. *Courting Justice: Gay Men and Lesbians v. the Supreme Court.* New York: Basic Books, 2001.

Pell, John. *Ethan Allen.* Boston and New York: Houghton Mifflin Company, 1929.

Rawls, John. *Justice as Fairness.* Cambridge, Mass.: The Belknap Press of Harvard University Press, 2001.

Resch, Tyler, ed. *The Bob Mitchell Years.* Rutland, Vt.: The Rutland Herald, 1994.

Robinson, Rowland E. *Out of Bondage and Other Stories.* Rutland, Vt.: Chas. E. Tuttle Company, 1936.

Shilts, Randy. *And the Band Played On.* New York: St. Martin's Press, 1987, 1988.

Shilts, Randy. *Conduct Unbecoming: Lesbians and Gays in the U.S. Military, Vietnam to the Persian Gulf.* New York: St. Martin's Press, 1993.

Shilts, Randy. *The Mayor of Castro Street: The Life and Times of Harvey Milk.* New York: St. Martin's Press, 1982.

Sullivan, Andrew. *Same-Sex Marriage: Pro and Con.* New York: Vintage Books, 1997.

Walters, Suzanna Danuta. *All the Rage: The Story of Gay Visibility in America.* Chicago: The University of Chicago Press, 2001.

INDEX